Gatekeepers of Global Commerce

Rules of Origin and International Economic Integration

Antoni Estevadeordal
and *Kati Suominen*

Inter-American Development Bank

Produced by the IDB Office of External Relations

Cataloging-in-Publication data provided by the
Inter-American Development Bank
Felipe Herrera Library

Estevadeordal, Antoni.

Gatekeepers of global commerce : rules of origin and international economic integration / Antoni Estevadeordal and Kati Suominen.

p. cm.
Includes bibliographical references.
ISBN: 978-1-59782-076-9

1. Certificates of origin. 2. Tariff preferences. 3. International economic integration. I. Suominen, Kati. II. Inter-American Development Bank.

HJ6617 .E873 2008
364.133 E873—dc22 LCCN: 2008929754

Table of Contents

Preface

Since the 1990s, countries in Latin America and the Caribbean and around the world have formed dozens of regional trade agreements (RTAs) to complement their unilateral and multilateral trade liberalization strategies. RTAs have transformed the international economic landscape: they regulate an estimated one-half of global trade and nearly all trade in the Americas. Some of the region's most prolific integrators, such as Chile and Mexico, have formed RTAs with all of their main trading partners.

The hard-won RTAs have provided their members with a crucial preferential edge in foreign markets and created opportunities for economies of scale, helping to attract foreign direct investment, fueling growth and development, and paving the way for further cross-border cooperation. However, RTAs are incredibly complex and include trade disciplines that may not necessarily serve liberalizing ends. One such discipline is rules of origin. Indeed, rules of origin are widely viewed as "hidden protectionism," as an obscure and opaque trade policy instrument that can work to offset the benefits of RTA-inspired tariff liberalization.

The Inter-American Development Bank has an extensive record of policy advice and technical support for the countries of Latin America and the Caribbean in the negotiation and implementation of RTAs. Such efforts have been buttressed by rigorous analytical work on RTAs and their implications. Over the years the Bank has emerged as a global leader in analyzing the structure and effects of RTAs in general, and rules of origin in particular.

Gatekeepers of Global Commerce: Rules of Origin and International Economic Integration is a collection of various contributions on rules of origin made by the Bank's Integration and Trade Sector since 2000. Many of the volume's chapters have appeared in peer-reviewed journals, and by now they have been presented in more than two dozen countries across four continents. Together, these chapters provide a comprehensive examination of the political economy and trade and economic effects of rules of origin and put forth a succinct policy roadmap for countries around the world, including those in the Americas, to follow in attenuating the potential negative implications of this complex trade discipline.

Santiago Levy Algazi
Vice President for Sectors and Knowledge, IDB

Antoni Estevadeordal
Manager, Integration and Trade Sector, IDB

CHAPTER 1

Introduction

Antoni Estevadeordal and Kati Suominen

Preferential trading arrangements (PTAs) have proliferated spectacularly around the world over the past two decades.[1] The number of PTAs in force soared from 50 in 1990 to some 200 in 2007; the dozens of ongoing PTA negotiations are expected to raise that number to near 400 by the end of 2010. PTAs are increasingly consequential to the global economy: some one-half of global trade flows between PTA partners, and every country in the world but one—Mongolia—belongs to at least one PTA. Most countries are signatories to several PTAs simultaneously; some, such as Mexico and the United States, belong to more than a dozen PTAs at once.

A major transformation in the postwar international political economy, PTAs have sparked a contentious policy debate about their endgame—whether they are trade creating or trade diverting, whether they are a deviation from or a pathway to global free trade. This is unsurprising: conferring preferential treatment on their members to access and operate in each others' markets, PTAs provide a market access edge to the insiders, discriminating against outsiders. As such, many have conceived PTAs as flying directly against the most-favored nation (MFN) principle, the bulwark of the multilateral trading system in the past six decades. In a reflection of these concerns, negotiators of the ongoing Doha Trade Round negotiations of the World Trade Or-

[1] PTAs include free trade agreements, customs unions, common markets, and single markets.

ganization (WTO) raised PTAs as a systemic issue and priority in the multilateral talks.[2]

Complicating efforts to deal with—and get a handle on—PTAs is the fact that PTAs expanded remarkably in the past two decades to cover a colorful mosaic of trade disciplines—such as provisions on market access for goods and services, standards, safeguards, government procurement, investment, and labor regulations. This has not only broadened the political constituencies and coalitions with an interest in the shape of PTAs; it has started diversifying the academic literature and policy debates on preferential trade.

Perhaps the most discussed—yet also the most poorly understood—PTA discipline is rules of origin (RoO). This is for a good reason: remaining in place even after preferential tariffs have been phased out, RoO are potentially the main agent of discrimination embedded in PTAs.

RoO define the processes to be performed and/or inputs to be incorporated into a final product within a particular PTA area in order for the product to qualify for PTA-conferred preferential tariff treatment. The purpose of RoO is to curb trade deflection—to avoid the transshipment of products from non–PTA members through a low-tariff PTA partner to a high-tariff one and, as such, to preclude outsiders from free-riding on the preferential market access granted to agreement insiders.[3] RoO are thus crucial gatekeepers of global commerce: a product shipped from an exporting PTA member must meet the applicable rule of origin in order to receive preferential treatment from the importing member. Since a failure to meet the RoO disqualifies an exporter from the PTA-conferred

---

[2] The Doha Declaration states that "We also agree to negotiations aimed at clarifying and improving disciplines and procedures under the existing WTO provisions applying to regional trade agreements. The negotiations shall take into account the developmental aspects of regional trade agreements."

[3] RoO are inherent to free trade agreements in which the member states' external tariffs diverge or in which the members wish to retain their individual tariff policies vis-à-vis the rest of the world. RoO are also widely used in customs unions, either as a transitory tool in the process of moving toward a common external tariff (CET) or as a more permanent means of covering product categories for which reaching agreement on a CET is difficult, because of, for instance, large tariff differentials between the member countries.

preferential treatment, RoO can and must be seen as a central market access instrument reigning over preferential trade.

But what renders RoO particularly relevant is that they are hardly a neutral instrument: given that RoO can serve as an effective means of deterring transshipment, they offer a temptation for political economy uses well beyond the efforts to avert trade deflection. Although RoO can become too restrictive through honest mistakes in negotiators' efforts to gauge and limit trade deflection, their design is subject to intense lobbying by protectionist interests, in particular. Often negotiated at up to 8- or 10-digit levels of disaggregation, RoO, like tariffs, make a superbly targetable instrument. Moreover, that RoO are generally defined in highly technical terms rather than assigned a numerical value entails that they can be tailored for each individual product differently and that they are not nearly as immediately quantifiable and comparable across products as tariffs are. RoO are thus essentially a valve that can be tightened or loosened to cut or expand the flow of trade between PTA areas and the rest of the world.

It is the use of RoO as a political economy instrument that helps account for the choice of RoO to govern preferential economic exchange—for the integrating governments' willingness to expend time and resources on the tedious, technical, and often highly contentious crafting of RoO protocols. After all, governments could completely forego using RoO by entering into a customs union or by excluding potentially trade-deflecting economic sectors from a PTA's coverage. Yet the bulk of PTAs employ RoO, and RoO of widely different types and in widely different combinations.

The implications of the political economy of RoO have not escaped analysts: RoO are widely considered a trade policy instrument that can work to offset the benefits of tariff liberalization.[4] Arbitrating the market

---

[4] Most prominently, RoO can be employed to favor intra-PTA industry linkages over those between a PTA and the rest of the world and, as such, to indirectly protect PTA-based input producers vis-à-vis their extra-PTA rivals (Krueger, 1993; Krishna and Krueger, 1995). As such, RoO are akin to a tariff levied by an importing country on an intermediate product (Falvey and Reed, 2000; Lloyd, 2001) and can be used by one PTA member to secure its

access of goods in the global economy, they are deemed to reverberate to firms' export, outsourcing, and investment decisions around the world. Notably, the relevance of RoO as gatekeepers of commerce can accentuate over time: their real effect kicks in when their preferential tariff liberalization is deep and the preferential margins—the gap between multilateral and preferential tariffs—they offer are wide enough for traders to have incentives to choose the PTA channel (and compliance with RoO) over the use of the MFN channel (and foregoing RoO altogether). By implication, it is multilateral trade liberalization that would obliterate the importance of RoO in world trade.

Notwithstanding RoOs' relevance in the manifold ongoing PTA negotiations, policy discussions, and the multilateral trade agenda, the global RoO panorama has until recently remained largely unexplored. The compilation in Cadot et al. (2006) is an important step forward; however, still scarce are rigorous empirical studies on both the political economy and the economic effects of RoO. The handful of existing studies remain by and large dispersed across economics and law journals.

The purpose of this book is to mend this gap. We bring together a set of empirical assessments of RoO that we have published and presented, at times with colleagues, over the past few years. In essence a "RoO reader," this book aims to contribute to a comprehensive view of the structure and effects of rules of origin in the global economy. As such, it is hoped to inform both the negotiation of new RoO regimes and the ongoing policy debate on RoO negative effects—and PTAs in general.

The next chapter, coauthored with Jeremy Harris, presents an analytical map of the uses of RoO in PTAs around the world. There are four main findings. The first is the bewildering assortment of RoO types and combinations. Empirically, there are more than 200 product-specific RoO permutations in the world's PTAs, and some of the most complex regimes, such as that of the North American Free Trade Agreement (NAFTA),

---

PTA partners' input markets for the exports of its own intermediate products (Krueger, 1993; Krishna and Krueger, 1995). Furthermore, given that RoO hold the potential for increasing local sourcing, governments can use RoO to encourage investment in sectors that provide high value added or jobs (Jensen-Moran, 1996; Hirsch, 2002).

employ up to 80 different RoO. Second, nonetheless, there are clear RoO families centered around the United States, European Union, and Mexico, in particular, which suggests effort to stick to a RoO blueprint among some of the world's most prolific PTA negotiators. These blueprints are proliferating around the world, both with U.S. and European PTAs and as copied into PTAs among countries in Asia and in Africa.

Third, the European and U.S. RoO models are among the most restrictive, and particularly so in agricultural products, textiles, and apparel. However (and fourth), U.S. agreements have become less restrictive over time, and the more recent intra-Asian agreements tend to be less restrictive and complex than their counterparts in Europe and the Americas.

Chapters 3 and 4 focus on the political economy of RoO in NAFTA and the EU-Mexico Free Trade Agreement, respectively. We find that tariffs and restrictiveness of RoO are driven by the same political economy dynamics and that RoO play an independent role in arbitrating preferential tariff liberalization. Producers that lobby for the most-demanding RoO also lobby for, and obtain, the longest tariff phaseouts. The policy implication of these findings are clear: stringent RoO and long phaseouts are the price integrationist forces will need to pay not only for PTA formation, but for forgoing manifold exclusions and building a meaningful, comprehensive, and liberalizing PTA.

Chapters 5 and 6 turn to RoOs' economic effects. Chapter 5 focuses on the trade effects of in some 100 PTAs, finding that restrictive and selective RoO discourage trade flows. At the sectoral level, both restrictive RoO and selectivity in RoO in final goods encourage trade in intermediate goods—which can mean that restrictive RoO engender trade diversion in inputs. However, some regime-wide RoO—RoO that apply similarly to all sectors in a given PTA yet vary across PTAs, such as cumulation and de minimis—bring flexibility in the application of product-specific RoO and thus facilitate trade. As such, various regime-wide RoO provisions can counteract restrictive product-specific RoOs' negative effects on trade. We also find that the negative effects of RoO dissipate over time: "RoO learning" among economic actors appears to replace "RoO interference."

Chapter 6, coauthored with José Ernesto López-Córdova, pioneers in analyzing the *investment* effects of RoO. We focus on the NAFTA RoO and Mexico, finding both that foreign direct investment in post-NAFTA Mexico has flowed into sectors with flexible RoO and that flexible RoO in downstream industries encourage investment upstream. These results suggest that NAFTA-era investment in Mexican final and intermediate goods industries has come from efficient, globally competitive firms thriving on flexible RoO.

Less well understood than the trade and investment effects of a given RoO regime or set of regimes are the effects of divergent RoO *across* regimes. Hypothetically, if the various agreements carry widely distinct RoO, they can impose undue transaction costs on traders, investors, and governments dealing in several PTA markets simultaneously (in comparison to those in the counterfactual case, where rules in the various PTA are exactly the same).

Chapter 7, again coauthored with Jeremy Harris, operationalizes RoO divergence, finding marked differences across RoO regimes around the world. On average, RoO on any given product will coincide for only about one-third of all PTAs. Nonetheless, there are clear RoO families centered on the United States (as well as Canada and Mexico) and the European Union. Within each of these families, the differences in RoO are much narrower—which suggests potential for some form of regional "RoO convergence." The chapter concludes with a set of policy recommendations for making RoO more amenable for global trade and investment, including through "multilateralizing" RoO while also promoting regional convergence among the main RoO regimes.

References

Cadot, Olivier, Antoni Estevadeordal, Akiko Suwa-Eisenmann, and Thierry Verdier. 2006. *The Origin of Goods: Rules of Origin in Regional Trade Agreements*. Oxford: Oxford University Press.

Falvey, Rod, and Geoff Reed. 2000. "Rules of Origin as Commercial Policy Instruments." Research Paper No. 2000/18. Nottingham, U.K.: Centre for Research on Globalization and Labor Markets, University of Nottingham.

Hirsch, Moshe. 2002. "International Trade Law, Political Economy and Rules of Origin: A Plea for a Reform of the WTO Regime on Rules of Origin." *Journal of World Trade* 36(2):171–89.

Jensen-Moran, Jeri. 1996. "Trade Battles as Investment Wars: The Coming Rules of Origin Debate." *Washington Quarterly* 19(1):239–53.

Krishna, Kala, and Anne O. Kruger. 1995. "Implementing Free Trade Areas: Rules of Origin and Hidden Protection." In Alan Deardorff, James Levinsohn, and Robert Stern (eds.), *New Directions in Trade Theory*. Ann Arbor: University of Michigan Press.

Krueger, Anne O. 1993. "Free Trade Agreements as Protectionist Devices: Rules of Origin." NBER Working Paper No. 4352. Cambridge, MA: National Bureau of Economic Research.

Lloyd, Peter J. 2001. "Rules of Origin and Fragmentation of Trade." In Leonard K. Cheng and Henryk Kierzkowski (eds.), *Global Production and Trade in East Asia*. Boston: Kluwer Academic.

PART I
RULES OF ORIGIN AROUND THE WORLD

CHAPTER 2

Structure, Restrictiveness, and Trends in Rules of Origin around the World*

Antoni Estevadeordal, Jeremy Harris, and Kati Suominen

The recent wave of preferential trading agreements has carried with it a colorful mosaic of trade disciplines—such as provisions on market access for goods and services, standards, safeguards, government procurement, and investment—to govern economic relations between PTA partners. However, there are as yet only a handful of rigorous efforts to disaggregate PTAs into their components parts.[1] This, in turn, implies that (1) very little is known about the compatibility of PTAs with one another or with the multilateral World Trade Organization Agreements; (2) the political economy sources of PTAs' formats remain only partially explored; and (3) analysts have yet to disentangle the respective economic effects of the different PTA disciplines from one another, let alone from the effects of variables beyond PTAs.

The lack of understanding of the various component parts of the rapidly burgeoning PTA universe severely undercuts the credibility and usefulness of the arguments of both those who view PTAs as discriminatory instruments hostage to protectionist interests obstructing global

---

* This chapter is a shortened and modified version of Estevadeordal, Harris, and Suominen (2007) and Estevadeordal and Suominen (2006).

[1] The few existing mappings of PTA disciplines include those found in WTO (2002a, 2002b), IDB (2002), Suominen (2004), and papers prepared for the WTO/HEI/NCCR Trade/CEPR Conference "Multilateralizing Regionalism," 10–12 September 2007, Geneva.

trade liberalization and those who see PTAs as holding a liberalizing logic conducive to multilateral opening.

The purpose of this chapter is to break new ground in dissecting PTAs by focusing on rules of origin, a crucial yet poorly understood market access discipline included in virtually every PTA. We present a global mapping of the existing RoO regimes and present an analytical coding scheme for the types of product-specific and regime-wide RoO employed in these regimes.

The most immediate contribution of this chapter is to advance the understanding of the RoO regimes around the world. However, we also hope to inspire further work aimed at disaggregating PTAs into their component parts—a task that is absolutely crucial for understanding the implications of regionalism to the global economic system, as well as for crafting nuanced, well-informed, and fruitful policy prescriptions concerning PTAs.

The following section lays out the different types of product-specific and general RoO employed in RoO regimes around the world. The chapter's third section examines the prevalence of the different types of RoO in 100 integration schemes from around the world. The fourth section puts forth analytical measurements of the degree of restrictiveness of product-specific RoO and strives to provide explanations for the variations in RoO restrictiveness across PTAs and in time. The fifth section analyzes the flexibility that regime-wide RoO instill in the application of product-specific RoO. The final section concludes.

Types of Preferential Rules of Origin

There are two types of rules of origin, nonpreferential and preferential. Nonpreferential RoO are used to distinguish foreign from domestic products in establishing antidumping and countervailing duties, safeguard measures, origin-marking requirements, or discriminatory quantitative restrictions or tariff quotas, as well as in the context of government procurement. Preferential RoO, meanwhile, define the conditions under which an importing country will regard a product as originating in an exporting country that receives preferential treatment from the importing country. PTAs thus employ RoO to determine whether a good qualifies for preferential treatment when exported from one member state to another.

Both nonpreferential and preferential RoO regimes have two dimensions: sectoral, product-specific RoO and general, regime-wide RoO. We discuss each in turn.

Product-Specific RoO

The Kyoto Convention recognizes two basic criteria for determining origin: *wholly obtained or produced* and *substantial transformation*.[2] The "wholly obtained or produced" category applies only to individual PTA members and asks whether particular commodities and related products have been entirely grown in or harvested or extracted from the soil in the territory of that member or have been manufactured within the member's territory entirely from commodities or products that meet the foregoing criterion. The origin requirement is met if a product or commodity does not use any second-country components or materials. Most countries apply this strict and precise definition of "wholly obtained or produced."

The substantial transformation criterion is more complex, involving four main components that can be used as stand-alones or in combinations with each other to meet RoO requirements. The precision with which these components define origin in PTAs today contrasts sharply with the vagueness of the substantial transformation criterion as used by the United States from 1908 until the inception of the Canada-U.S. Free Trade Agreement (CUSFTA) in 1989 and, subsequently, NAFTA in 1994 (Reyna, 1995: 7).[3]

The first component of the substantial transformation criterion is a change in tariff classification (CTC) for a manufactured good from the classification for the inputs from extra-PTA parties used in the process of producing the good. Meeting the substantial transformation criterion via

---

[2] The Revised Kyoto Convention is an international instrument adopted by the World Customs Organization (WCO) to standardize and harmonize customs policies and procedures around the world. The WCO adopted the original convention in 1974. The revised version was adopted in June 1999.

[3] The old criterion basically required the emergence of a "new and different article" as a result of the manufacturing process applied to the original article. It was, however, much criticized for allowing—and indeed requiring—subjective and case-by-case determinations of origin (Reyna, 1995: 7).

a CTC may require that the product alter its chapter (2 digits under the Harmonized Commodity Description System, or Harmonized System [HS]), heading (4 digits), subheading (6 digits), or item (8–10 digits) in the exporting PTA member. A change in heading is a particularly common requirement, either as a stand-alone or in tandem with other RoO criteria.

The second component is an exception attached to a particular CTC (ECTC). An ECTC generally prohibits the use of nonoriginating materials from a particular Harmonized System subheading, heading, or chapter in goods that qualify as meeting requirements via the substantial transformation criterion.

The third component is value content (VC), which requires the product to acquire a certain minimum local value (usually between 30 and 60 percent) in the exporting country in order to meet RoO requirements. The value content requirement can be expressed in three main ways: as a minimum percentage of the product's total value that must have been added in the exporting country (domestic or regional value content, RVC); as a minimum difference between the value of the final good and the costs of the imported inputs (import content, MC); or as a value of parts (VP), whereby originating status is granted to products having a minimum percentage of originating parts out of the total.

The fourth component of the substantial transformation criterion is technical requirement (TECH), in which the product must undergo certain manufacturing operations in the originating country to meet RoO requirements. TECH essentially prescribes or prohibits the use of certain inputs and/or the employment of certain processes in the production of the good.[4] It is a particularly prominent feature in RoO governing textile products.

Adding analytical complexity albeit administrative flexibility is that many RoO regimes provide two alternative routes to fulfilling RoO for a given product, such as a change in HS chapter or, alternatively, a change in HS heading plus an RVC requirement.

---

[4] TECH can be highly discretionary given the lack of classification tools for objectively guaranteeing sufficient transformation in the production of a good.

Regime-Wide RoO

In addition to the differences in product-specific RoO, RoO regimes vary by the types of general RoO they employ—including in the degree of de minimis included, whether or not the roll-up principle is used, and the type of cumulation employed.

First, most PTAs contain a de minimis rule, which allows for a specified maximum percentage of nonoriginating materials to be used without the inclusion of these materials affecting origin. The de minimis rule inserts leniency in the CTC and TECH components by making it easier for products with nonoriginating inputs to qualify as originating under the substantial transformation criterion. De minimis provisions allow goods to qualify as originating despite having some minimal content of nonoriginating inputs that do not meet CTC requirements.

Second, the roll-up or absorption principle allows materials to acquire origin by meeting specific processing requirements to be considered originating when used as input in a subsequent transformation. That is, when roll-up is allowed, nonoriginating materials are not taken into account in the calculation of the value added of a subsequent transformation.

Third, cumulation allows producers in one PTA member to use materials from other PTA members without a final product's losing its preferential status. Here, we develop a more-simplified taxonomy of cumulation types than is generally used in the literature.

There are three basic types of cumulation. Bilateral cumulation operates between two PTA partners and permits each to use products that originate in the other PTA partner as if they were its own when seeking to qualify for the PTA-conferred preferential treatment in that partner. It refers to provisions that permit goods that qualify as originating in any one signatory country to be considered as such when incorporated into a subsequent product in another signatory country. Bilateral cumulation is included in basically all PTAs. For our purposes, bilateral cumulation can be based on either products or processes (full cumulation).[5] A second

[5] The distinction between cumulation based on products and that based on processes is significant, but it is not essential to our later policy analysis.

type of cumulation, extended cumulation, allows some use of inputs from nonsignatories. It is the mechanism by which the spaghetti bowl problem (see Chapter 7) can begin to be ameliorated.[6] A third type of cumulation, diagonal cumulation, is a special case of extended cumulation.[7]

Whereas de minimis, roll up, and cumulation allow for leniency in the application of RoO, three provisions found in PTAs may have the opposite effect and increase the stringency of RoO.

First, most PTAs include a list indicating operations performed on products or product inputs that are in all circumstances considered insufficient to confer origin, such as preservation during transport and storage, as well as simple operations of cleaning, sorting, painting, packaging, assembling, and marking and labeling.

Second, many PTAs prohibit duty drawback—that is, they preclude a PTA partner from refunding tariffs paid by another PTA partner on nonoriginating inputs that are subsequently included in a final product that is exported to the first PTA partner. Many developing countries employ drawback to attract investment and to encourage exports; however, drawback in the context of a PTA is viewed as providing a cost advantage to PTA-based producers that gear their final goods to export over producers selling their final goods in the domestic market.[8] Elimination of duty drawback entails an increase in the cost of nonoriginating components for PTA-based final goods producers. As such, it may, in the presence of cumulation, encourage intra-PTA producers to shift to suppliers in the cumulation area (WTO, 2002a).

Third, the complexity of a PTA's method for certifying origin of goods can increase administrative costs to exporters. The main methods

---

[6] See also Cornejo and Harris (2007) for an extended discussion of this idea. We discuss these implications in the multilateral context in "Regime-Wide Measures: 'Flexibilizing' Restrictive RoO."

[7] To be sure, nonmembers of a cumulation area may view the cumulation system as introducing another layer of discrimination by virtue of its providing incentives to the member countries to outsource from within the cumulation zone at the expense of extrazone suppliers.

[8] Cadot, de Melo, and Olarreaga (2001) show that duty drawback may have a protectionist bias in that it diminishes producers' interest in lobbying against protection of intermediate products.

for certifying origin are self-certification by exporters, certification by the exporting-country government or an industry umbrella group to which the government has delegated the task of issuing the certificate, and a combination of "private" self-certification and "public" governmental certification. The more numerous the bureaucratic hurdles and the higher the costs for an exporter to obtain an origin certificate, the lower the incentives to seek PTA-conferred preferential treatment.

Rules of Origin around the World

Product-Specific RoO

Europe: The Pan-Euro System

The RoO regimes employed across the EU's PTAs are highly uniform, largely because of the European Commission's drive in the 1990s to harmonize the EU's RoO protocols with those of the European Free Trade Association (EFTA) countries that dated from 1972 and 1973, as well as across the EU's PTAs forged in the early 1990s in the context of the European agreements with Bulgaria, the Czech Republic, Estonia, Hungary, Latvia, Lithuania, Poland, Slovakia, and Romania.[9] This harmonization work culminated in 1997 in the launch of the Pan-Euro system, which established identical RoO protocols across the EU's existing PTAs, providing for cumulation among the participating countries. The commission's Regulation 46 of January 1999 reiterates the harmonized protocols, outlining the so-called single-list RoO.

The Pan-Euro RoO are highly complex, combining change in tariff classification mainly at the heading level with exceptions, value content rules, and technological requirements and varying markedly across products. However, the harmonized RoO do not represent a dramatic break with those of the pre-1997 era.[10]

---

[9] See Driessen and Graafsma (1999) for a review.

[10] For example, RoO for nearly 75 percent of the products (in terms of tariff subheadings) covered in the Pan-Euro and original EU-Poland RoO protocols published in 1993 are identi-

The Pan-Euro RoO have been incorporated in the Euro-Mediterranean Association Agreements between the EU and the various southern Mediterranean countries; their system of cumulation operates among the regional countries that have signed bilateral agreements with one another. The so-called Pan-Euro-Med cumulation zone covers the 27 EU members and is gradually incorporating 15 other countries or territories.[11]

Also the EU's Stabilization and Association Agreements with Albania, Bosnia and Herzegovina, Croatia, the former Yugoslav Republic of Macedonia, and Serbia and Montenegro employ the Pan-Euro RoO, as do the EU's extraregional PTAs with South Africa, Mexico, and Chile (Estevadeordal and Suominen, 2003). RoO of the EU's Generalized System of Preferences (GSP) and the 2000 Cotonou Agreement with the African, Caribbean, and Pacific (ACP) developing countries are nearly identical to the Pan-Euro rules. EFTA's recently concluded PTAs with Mexico and Singapore also follow the Pan-Euro model, albeit providing an additional alternative rule in selected sectors—such as plastics, rubber, textiles, iron and steel products, and some machinery products.

The Americas: RoO Poles

There is more variation across RoO regimes in the Americas. Nevertheless, distinct RoO families can be identified (Garay and Cornejo, 2002, and Estevadeordal and Suominen, 2005). One extreme consists of the traditional

---

cal. Both the new and the old versions combine CTC with VC and/or TECH. Indeed, EU RoO feature remarkable continuity: the RoO of the European Community–Cyprus PTA formed in 1973 are strikingly similar to those used today. One notable difference between the older and the newer protocols is that the latter allow for an optional way of meeting RoO requirements for about 25 percent of the products covered, whereas the former mostly specify only one way of meeting the RoO requirements. The second-option, alternative RoO, much like the first-option RoO, combine different RoO criteria; however, the most frequently used alternative rule of origin is a stand-alone import content criterion.

[11] The Pan-Euro-Med system of cumulation operates between the EU and the member states of the European Free Trade Association (Iceland, Liechtenstein, Norway, and Switzerland) and Turkey, and countries that signed the Barcelona Declaration, namely, Algeria, Egypt, Israel, Jordan, Lebanon, Morocco, Syria, Tunisia, and the Palestinian Authority of the West Bank and Gaza Strip. The Faroe Islands have been added to the system as well.

trade agreements such as the Latin American Integration Association (LAIA), which uses a general rule applicable across the board for all tariff items (a change in tariff classification at the heading level or, alternatively, a regional value added of at least 50 percent of the FOB export value of the final good) plus a handful of specific rules applicable to specific products. The LAIA model is the point of reference for RoO used in the Andean Community and Southern Common Market (MERCOSUR), as well as the agreements between the two groupings. The Caribbean Community (CARICOM) rules of origin are also based on a general change in heading requirement, though the exceptions to this general rule have a flavor more reminiscent of the Pan-Euro rules and their predecessors.

At the other extreme lie the so-called new-generation PTAs such as NAFTA, which is used as a reference point for subsequent U.S. and Canadian agreements in the hemisphere (the U.S.-Chile, U.S.-Colombia, U.S.-Peru, Chile-Canada, Canada–Costa Rica FTAs and the U.S.–Central America–Dominican Republic Free Trade Agreement, or CAFTA), as well as many of Mexico's agreements, including the Mexico–Costa Rica, Mexico-Chile, Mexico-Bolivia, Mexico-Nicaragua, Mexico–Northern Triangle (El Salvador, Guatemala, and Honduras), and Mexico-Colombia-Venezuela (or G3) PTAs. The RoO regimes in these agreements may require a change in chapter, heading, subheading, or item, depending on the product in question. In addition, the rules for many products combine a requirement for a change in tariff classification with an exception, a regional value content requirement, or a technical requirement.

The RoO regime of the Central American Common Market (CACM) can be seen as located between those of MERCOSUR and NAFTA: it employs chiefly change in tariff classification requirements alone, but in more precise and diverse ways than MERCOSUR, in that it requires the change to take place at the chapter, heading, or subheading level, depending on the product in question. CAFTA coexists with the CACM's market access mechanisms under the so-called multilateralism principle, which allows Central American producers to choose between the CACM and CAFTA market access regimes when exporting to the other Isthmus markets. There is a third set of RoO as an option for trade between CACM countries and the Dominican Republic.

Notably, unlike the EU's extraregional PTAs, which follow the Pan-Euro system, U.S. bilateral PTAs with extrahemispheric partners—Jordan and Israel—diverge markedly from the NAFTA model, operating on VC requirements alone. U.S. agreements with Morocco, Bahrain, and Oman also use VC requirements almost exclusively, except in the case of textile products, for which NAFTA-style change in tariff classification rules are applied.

Transpacific Agreements

PTAs in the Americas are shaping the RoO regimes negotiated between countries of the Americas and Asia. U.S. agreements with Singapore, Australia, and Korea are complex and have RoO that resemble those of CAFTA; meanwhile, RoO in the Chile-Korea FTA follow the model of U.S.-Chile RoO. However, these transpacific agreements are less complex overall than their counterparts in the Americas, featuring a strong change in heading requirement. Peru's agreement with Thailand, Chile's agreement with Japan, and the P4 agreement (among Brunei, Chile, New Zealand, and Singapore), as well as Mexico's agreement with Japan, follow the detailed, selective model of these countries' agreements with the United States. Chile's agreement with China stands in contrast, applying an across-the-board VC rule, with a handful of exceptions where change in chapter or change in heading requirements are applied.

Meanwhile, further European moves into Asia, such as in planned agreements with the Association of Southeast Asian Nations (ASEAN) and India, will likely bring the Pan-Euro model into the region even more to accompany the U.S. model.

Asia: Multiple Influences

Some of the main integration schemes in Asia—the ASEAN Free Trade Area, the ASEAN-China and ASEAN-Korea agreements, the Agreement on Trade Negotiations among Developing Member Countries of the Economic and Social Commission for Asia and the Pacific (Bangkok Agreement), the Australia-Singapore Free Trade Agreement, and

South Pacific Regional Trade and Economic Cooperation Agreement (SPARTECA)—carry an across-the-board VC rule with relatively few exceptions. However, the proliferation of PTAs in Asia has brought complexity to the region's RoO theater, especially as these countries have entered into agreements with extraregional partners.

The RoO of the Japan-Singapore Economic Partnership Agreement (JSEPA) are complex, as evinced by the more-than-200-page RoO protocol. However, much as in the Chile-Korea PTA, many of the Japan-Singapore RoO are based on a simple change in heading criterion, which makes the regime much less complex when contrasted with the Pan-Euro and NAFTA models. Furthermore, for many products JSEPA introduces an alternative, usually Pan-Euro-type, freestanding VC rule, which instills generality and flexibility into the agreement. Japan's agreements with Malaysia and Thailand, on the other hand, repeat the more complex set of rules seen in Japan's agreement with Mexico.

The Australia–New Zealand Closer Economic Relations Trade Agreement (ANZCERTA) recently replaced its across-the-board VC rule with a set of rules that are quite similar to those established in the U.S.-Australia regime. Australia and New Zealand have also entered into separate agreements with Thailand that carry a similar set of rules.

Africa and the Middle East

The relative complexity of RoO in Europe, in the Americas, and, increasingly, in Asia stands in contrast to the generality of RoO in many African and Middle Eastern PTAs. The Economic Community of West African States (ECOWAS) and the Common Market for Eastern and Southern Africa (COMESA) in Africa and the Gulf Cooperation Council (GCC) in the Middle East are based on an across-the-board VC rule with an RVC requirement that ranges from 30 percent (ECOWAS) to 40 percent (COMESA). Some of the agreements allow, or, indeed, require, RoO to be calculated on the basis of import content. Most of these regimes also specify an alternative RoO based on the CTC criterion; most often the alternative involves a change in heading or, in the case of ECOWAS with its relatively low RVC requirement of 30 percent, change in subheading.

However, the Southern African Development Community (SADC) RoO approximate the Pan-Euro model both in *types* of sectoral RoO and in sectoral selectivity. Moreover, there have been some initiatives to renegotiate COMESA RoO toward a more complex mold.

Nonpreferential RoO

Nonpreferential RoO are used for purposes distinct from those of preferential rules. Even if a country did not have any preferential RoO at all, it would still apply some type of nonpreferential RoO. Unlike preferential RoO, which have thus far escaped multilateral regulation, nonpreferential RoO have been undergoing a process of harmonization since 1995 as mandated by the Uruguay Round's Agreement on Rules of Origin (ARO). Indeed, the rapid evolution of the preferential RoO panorama stands in contrast to the glacial progress made in harmonizing nonpreferential RoO. The harmonization work, propelled precisely by growing concerns about the divergent national RoOs' effects on trade flows, has been carried out under the auspices of the Committee on Rules of Origin of the World Trade Organization and the Technical Committee on Rules of Origin of the Brussels-based World Customs Organization (WCO). The WCO has been responsible for the technical part of the work, including discussions on the RoO options for each product under consideration.

The harmonization drive was initially scheduled for completion by July 1998. However, the deadline has been extended several times since then, and the work is not yet finished. As of now, the pending product-specific issues involve some 30 products. There are also two major issues that have yet to be resolved: use of the value-added versus the change in tariff classification principle in assembly in Harmonized System Chapters 84–90, and implementation issues, particularly the use of the harmonized nonpreferential RoO in antidumping cases.[12]

---

[12] ARO states that nonpreferential rules are to be the basis for antidumping actions. However, some WTO members, such as the United States, Korea, and Japan, have argued that the calculation of the margin of dumping in antidumping cases—the wedge between the price of the exported good and its value in the domestic market—is per the Agreement on Anti-Dumping, based on the concept of exporting country and not on

Although the ARO is centered on nonpreferential RoO, its Common Declaration with Regard to Preferential Rules of Origin spells out a requirement for its signatories to keep the WTO Secretariat informed about their preferential RoO. In their current structure, the nonpreferential RoO negotiated under the ARO approximate the Pan-Euro and NAFTA models in sectoral specificity, yet are less demanding than either of the two main RoO regimes. However, since the final agreement has yet to be reached, the ultimate degree of complexity and restrictiveness of the harmonized nonpreferential RoO remains to be evaluated.

Depicting Product-Specific RoO around the World

This subsection maps out RoO regimes around the world according to their various components discussed previously. Figure 2.1 focuses on the first RoO component and a staple of most RoO regimes, the change in tariff classification component, in the RoO regimes of 26 selected PTAs, as well as the current status of the nonpreferential negotiations in regard to this component.[13]

There are some clear families. The Andean Community, as well as MERCOSUR and its agreements with other South American countries, makes very extensive use of the change in heading requirement, whereas U.S., Mexican, and most Chilean agreements use a mix of CTC requirements at a variety of levels (heading, subheading, etc.). RoO built upon the NAFTA RoO regime are based on change in heading and change in chapter requirements in relatively even numbers. The formats of the U.S.-Chile FTA and CAFTA stand somewhat apart from that of NAFTA in requiring only change in subheading for a substantial number of tariff lines. Meanwhile, the Chile-CACM FTA diverges from the NAFTA model in its marked change in heading requirement, as do the Japan-Singapore

---

the country of origin. Many members also resist the application of harmonized RoO in antidumping actions because of the changes and constraints this would impose on their domestic antidumping legislations.

[13] The figure is based on the rule of origin that is listed first when two or more possible RoO are provided for a particular product category.

Figure 2.1 | Distribution of CTC Components by Agreement, Selected PTAs

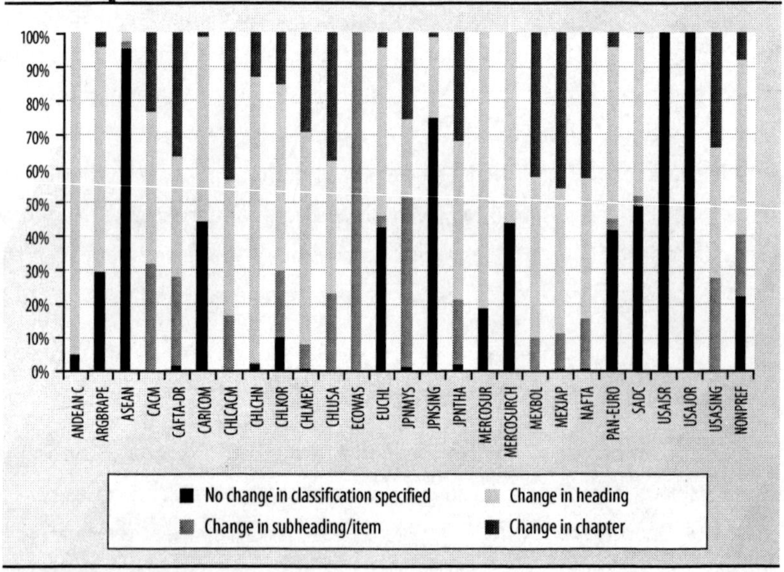

Source: Authors' calculations on the basis of PTA texts. NONPREF=nonpreferential tariffs. See Appendix 2.1 for a key to other abbreviations used in the figure.

and Chile-Korea PTAs. In contrast, the change in heading requirement dominates EU RoO.

The Japan-Singapore agreement relies on a default wholly obtained rule for products with no other rule specified in the agreement annex, and then otherwise heavily employs a change in heading requirement. In contrast, the ASEAN employs CTC requirements for a very small number of products in its agreements, and not at all in its agreements with China and Korea. The regimes employed by SADC and the EU depend on a fairly even split between change in heading and non-CTC rules. Appendix Table 2A.1 presents a disaggregated description of the different criteria combinations.

Another notable difference among the various PTAs is that some, such as the Bangkok Agreement, employ the VC component across sectors, completely foregoing the use of the CTC component. The

Table 2.1 VC Components by Agreement

	Regional value content/buildup	Build-down	Maximum imported content	Factory cost	Net cost
Andean Community			50–55		
Argentina-Brazil-Peru			50		
Argentina-Colombia			40–55		
Argentina-Ecuador			40–55		
Argentina-Venezuela			40–55		
ASEAN	40				
ASEAN-China	40		60		
ASEAN-Korea	35–70	40			
Australia-New Zealand	35–55	30–45		45–60	
Australia-Singapore	30–50				
Australia-Thailand	40–55				45
Bangkok			50		
Brazil-Colombia			40–55		
Brazil-Ecuador			40–55		
Brazil-Venezuela	55		40–50		
CAFTA-Dominican Republic	30–65	25–55			35
Canada-Costa Rica	30–60				20–30
CARICOM			30–65		
Chile-Canada	30–65				20–55
Chile-China	40–50				
Chile-Ecuador			50		
Chile-Korea	45–80	30			
Chile-CACM	20–30				
Chile-Mexico	32–50				26–40
Chile-Peru		50	50		
U.S.-Chile	40–65	30–55			
Chile-Colombia	30–70				
COMESA			60	35	
ECOWAS				30	
EU-Chile				20–50	
EU-Mexico				20–60	
G3	35–60				

(continued on next page)

Table 2.1 ▌ VC Components by Agreement *(continued)*

	Regional value content/buildup	Build-down	Maximum imported content	Factory cost	Net cost
Japan-Malaysia	40–60				
Japan-Singapore	40–60				
Japan-Thailand	40				
MERCOSUR	60		40		
MERCOSUR-Bolivia	60	40	40		
MERCOSUR-Chile	60	40			
Mexico-Bolivia	50				40–60
Mexico-Costa Rica	50				40–60
Mexico-Japan	50–90				
Mexico-Nicaragua	50				40–41.66
Mexico-Northern Triangle	50				
Mexico-Uruguay	50–55		50		40–50
NAFTA	30–80				25–70
P4	45–50				
Peru-Thailand	35–60				
Paraguay-Colombia			50		
Paraguay-Ecuador			50–60		
Paraguay-Peru			50		
Paraguay-Venezuela			50		
SADC	40–65				30–65
SAFTA	25–60		60		
Thailand-India	20–40				
Thailand-New Zealand	50				
Uruguay-Colombia			50		
Uruguay-Ecuador			50		
Uruguay-Peru			50		
Uruguay-Venezuela			50		
U.S.-Australia	45–65	35–50			50
U.S.-Bahrain	35				
U.S.-Colombia	35–65	20–65			35
U.S.-Israel	35				
U.S.-Jordan	35–60				

(continued on next page)

Table 2.1 ▌ VC Components by Agreement *(continued)*

	Regional value content/buildup	Build-down	Maximum imported content	Factory cost	Net cost
U.S.-Korea	30–60	30–55			35
U.S.-Morocco	35				
U.S.-Panama	30–65	20–55			35
U.S.-Peru	30–65	20–65			35
U.S.-Singapore	40–65	30–55			

Source: Authors' calculations on the basis of PTA texts.

EU does this in about a quarter of its RoO.[14] Table 2.1 focuses on the level of the VC component in the tariff subheadings governed by VC (including combinations of VC with CTC, and VC when employed as an alternative to a CTC criterion) in various RoO regimes, as well as the different methods set forth for calculating VC. The typical level of VC required is 40–50 percent, whether defined as maximum import content or as RVC. However, in the U.S.-Chile PTA, CAFTA, and the Chile-CACM PTA, RVC is generally set at lower levels of 30–35 percent; conversely, for some products in the Pan-Euro and SADC regimes, the permitted value of nonoriginating inputs is as low as 15–30 percent of the price of the final product (roughly equivalent to a 70–85 percent RVC requirement). Differences in the method of calculating the value of inputs can have crucial implications for the exporters' capacity to meet the RoO.

The various RoO employed in regimes around the world yield more than 200 potential combinations of RoO criteria. Figure 2.2 analyzes the number of RoO permutations employed by the various regimes around the

[14] More than 80 percent of these RoO are based on the wholly obtained criterion, used particularly for agricultural products, or on an import content rule that imposes a ceiling of 40–50 percent on nonoriginating components of the ex-works price of a final product. Stand-alone import content RoO are used particularly frequently for optics, transportation equipment, and machinery and electrical equipment.

Figure 2.2 RoO Permutations

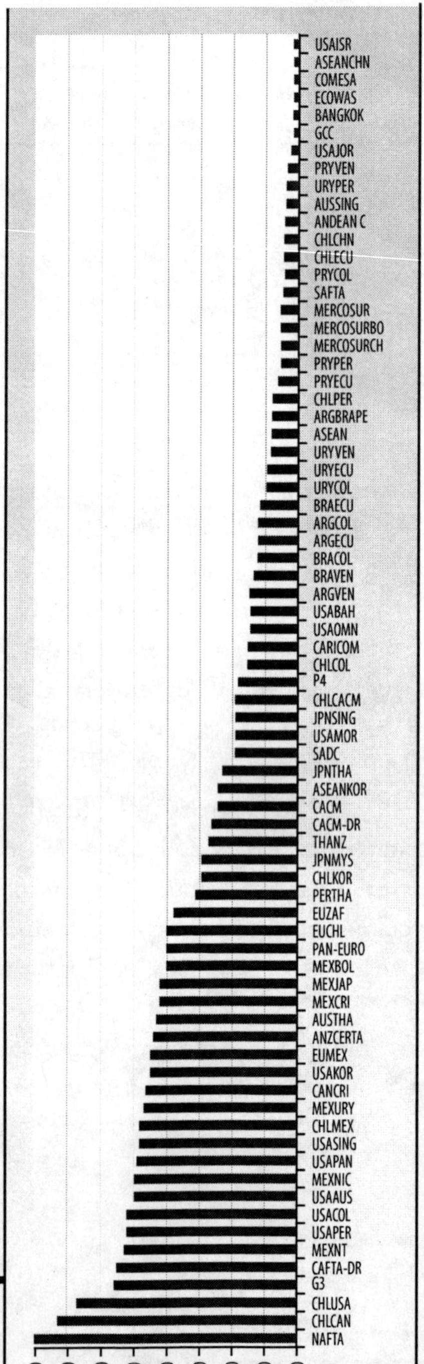

Source: Authors' calculations on the basis of PTA texts. See Appendix 2.1 for a key to the abbreviations used in the figure.

world.[15] NAFTA emerges as the most complex of the agreements in the sample in terms of number of permutations of criteria employed, followed by the two agreements most closely modeled on it, those of Canada and the United States with Chile. Among the remainder, other agreements modeled on NAFTA as well as the EU's agreements are generally the most complex. Agreements within South America, Africa, and Asia are generally the simplest.

Regime-Wide RoO

Besides product-level RoO, the different RoO regimes can be compared according to their general, regime-wide RoO: those that apply similarly to nearly all goods with a regime. Table 2.2 contrasts the various RoO regimes according to three key regime-wide RoO—de minimis, cumulation, and certification.

De Minimis

EU RoO regimes feature a higher de minimis (at 10 percent) than NAFTA and some other PTAs in the Americas, although most of the newer PTAs (U.S.-Chile, CAFTA, U.S.-Colombia, U.S.-Peru) also apply the same de minimis level as Pan-Euro. Meanwhile, there is no de minimis rule in MERCOSUR's FTAs or in most agreements in Asia and Africa.

The de minimis principle does have exceptions, however, in most regimes that employ it: for example, the EU's de minimis does not apply to textiles and apparel, except for allowing an 8 percent de minimis of the total weight of textile materials in mixed-textiles products. In the EU–South Africa agreement, de minimis is set at 15 percent but excludes fish and crustaceans and tobacco products, as well as certain meat products and alcoholic beverages. NAFTA de minimis is also calculated based on weight rather than value for textiles and apparel, and it does not provide

[15] Permutations are based on Harris's (2007) categorizations of change in classification, addition, exception, value test, technical requirement, and alternative criteria components (see Appendix 2.3).

Table 2.2 | Regime-Wide RoO in Selected PTAs

PTA	De minimis	Extended cumulation	Certification method
Andean Community	None	No	Public (or delegated to a private entity)
ANZCERTA	10%	No	Public (or delegated to a private entity)
ASEAN	None	No	Public (or delegated to a private entity)
ASEAN–China	None	No	Public (or delegated to a private entity)
ASEAN–Korea	10 (10% of weight in Chapters 50–63)	No	Public (or delegated to a private entity)
Australia–Thailand	10%	No	Public (or delegated to a private entity)
Bangkok	None	No	Public (or delegated to a private entity)
CACM	10 (10% of weight in Chapters 50–63)	No	Self-certification
CACM–Chile	8% (not Chapters 1–27 unless CS)	No	Self-certification
CAFTA–Dominican Republic	10% (Not Chapters 4 and 15)	Possibly Chapter 62 (with Canada and Mexico)	Self-certification
Canada–Costa Rica	10% (except in Chapters 10 to 24; 10% of weight in Chapters 50–63)	No	Self-certification
Canada–Chile	9% (except in agricultural and industrial products; 9% of weight in Chapters 50–63)	No	Self-certification
Canada–Israel	10% (except in agricultural and industrial products; 7% of weight in Chapters 50–63)	Yes (with U.S.)	Self-certification
CARICOM	None	No	Public (or delegated to a private entity)
Chile–China	8%	No	Public (or delegated to a private entity)
Chile–Colombia	10% (except in agriculture and processed agriculture products; 10% of weight in textiles).	No	Public; limited self-certification

(*continued on next page*)

Table 2.2 Regime-Wide RoO in Selected PTAs *(continued)*

PTA	De minimis	Extended cumulation	Certification method
Chile–Ecuador	None	No	Public; limited self-certification
Chile–Korea	8% (not Chapters 1–24 unless CS; 8% of weight in Chapters 50–63	No	Self-certification
Chile–Peru	None	No	Public; limited self-certification
COMESA	2%	No	Two-step private and public
ECOWAS	None	No	Public (or delegated to a private entity)
EU–Chile	10% (except in Chapters 50–63)	No	Public; limited self-certification
EU–Mexico	10% (except in Chapters 50–63)	No	Public; limited self-certification
EU–South Africa	15% (10 for Chapters 3 and 24) (not Chapters 50 to 63)	Yes with ACP (full with SACU)	Public; limited self-certification
G3	7 (7% of weight in Chapters 50–63)	No	Two-step private and public
GCC	None	No	Public (or delegated to a private entity
Japan–Malaysia	To be determined	Limited products from ASEAN	Public (or delegated to a private entity)
Japan–Thailand	To be determined	Limited products from ASEAN	Public (or delegated to a private entity)
Japan–Singapore	To be determined	No	Public (or delegated to a private entity)
MERCOSUR	None	No	Public (or delegated to a private entity)
MERCOSUR–Bolivia	None	Yes (Bolivia may cumulate from LAIA)	Public (or delegated to a private entity)
MERCOSUR–Chile	None	No	Public (or delegated to a private entity)
MERCOSUR–Colombia–Ecuador–Venezuela	None	Yes (within MERCOSUR and Andean Community)	Public (or delegated to a private entity)
MERCOSUR–Peru	None	Yes (within MERCOSUR and Andean Community)	Public (or delegated to a private entity)

(continued on next page)

Table 2.2 ▌ Regime-Wide RoO in Selected PTAs *(continued)*

PTA	De minimis	Extended cumulation	Certification method
Mexico–Nicaragua	7% (except Chapters 01–27 and 50–63)	No	Self-certification
Mexico–Northern Triangle	7% (except Chapters 01–27 and 50–63)	No	Self-certification
Mexico–Uruguay	8% (except Chapters 01–27 and 50–63)	No	Self-certification
Mexico–Bolivia	7% (not Chapters 1–27 unless CS; not Chapters 50–63)	No	Self-certification
Mexico–Chile	8% (except in agricultural and industrial products; 9% of weight in Chapters 50–63)	No	Self-certification
Mexico–Costa Rica	7% (except in Chapters 4–15 and Headings 0901, 1701, 2105, 2202)	No	Self-certification
NAFTA	7% (except in agricultural and industrial products; 7% of weight in Chapters 50–63)	No	Self-certification
P4	10%	No	Self-certification
Pan-Euro	10% (8–10% of weight in textiles)	Yes (full in EEA)	Public; limited self-certification
Peru–Thailand	10%	No	Public (or delegated to a private entity)
SAFTA	None	No	Public (or delegated to a private entity)
SADC	10% (not Chapters 50–63, 87, 98)	No	Two-step private and public
Singapore–Australia	2%	No	Public (or delegated to a private entity)
Thailand–New Zealand	10%	No	Self-certification
U.S.–Korea	10% (by weight in textiles; except in agriculture and processed agriculture products)	No	Self-certification

(continued on next page)

Table 2.2 Regime-Wide RoO in Selected PTAs *(continued)*

PTA	De minimis	Extended cumulation	Certification method
U.S.–Panama	10% (by weight in textiles; except in agriculture and processed agriculture products)	Possibly for Chapter 61 or 62	Self-certification
U.S.–Colombia	10% (by weight in textiles; except in agriculture and processed agriculture products)	Possibly with Peru	Self-certification
U.S.–Peru	10% (by weight in textiles; except in agriculture and processed agriculture products)	Possibly with Colombia	Self-certification
U.S.–Australia	10% (except in agriculture and processed agriculture products)	No	Self-certification
U.S.–Bahrain	None	Possibly with regional counties	Self-certification
U.S.–Chile	10% (by weight in textiles; except in agriculture and processed agriculture products)	No	Self-certification
U.S.–Israel	None	Yes (West Bank and Gaza)	Self-certification
U.S.–Jordan	None	QIZ cumulation from Israel	Self-certification
U.S.–Singapore	10% (except in various agriculture products; 7% of weight in Chapters 50–63)	ISI*	Self-certification

* (Integrated Sourcing Initiative. Primarily IT products need not meet any rule of origin if shipped directly between the signatories.)

Source: Authors' calculations on the basis of PTA texts.

for dairy products; edible products of animal origin; citrus fruit and juice; instant coffee; cocoa products; and some machinery and mechanical appliances, such as air conditioners and refrigerators (Reyna, 1995: 115–17). Many of the same exceptions appear in subsequent U.S., Canadian, and Mexican FTAs.

Cumulation

The EU's Pan-European system of cumulation, applied since 1997, draws a clear distinction between the EU RoO regimes, on the one hand, and most RoO regimes elsewhere in the world, on the other. In concrete terms, the Pan-European system enables producers to use components originating in any of the participating countries without losing the preferential status of the final product. This provision is only available, however, when all of the countries supplying components for the final product also have PTAs in force with all of the other countries contributing to the final product, which in many instances is not yet the case. The European Economic Association (EEA) agreement between the EU and EFTA signatories also permits full cumulation.

The EU's agreements with extraregional partners do not form part of the Pan-Euro system, yet in some cases they do allow for extended cumulation. The EU–South Africa PTA allows both parties to cumulate diagonally with the ACP states. In addition, it incorporates the "single-territory" concept, whereby South Africa can count work or processing carried out within the Southern African Customs Union (SACU) area as if it had been performed in South Africa (but not as if it had been performed in the EU).

The EU's agreements with Mexico and Chile, on the other hand, do not include provisions for cumulation from any countries other than the direct signatories. The hypothetical reasons why these two agreements, despite their not employing the Pan-Euro system of cumulation, still adopted the Pan-Euro RoO, which include the EU's desire to minimize transaction costs for its customs verifying the origin of goods and exporters operating in multiple PTA theaters at once, and/or the parties' hypothetical desire to enable rapid accession to the Pan-Euro system of cumulation at a future date (as identical RoO would be required for such accession).

There are various examples of extended cumulation that is not complete enough to be properly considered diagonal. In SPARTECA, Australia and New Zealand allow members of the Pacific Islands Forum (formerly the South Pacific Forum) to cumulate among themselves and still receive preferential treatment. The forum islands may not, however, cumulate inputs from New Zealand for exports to Australia and receive preferential treatment, or vice versa, as trade between Australia and New Zealand is governed by ANZCERTA (which does not provide for cumulation of inputs originating in forum countries).[16]

For reasons probably more political than economic, cumulation in U.S. agreements with Israel and Jordan is similarly tangled and limited. The U.S.-Israel PTA permits cumulation of inputs from the West Bank and the Gaza Strip, but not Jordan. Prior to the negotiation of a PTA with Jordan, the United States established a classification of "qualifying industrial zones" (QIZ) with Jordan and also with Egypt. This classification allowed for cumulation of inputs from Israel, the West Bank, and Gaza, but not from Jordan (for Egyptian imports) and Egypt (for Jordanian imports). The subsequent PTA between Jordan and the United States includes rules that permit cumulation only bilaterally, but the QIZ program remains in effect, allowing continuation of the cumulation of inputs from Israel and the Palestinian territories. The QIZ, however, are still a unilateral concession of the United States, not a bilateral treaty obligation.

The Canada-Israel FTA permits cumulation with the two countries' common PTA partners as of the agreement's entry into force, a set of countries that includes the United States and no other. This extension of cumulation most likely accommodates existing integration of Canadian industry with U.S. suppliers.

CAFTA provides for cumulation of inputs from Canada and Mexico in the production of garments of woven fabric (HS Chapter 62) in CAFTA signatories. The provisions governing cumulation are subject to negotiation of origin verification protocols different from those in NAFTA as well as adjustments to the rules in the agreements of the Central American countries with Mexico. Thus far, Mexico has participated actively in the negotiation and implementation of these adjustments whereas Canada has shown less interest. Similar provisions are available to the Dominican Republic for a transition period, by

[16] The ANZCERTA rules were completely renegotiated in 2006, with the new rules going into force in 2007.

the end of which it must negotiate a PTA with Mexico in order for the provisions to remain in effect.[17]

There are also efforts at extended cumulation elsewhere in Latin America. One case in point is the recent agreements between MERCOSUR and the Andean Community. Although these agreements share text with a common origin, including a provision for cumulation that includes all nine countries (including Bolivia), the product-level rules were negotiated bilaterally, resulting in 16 full sets of rules. Because these rules are not uniform across these bilateral relationships, there are many opportunities for "triangulation" whereby minor processes undertaken in one country can confer origin for purposes of export to a given partner when those same processes would not confer origin for the same partner if undertaken in a third member of the group.[18] Although there have been some initial attempts to mitigate this problem, no clear solution has yet emerged.

Singapore's PTAs incorporate the outward-processing (OP) concept, tailored to accommodate Singapore's unique economic features and its access to low-cost processing in neighboring countries (see Estevadeordal and Suominen, 2006). The U.S.-Singapore FTA also incorporates the Integrated Sourcing Initiative (ISI), which provides further flexibility in sourcing. Japan's agreements with Malaysia and Thailand include rules that specifically allow cumulation of inputs from ASEAN. Application of these rules is concentrated in just a few agricultural products and in textiles and apparel.

Certification

The purpose of origin certification procedures is to ensure that preferences are granted only to goods originating in a particular country, according to the rules of the country receiving the goods. Certificates thus provide a check on the accuracy and veracity of claims for preferential treatment.

---

[17] The beginning of these negotiations has already been announced.

[18] See Table 8 of Cornejo and Harris (2007) for an analysis of the differences in the product-level rules in these agreements.

The method used for certifying origin is important insofar as it is effective in achieving this objective at a minimum possible administrative cost.

The method employed for certifying origin varies across PTAs. Three fundamental systems can be identified, according to the entity responsible for certifying origin. The official certifying entity can be either an interested party or a third party, which in turn can be either the exporting country's government or a designated private entity. Interested parties include the producer, exporter, and importer of the goods being certified (in many cases these three may be one and the same). Designated private entities are generally chambers of commerce or other industry associations.

EU RoO regimes require a movement certificate issued by the government of the country from which the goods are being exported; the exporter or its competent agency must apply for the certificate. However, under the EU regimes, customs authorities of exporting countries may authorize an alternative method of certification, the invoice declaration, for exporters that make frequent shipments (*approved exporters*). The fact that these regimes provide for the authorization of interested-party certification implies that there are recognized cost savings in avoiding the governmental certification process. The requirement for authorization to use the alternate certification method, however, may in some cases serve as something of a barrier to entry for new exporters.

Meanwhile, NAFTA and a number of other FTAs in the Americas as well as the Chile-Korea FTA rely on certification by interested parties, which entails that an exporter's signing of a certificate of origin suffices as an affirmation that the items covered by it qualify as originating. In CAFTA, an importer claiming preferential tariff treatment for a good, rather than the exporter, is the party ultimately responsible for declaring that the good is originating. Although this system places the burden of proof on importers and is thus the simplest and least costly for exporters, it opens the door to more potential fraud and abuse. As such, the cost to customs of establishing and operating an effective origin verification regime may be more significant under RoO that rely on this method.

Agreements based on the LAIA model, such as MERCOSUR and that of the Andean Community, as well as CARICOM, the ASEAN Free Trade Area, ANZCERTA, South Asia Free Trade Agreement

(SAFTA), the Bangkok Agreement, the Japan-Singapore PTA, and the ECOWAS agreement require certification by a public body or a private umbrella entity approved by the government as a certifying agency. The exporter is required to furnish the certifying agency with a legal declaration of a product's origin, which is then certified. This method has the advantages of review by a relatively disinterested third party, as well as the potential that certifying entities will be more familiar with production processes than government agents may be, though this method presents costs to traders similar to those involved in the governmental certification method.

Analytical Coding Methodology for Rules of Origin in PTAs

This section presents a methodology for measuring (1) the relative restrictiveness of the product-specific RoO governing different economic sectors in various preferential trade agreements and (2) the degree of flexibility instilled in the various RoO regimes by the different regime-wide RoO, such as de minimis and drawback. We subsequently compare RoO regimes according to the values yielded by these two analytical measures.

Restrictiveness and Complexity

The capacity of RoO to affect economic decisions depends on the degree to which they restrict the options of economic actors and the size of the tariff preference to which compliance with these rules gives access. The degree to which RoO restrict the options of producers/exporters we refer to as their "restrictiveness." Two concepts related to preferential trade agreements—input pool and geographical pool—are key to understanding RoO restrictiveness.

In regard to input pool, an agreement's RoO establish, for each product the agreement covers, which of its inputs and/or what fraction of its inputs may be "nonoriginating" in order for the product to retain access to the preferential tariff treatment established by the agreement. The fewer restrictions, whether qualitative or quantitative, placed on the use of nonoriginating inputs, the more "open" the preferential bloc is to the rest of the world. The more open a RoO regime is, the bigger is its input pool.

As for geographical pool, any origin regime (implicitly or explicitly) establishes the list of countries whose products can be considered originating for purposes of the agreement (this might also be referred to as the "cumulation zone"). In most PTAs, this list is simply the direct signatories of the agreement. Some agreements, however, also specify additional countries whose products may be treated as originating when used as inputs in one or more direct signatories. Subregional integration groups receive such treatment in the EU's GSP scheme, as do the bilateral agreements that make up the Pan-Euro cumulation system. The longer the list of countries whose products qualify as originating in the origin regime of a given PTA, and the larger those countries are, the larger the agreement's implicit geographical pool.

Rules of origin thus determine both the openness of a bloc and its size, which, in turn, play a role in defining its restrictiveness. Increasing a given bloc's openness or size—its input or geographical pool—can be expected to reduce the distortions caused by the origin regime that governs the bloc.

Measuring Restrictiveness

How can restrictiveness be measured? A rule of origin is more restrictive to the degree that it permits less use of inputs from outside the applicable cumulation zone, where the cumulation zone is the set of countries whose products can be considered originating when used as inputs in later production. Restrictiveness defined in this way is the most easily observed, as the means of observation is expressed in the text of the rule itself.

Two existing measures of restrictiveness are based on this idea. The first is that of Estevadeordal (2000), which constructs a categorical variable ranging from 1 (least restrictive) to 7 (most restrictive) on the basis of NAFTA RoO. This index can be conceptualized as an indicator of how demanding a given RoO is for an exporter. The observation rule for the index is based on two assumptions: (1) change at the level of chapter is more restrictive than change at the level of heading, change at the level of heading is more restrictive than change at the level of subheading, and so on; and (2) VC technical requirements (such as chemical transformations) attached to a given CTC add to RoOs' restrictiveness. Several other studies, such as Cadot et al. (2006), Suominen (2004), and Portugal-Perez (2006), have applied variations of Estevadeordal's index.

The second measure is that of Harris (2007). It presents a significant overhaul of Estevadeordal's methodology, applying similar logic but much more precisely capturing details of the variation across products and across agreements in the definition of rules of origin.[19] Appendix 2.3 provides a detailed explanation of the calculation of Estevadeordal's and Harris's indices.

Figure 2.3 reports the restrictiveness of RoO as calculated at the 6-digit level of disaggregation in selected PTAs by using the two measures, and Figure 2.4 displays RoO regimes' selectivity (standard deviation in RoO restrictiveness) by engaging the two measures. EU, Mexican, Chilean, and U.S. agreements are found to be among the most restrictive. Agreements in Asia are revealed to be less restrictive, in part because of their tendency to set across-the-board VC rules. The Japan-Singapore PTA is somewhat exceptional in that it applies a highly restrictive wholly obtained rule in product categories for which no RoO is specified in the agreement's origin annex.

Estevadeordal's and Harris's measures produce meaningfully different rankings for the regimes joining MERCOSUR and Andean Community countries, largely because Harris's methodology assigns lower values to rules that present alternative qualification criteria. Such criteria are especially prevalent in these agreements, which otherwise have similar

[19] Given that these measures of restrictiveness are a function of ex ante restrictiveness rather than the effective restrictiveness following the implementation of the RoO, the methodology of both—much like that of Garay and Cornejo (2002)—is particularly useful for endogenizing and comparing RoO regimes. The methodology allows RoO to be analyzed in terms of their characteristics rather than their effects, that is, their observed rather than their effective restrictiveness.

Figure 2.3 Restrictiveness (Index Values) of RoO

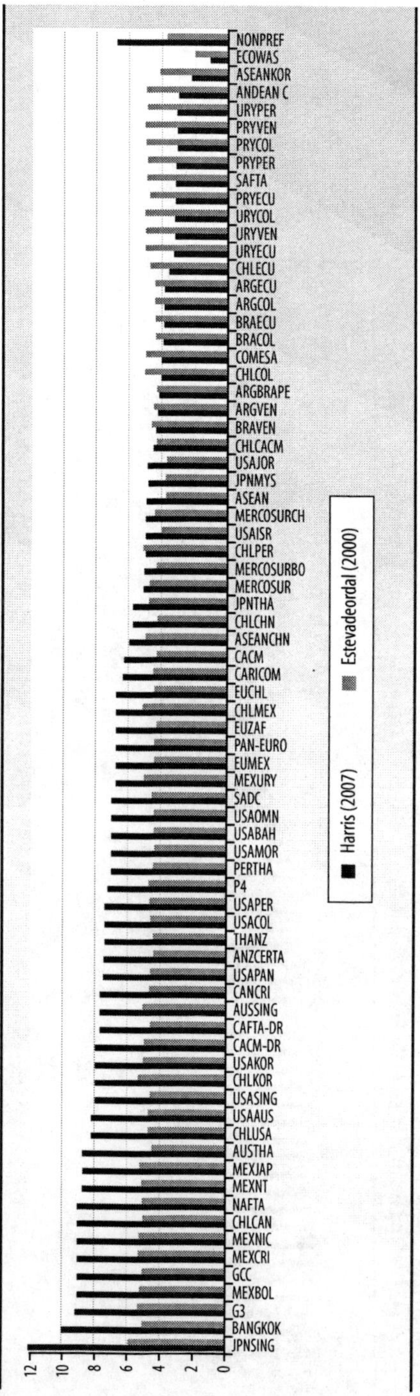

Source: Authors' calculations on the basis of PTA texts. See Appendix 2.1 for a key to abbreviations used in the figure.

Figure 2.4 Selectivity of Product-Specific RoO in Selected RoO Regimes (standard deviation of RoO restrictiveness)

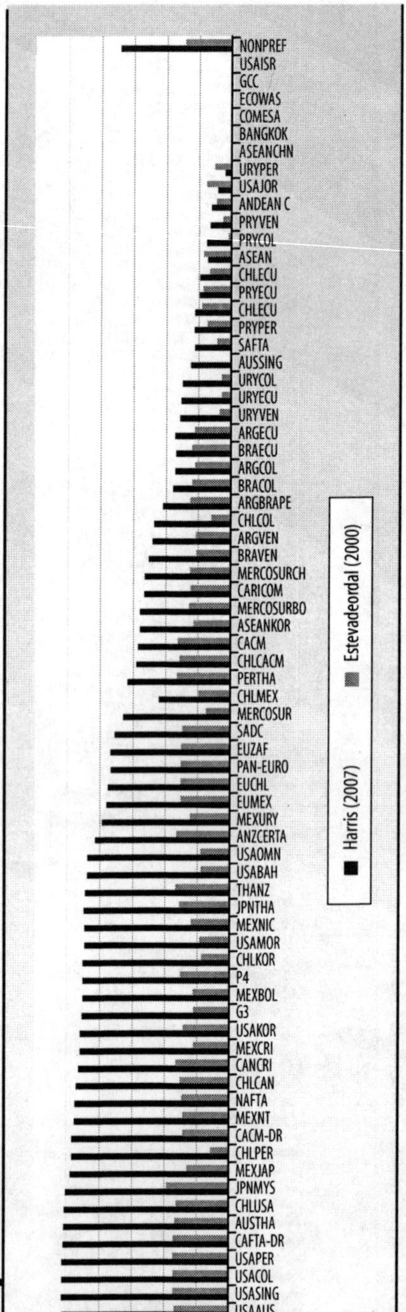

Source: Authors' calculations on the basis of PTA texts. NONPREF=nonpreferential tariffs. See Appendix 2.1 for a key to other abbreviations used in the figure.

rules across products, with the result that this methodological decision produces such different results.

Table 2.3 catalogues sectoral restrictiveness. The table shows particularly high restrictiveness scores for agricultural products and textiles and apparel in each regime, which is consistent with Estevadeordal (2000), Suominen (2004), and Harris (2007) in that the restrictiveness of RoO is driven by the same political economy variables that arbitrate the level of tariffs, particularly in the EU and the United States. Nonpreferential RoO exhibit similar patterns across sectors, communicating the operation of political economy dynamics also multilaterally. Suominen (2004) finds that when the sectoral restrictiveness values are weighted with trade (i.e., when greater "weight" or relevance is assigned to the restrictiveness values in sectors with large trade flows), the outcome is very similar—which may in and of itself be an indication that stringent RoO stifle commerce.[20]

As for the selectivity of RoO, the MERCOSUR model, pertinent to MERCOSUR-Chile and MERCOSUR-Bolivia FTAs, is more general, yet still exhibits more cross-sectoral variation in the restrictiveness of its RoO, than the LAIA model, which is marked by across-the-board change in heading RoO. The generality of the LAIA model is replicated in most Asian and African RoO regimes. However, some newer agreements—such as the Chile-Korea FTA and the SADC agreement—feature high levels of cross-sectoral variation in RoO.[21]

---

[20] See Suominen (2004) for weighted RoO.

[21] Two interesting points arise from these patterns. First, while NAFTA ranks first in Figure 2.2 based on the number of different combinations of qualification criteria, the more recent U.S. agreements (with Panama, Australia, Singapore, Colombia, Peru, Central America, and Chile) feature higher standard deviations of the restrictiveness index. This implies that NAFTA's 80 permutations all group tightly around a more restrictive mean, whereas subsequent agreements must feature a significant relaxing of the restrictiveness of the rules governing many products, resulting in a lower average restrictiveness as well as a higher standard deviation.

Second, the Japan-Singapore FTA ranks first in standard deviation of the restrictiveness index, but in the middle based on the number of rule combinations. This is due to that agreement's specification that all products for which the agreement's annex specifies no specific rule must be wholly obtained.

Table 2.3 ▌ Average Restrictiveness by HS Section in Selected Preferential and Nonpreferential Agreements

HS Section	Andean Community	Argentina-Brazil-Peru	ASEAN	Australia-Singapore	CACM	CAFTA-DR	CARICOM	Chile-China	Chile-Korea	Chile-Mexico	U.S.-Chile	ECOWAS	EU-Chile	Japan-Malaysia	Japan-Singapore	Japan-Thailand	MERCOSUR	MERCOSUR-Chile	Mexico-Bolivia	Mexico-Japan	NAFTA	Pan-Euro	SADC	U.S.-Israel	U.S.-Jordan	U.S.-Singapore	Nonpreferential
1. Live animals	3.0	3.0	5.0	7.0	9.2	9.0	13.6	8.0	10.5	8.4	8.7	1.0	13.6	9.9	16	9.8	3.2	3.1	8.8	9.9	8.5	13.6	16	5.0	5.0	8.6	11.9
2. Vegetable products	3.0	3.0	5.0	7.0	8.4	7.8	10.2	8.0	8.4	8.0	8.2	1.0	11.1	8.0	16	7.8	3.0	3.0	8.0	8.0	7.8	11.1	12.7	5.0	5.0	7.9	14.2
3. Fats and oils	3.0	8.3	5.0	7.0	9.0	8.0	4.70	8.0	11.0	8.1	13.6	1.0	5.0	7.8	16	8.1	6.9	4.2	13.9	8.5	13.6	5.0	5.5	5.0	5.0	13.6	6.0
4. Food, beverage, and tobacco	3.0	7.8	5.0	7.0	8.0	8.6	6.0	6.5	8.2	8.5	9.3	1.0	7.0	10.7	15.6	10.5	4.7	4.4	10.4	11.3	8.4	7.3	5.6	5.0	5.0	8.5	7.5
5. Mineral products	3.0	3.0	5.0	7.0	7.6	6.2	5.9	5.7	7.5	8.6	5.3	1.0	5.1	2.8	14	6.4	3.1	3.0	8.6	8.7	8.6	5.1	6.0	5.0	5.0	5.4	10.4
6. Chemicals	3.0	4.5	5.0	7.0	5.3	3.1	5.2	5.6	4.0	5.0	3.2	1.0	6.7	2.3	10.3	2.6	7.6	3.7	6.1	5.3	5.8	6.7	6.0	5.0	5.0	3.1	4.8
7. Plastics	3.0	3.0	5.0	7.4	6.7	4.5	4.8	5.6	4.1	8.7	6.9	1.0	5.2	3.0	11	3.1	3.0	4.1	8.8	10.1	10.2	5.2	10.7	5.0	5.0	3.6	6.2
8. Leather goods	3.0	3.0	4.9	9.1	5.6	6.6	6.2	5.0	6.9	9.9	7.9	1.0	6.0	10.8	15.3	9.7	3.0	3.0	8.8	5.0	7.2	4.5	5.8	5.0	4.9	7.5	5.9
9. Wood products	3.0	3.0	4.1	7.0	5.8	6.1	7.4	5.9	6.1	7.0	6.0	1.0	5.4	6.0	14.6	6.6	3.0	3.0	6.7	7.1	6.5	5.4	6.1	5.0	5.0	6.1	5.3
10. Pulp and paper	3.0	3.0	5.0	7.0	5.3	8.5	6.0	5.9	6.4	7.6	8.6	1.0	6.2	1.0	7.7	5.3	3.7	4.3	8.0	8.0	9.5	6.2	6.1	5.0	5.0	6.2	6.1
11. Textiles and apparel	3.0	4.5	4.0	9.9	8.0	16.0	6.1	6.0	14.9	3.0	16.1	1.0	4.0	12.9	4.9	12.4	7.4	7.8	16	16.0	16.1	4.0	2.9	5.0	4.0	16.3	6.9
12. Footwear	3.0	3.5	4.8	9.2	10	8.6	8.6	5.5	12.0	12.3	11.2	1.0	6.8	8.1	13.1	8.7	3.7	5.9	12.3	14.2	14.4	6.8	6.9	5.0	4.8	9.7	6.8

(continued on next page)

Table 2.3 ▌ Average Restrictiveness by HS Section in Selected Preferential and Nonpreferential Agreements *(continued)*

HS Section	Andean Community	Argentina-Brazil-Peru	ASEAN	Australia-Singapore	CACM	CAFTA-DR	CARICOM	Chile-China	Chile-Korea	Chile-Mexico	U.S.-Chile	ECOWAS	EU-Chile	Japan-Malaysia	Japan-Singapore	Japan-Thailand	MERCOSUR	MERCOSUR-Chile	Mexico-Bolivia	Mexico-Japan	NAFTA	Pan-Euro	SADC	U.S.-Israel	U.S.-Jordan	U.S.-Singapore	Nonpreferential
13. Stone and glass	3.0	3.0	5.0	7.1	6.7	9.2	5.6	5.3	10.0	10.0	9.1	1.0	5.1	3.3	12.6	3.5	3.1	3.3	9.8	9.9	9.7	5.1	5.6	5.0	4.9	9.3	5.6
14. Jewelry	3.0	3.0	5.0	7.6	6.5	7.5	5.8	5.0	9.4	9.4	9.0	1.0	5.7	4.0	14.0	5.5	3.0	3.0	10.6	9.4	9.2	5.7	5.8	5.0	5.0	9.0	6.7
15. Base metals	3.0	3.3	5.6	7.1	6.3	7.0	6.0	5.3	8.0	9.1	8.4	1.0	5.4	1.1	11.6	3.8	3.3	4.0	9.7	8.7	9.2	5.5	5.2	5.0	5.0	7.6	6.0
16. Machinery and electronic equipment	3.0	4.7	5.0	7.1	4.6	5.5	6.0	5.2	6.1	5.8	6.0	1.0	6.8	1.0	16.0	2.1	5.2	6.3	5.9	5.0	6.0	6.9	6.9	5.0	5.0	5.9	5.8
17. Transportation equipment	3.9	5.3	5.0	7.6	7.1	4.7	6.0	5.2	4.2	4.7	6.0	1.0	3.7	2.3	15.9	3.4	4.9	6.9	7.1	7.9	7.5	5.6	6.8	5.0	5.0	6.4	7.3
18. Optics	2.8	3.2	5.0	7.1	5.0	4.1	6.0	5.0	5.1	6.4	4.8	1.0	6.2	1.1	15.8	2.3	4.4	5.3	6.2	4.9	5.4	6.2	6.7	5.0	5.0	5.3	6.6
19. Arms and ammunition	3.0	3.0	5.0	7.0	6.0	6.1	6.0	6.0	5.6	6.3	6.1	1.0	6	1.0	6.5	3.0	3.0	3.0	6.3	6.1	6.1	6	5	5.0	5.0	6.5	7.2
20. Miscellaneous merchandise	3.1	3.0	4.8	7.2	5.0	5.8	5.9	5.5	6.0	6.7	6.5	1..0	5.5	1.5	12.0	3.1	3.1	5.2	6.9	6.9	6.4	5.5	5.5	5.0	5.0	6.6	6.3
21. Works of art	3.0	3.0	5.0	7.0	4.0	5.4	6.0	5.0	6.0	8.0	4.0	1.0	6.0	1.0	16.0	3.0	3.0	3.0	8.0	8.0	8.0	6.0	6.0	5.0	5.0	5.4	6.1

Source: Authors' calculations on the basis of PTA texts.

Explaining Sources of RoO Restrictiveness and Latest Trends

One of the main findings in the foregoing analysis is that RoO regimes based on NAFTA and the Pan-Euro RoO models are among the most restrictive and most selective in the world. In addition to the patterns emerging from the static analysis, two key trends can be discerned in RoO regimes over time.

First, at the global level, it is the so-called new-generation regimes of the 1990s that score the highest in the RoO restrictiveness and selectivity indices. What may account for this?

One possibility is that MFN liberalization and the growth of global trade have strengthened export lobbies, while antagonizing import-competing interests. Governments–under growing pressures from export interests to effect deeper trade liberalization–have had to develop targetable and effective tools, such as product-specific RoO, to compensate the potential losers from liberalization. In the context of NAFTA, for example, it could be argued that neither the agreement's deep preferences nor the sustained political support for it would have been possible without a stringent RoO regime. Earlier integration schemes, such as LAIA, were less liberalizing; as such, they managed the potential losers' concerns in the tariff schedules, which obviated the need to create a sturdy set of new compensation tools for the PTA. It would thus be no accident that the ambitious liberalization of today's PTAs is accompanied by restrictive RoO.

Another, complementary explanation is that the growing propensity toward fragmentation of global production presents a threat to import-competing intermediate goods providers, who, in turn, see an opportunity in stringent RoO to discourage final goods producers from outsourcing or shifting production abroad (Suominen, 2003). This notion implies that the very formation of PTAs could be driven by protectionist interests.

However, another trend is taking hold in PTAs in the Americas and transpacific PTAs: a reduction in restrictiveness of RoO based on the NAFTA model. Although RoO regimes may carry hidden protectionism, an examination of their evolution over the past few years in the Americas gives reasons for optimism.

First, NAFTA RoO have been undergoing a liberalization process.[22] The review process of the trilateral Working Group on Rules of Origin has completed RoO simplification covering such sectors as alcoholic beverages, petroleum/topped crude, esters of glycerol, pearl jewelry, headphones with microphones, chassis fitted with engines, photocopiers, chemicals, pharmaceuticals, plastics and rubber, motor vehicles and their parts, footwear, copper, various textile products, cocoa preparations, cranberry juice, ores, slag and ash, leather, cork, feathers, glass and glassware, copper and other metals, televisions, and automatic regulating or controlling instruments, among others. The reforms are estimated to extend to more than US$100 billion in trilateral trade.

Second, U.S. RoO regimes have progressively evolved toward a more liberal framework, from NAFTA to the U.S.-Chile PTA, to CAFTA, and then on to the U.S.-Colombia and U.S.-Peru agreements. The last three of these agreements incorporate simpler, more practical, and less restrictive product-specific rules of origin than NAFTA did.

Third, the various regimes designed after NAFTA are fairly similar vis-à-vis one another, in both the types of rules of origin specified and their level of restrictiveness. This can alleviate any potential transaction costs for NAFTA-model adherents that export under preferential terms to two or more NAFTA-model PTAs.

Fourth, the NAFTA-style regimes include terms that alleviate the restrictiveness of product-specific RoO, which in turn helps reduce the costs of compliance. Even more encouraging is the movement toward somewhat higher de minimis levels and the willingness to experiment with diagonal cumulation. As mentioned above, CAFTA stipulates that the member countries can use materials from Mexico or Canada for apparel as if they were CAFTA-originating.

---

[22] The initial set of revised NAFTA rules of origin took effect on 1 January 2003; see Canada Gazette (2003). In July 2004, the trade ministers of the NAFTA countries instructed the trilateral Working Group on Rules of Origin to extend the liberalization drive to all items with a zero most-favored nation tariff for all of the NAFTA members. The August 2007 joint declaration among the three NAFTA countries' heads of state at the Montebello Summit endorsed "an analysis of the free trade agreements that each country has negotiated subsequent to the NAFTA, beginning with those in the Western Hemisphere, including opportunities for innovative provisions on rules of origin" (Joint Statement, 2007).

Fifth, the NAFTA model has now been adopted in numerous free trade agreements. The current adherents will thus find it fairly easy to negotiate, adopt, and implement future free trade agreements. The costs of adjusting to RoO should thus have been incrementally diminishing for a good part of the hemisphere in the past decade.

Finally, negotiators on rules of origin throughout the Americas, and particularly on RoO in PTAs based on the NAFTA model, have proved their willingness to revise existing RoO regimes to make them more flexible. NAFTA's review of its own rules of origin is the clearest example, demonstrating commitment to keeping North America's rules of origin apace with changes in technology and the globalization of production and potentially marking a growing role of export interests in setting trade policy.

More generally, the precision of the NAFTA-model rules of origin can be viewed as superior to the vague definition and subjectivity of past rules of origin. Because the NAFTA regime is based on change in tariff classification requirements, it provides a fairer, more transparent, and more easily verifiable RoO model than regimes based on value content requirements, which paradoxically can be hard to meet in countries with low production costs; furthermore, such regimes are difficult to implement in the face of fluctuations in exchange rates and changes in production costs. Precise rules of origin do not need to be restrictive rules of origin; the ongoing NAFTA review process may well yield rules of origin that are both precise and flexible.

Furthermore, the seeming "RoO borrowing" from one agreement to another could enhance convergence between the NAFTA RoO and other RoO regimes around the world.

What might explain the trend toward loosening the restrictiveness of RoO? Besides the potential strengthening of export lobbies in the Americas since the mid-1990s, there are three potential explanations.

First, the NAFTA partners have had time to learn about the implications of different types of RoO. NAFTA was one of the first regimes in the world to carry RoO tailored individually for each product covered by the agreement; as such, both governments and business lobbies lacked information about RoO's effects when the NAFTA RoO were first negotiated. NAFTA-based exporters and producers are widely seen as having grown to find the agreement's RoO regime excessively restrictive.[23]

Second, the newer regimes may be endogenous to the prior ones. Countries integrating with the United States after Mexico did so—Chile, the Central American countries, Peru, and Colombia—may have sought terms more favorable than those obtained by Mexico in order to bring themselves rapidly to a par with prior U.S. partners in the U.S. preferential market.[24]

A third explanation negates the previous two: the diminished restrictiveness may have little to do with temporal dynamics and simply be the result of other variables, such as bilateral trade volumes and the types of goods produced by the different partners to the agreement. One hypothesis is that the same level of protection provided by a tough rule of origin in NAFTA may have been purchased with a less stringent rule of origin in other regimes. Detailed time-series data on the utilization rates of tariff preferences in the different NAFTA-model PTAs would help illuminate whether this is actually the case.[25]

Caveat to Restrictiveness: Geographical and Input Pools

The loosening of RoO in the Americas is encouraging. Moreover, it is important to note that restrictiveness on paper is one thing: a rule of origin that is restrictive according to the measures discussed in the previous subsection may not be so when the "real" input pool is considered. A major caveat to RoO restrictiveness is thus that RoO are "effectively restrictive" only to the extent that they limit both the input and geographical pools

[23] In theory at least, in cases in which stringent NAFTA RoO have resulted in motivating competitive extraregional producers to move production facilities to the NAFTA region, intraregional producers who initially favored restrictive RoO could also have grown disposed to loosening the RoO regime.

[24] Perhaps less plausibly, the fact that all recent FTAs in the Americas have been negotiated in the shadow of the Free Trade Area of the Americas (FTAA) process may have provided the NAFTA-model adherents with incentives to define a RoO model that is more acceptable to all countries of the hemisphere as the FTAA RoO regime. This, to be sure, assumes that adherents to the NAFTA model favor the adoption of the FTAA.

[25] The pattern would, however, not be universal, given that the EU has implemented the identical RoO regime across all its partners.

from which a producer can draw if it wants a product to have originating status, thus increasing the cost of production (by requiring firms to use higher-cost regional inputs).

The concept of effective restrictiveness is less observable than RoO on paper are, as it requires knowledge of the input-output structure of each product covered by the RoO regime as well as the scale and efficiency of regional production of the relevant inputs in each country within the regime's cumulation zone. However, this is the sense of restrictiveness that matters economically, both for the degree of liberalization achieved within a PTA and for the extent of impact on third parties. As such, it arbitrates the degree to which a producer can globalize production without foregoing the preferential access available in a PTA.

Imagine trade in roasted, ground coffee. In an agreement between the United States and Canada, a rule that requires that all coffee products be derived from originating beans would be highly restrictive, effectively canceling any preferential tariff treatment, as there is no significant production in either country of coffee beans. The same rule applied to trade between the United States and Colombia, on the other hand, though still binding on producers of specialized blends of coffee, would be significantly less onerous, as Colombia is a major global producer of coffee.

"Real" or effective restrictiveness thus depends on the availability of efficient input supplies in member countries of a PTA, which one would expect to be correlated with size of the integrating economies. This issue of the size of the cumulation zone is of crucial importance when the utility of connecting or multilateralizing RoO regimes is analyzed. However, since the effective restrictiveness of a particular rule of origin is so difficult to observe, any broad analysis must move forward with measures of observed restrictiveness (that is, restrictiveness as inferred from the text of the rule alone) as a useful proxy, bearing in mind that it is a proxy and not an ideal measure.

Figure 2.5 illustrates the relationship between a PTA's observed restrictiveness and the size of its cumulation zone, measured as the combined GDP of the agreement's member countries. A stylized fact that emerges clearly from examination of the figure is that observed restrictiveness is increasing in the size of the cumulation zone. Two alternative

Figure 2.5 | Restrictiveness versus Cumulation Zone

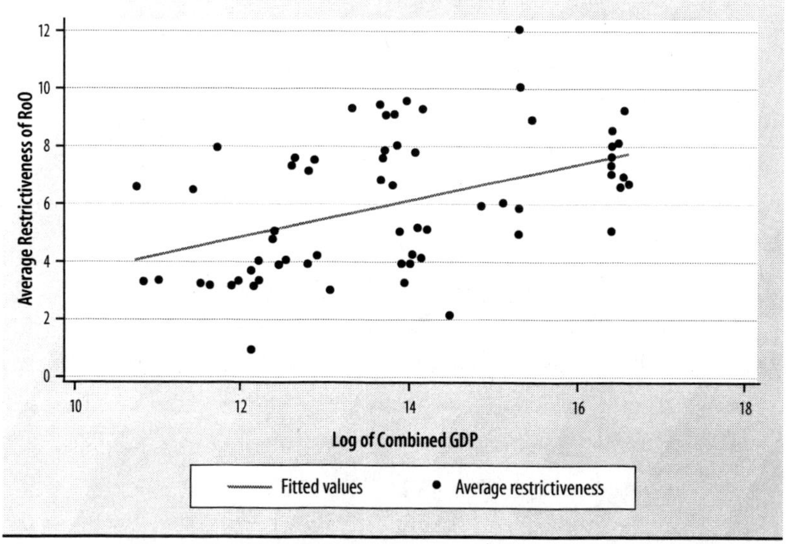

conclusions can be drawn from this. One is that large, dominant partners such as the United States and the European Union tend to dictate more restrictive rules of origin in their PTAs, whereas developing countries tend to negotiate less restrictive regimes. This interpretation is perhaps the most popular (see, for example, Cadot et al., 2006), and it certainly is not difficult to find anecdotal evidence to support it.

However, such a conclusion ignores the fact that observed restrictiveness is not strictly linked to effective restrictiveness across agreements. A rule with high observed restrictiveness in an agreement with the United States or Europe still allows a firm to source inputs from a vast partner country in the cumulation zone, and the likelihood of that rule's precluding the use of inputs from the global low-cost source is lower (though not necessarily zero) than in the case of a rule with the same level of observed restrictiveness in a PTA joining two small developing countries.

The alternative conclusion to be drawn is that a PTA's average effective restrictiveness may have no relationship, or even a negative relationship, with the economic size of the agreement's cumulation zone. This is because the greater availability of inputs implied by the larger economy of the cumulation zone results in rules with greater *observed* restrictiveness in fact having lower *effective* restrictiveness.

Selectivity of RoO Regimes

Selective RoO (RoO that vary in type within a regime) present a further caveat for the analysis of restrictiveness and divergence for a number of reasons.

First, more selective rules are more difficult to administer. If a country is party to several PTAs that each feature across-the-board rules (that is, each with zero selectivity), there will never be a problem of confusion as to what rule applies to a given product or an incentive to misclassify a product to take advantage of a different rule. In short, administration under zero selectivity is quite straightforward.

Compare this case to that of a country party to several PTAs that each feature selective, complex sets of rules of origin. Clearly, in such a case, the opposite will be true. Administering these rules of origin will require customs authorities to take much greater care with identification of the correct rule and with correct classification of the product (as well as correct classification of its inputs, if the rule is based on CTC).

Second, when overlapping regimes are more selective, the rules for a given product are more likely to vary across regimes, potentially requiring firms to adjust their sourcing strategies to accommodate different export markets. The resulting costs could be significant.

Selectivity of the RoO in a bilateral agreement could be hypothesized to be directly related to the complexity of the bilateral trade relationship (Harris, 2007). It is broadly recognized that the level of restrictiveness of rules of origin is generally affected by political economy variables. Regardless of the specific political economy model employed, the variables that will likely determine the rule of origin for a particular product in a specific PTA will focus on the levels of its production in the countries participating in the agreement as well as the scale and efficiency of production of its inputs both within and outside of the agreement's cumulation zone. Consequently, the number of products covered by a particular PTA for which the political economy pressures reach some minimum threshold for influencing the negotiations of the product-specific rule will depend on the number of products actively traded among the participating countries of the agreement.

Selectivity of a PTA's origin regime is thus dependent on the complexity of the pattern of trade among the members of the agreement (as measured by the number of HS subheadings in which products are traded). Figure 2.6 illustrates the degree to which this is observed in the data.

The strong outliers in this relationship are interesting cases. The points in the figure representing low numbers of traded subheadings and high variation in rules of origin are most notably the Mexico-Bolivia (85 products), U.S.-Morocco (527 products), and Canada-Costa Rica (1,050 products) FTAs. The U.S.-Morocco agreement features an across-the-board VC requirement, except for in the case of textiles and a small set of products that seem to have been of particular interest to Morocco (some fruits and vegetables, coffee, and some auto parts). A large difference in the restrictiveness of the general rule and the rules for those products identified for special treatment seems to be generating the especially high standard deviation figures for that agreement.

Figure 2.6 | Complexity of RoO and of Trade Patterns

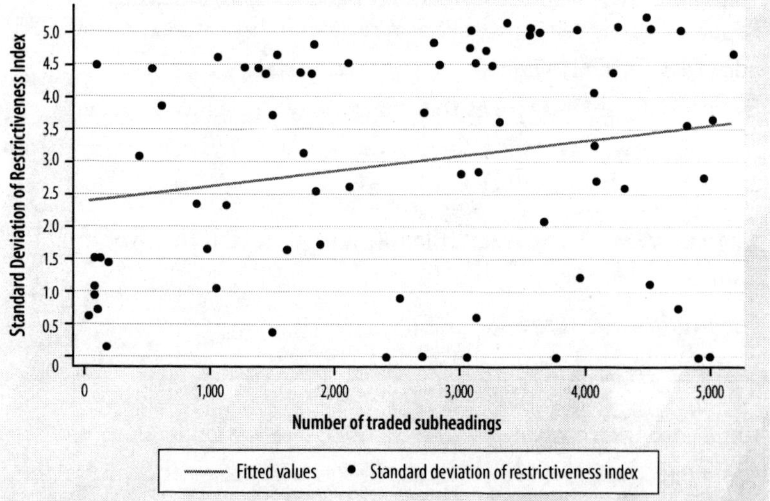

In the opposite corner of the figure, the notable outliers are the larger Asian agreements (the ASEAN, ASEAN-China, and Bangkok agreements) and the U.S.-Israel agreement. All of these agreements feature across-the-board VC rules, except the ASEAN agreement, which has a relatively small number of specific rules for products (primarily steel, textiles, and wood). The choice of an across-the-board VC regime is a bit harder to explain. One possible reason for such a choice might be that many of these countries maintain relatively low MFN tariffs or very limited preferential tariff liberalization, and so the levels of preference are quite low, necessitating only minimum rules. This interpretation is backed up by anecdotal evidence of relatively low preference utilization rates in ASEAN. In short, selectivity of rules of origin is increasing in the diversity of products traded among PTA members. The more product-specific interests there are to satisfy in the origin negotiations, the more different outcomes we are likely to find.

Restrictiveness and selectivity within RoO regimes imply that as regions of overlapping PTAs pursue convergence, forming groups of greater economic size and with a wider variety of traded goods, we should expect a tendency toward greater observed restrictiveness and selectivity. Both of these are potentially problematic for the international trading system. Greater observed restrictiveness, although not necessarily implying greater effective restrictiveness, still amounts to increasing barriers to trade among regions. Greater selectivity in origin regimes implies increasing difficulty of administration and thus greater potential uncertainty, especially in developing countries. Chapter 7 strives to establish ways to reduce selectivity within regimes—and induce some form of convergence in RoO across regimes.

Regime-Wide Measures: "Flexibilizing" Restrictive RoO

Facilitation Measures

Though it is possible to generate restrictiveness values for product-specific RoO, getting a complete picture of restrictiveness requires consideration of further, regime-wide RoO provisions. Indeed, as shown previously, most RoO regimes employ several regime-wide mechanisms, such as de minimis and cumulation, that can add flexibility to the application of the product-specific RoO and consequently attenuate their restrictiveness—and even render them nonbinding.

Suominen (2004) captures the combined effect of such mechanisms by developing a regime-wide "facilitation index" (Facil index) based on five components: de minimis, diagonal cumulation, full cumulation, drawback, and self-certification. The maximum index value of 5 results when the permitted level of de minimis is 5 percent or higher and when the processes represented by the other four variables are permitted by the RoO regime in question.

Figure 2.7 graphs the Facil index values for selected PTAs. The index values for Pan-Euro and NAFTA models are nearly at a par; the difference here is produced by coding NAFTA as allowing drawback, as it did for the first seven years. The Canada-Israel agreement is found to have the most "permissive" regimes, the former thanks to drawback and diagonal and full cumulation, and the latter because of self-certification, drawback, and cumulation with the United States. Meanwhile, many regimes with across-the-board RoO neither provide for de minimis nor feature many regime-wide provisions of flexibility; the regime-wide rule occurring most often in these PTAs is drawback. Indeed, that regimes with the most stringent RoO and the highest degree of sectoral selectivity in their RoO feature the highest facilitation values may evince counterlobbying by producers jeopardized by stringent product-specific RoO.

Figure 2.7 | Facil Index for Selected PTAs

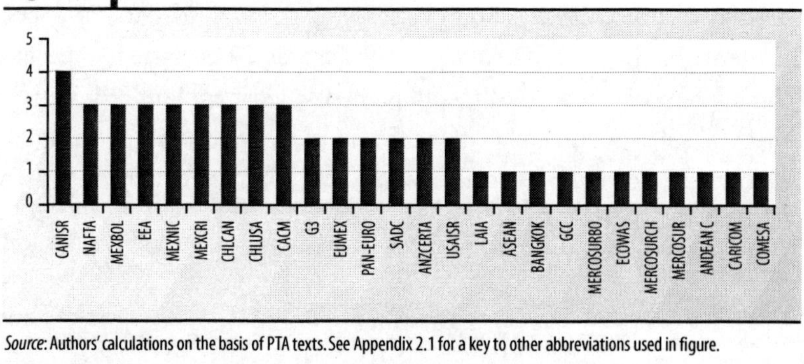

Source: Authors' calculations on the basis of PTA texts. See Appendix 2.1 for a key to other abbreviations used in figure.

In Chapter 5 we find that Facil components alleviate the negative trade effects of restrictive product-specific RoO. The regimes for several agreements have also experimented with innovative mechanisms to alleviate supply shortages and to aid developing member countries of the agreements in complying with the agreements' RoO.[26]

Further Agents of Flexibility

Many RoO regimes include further provisions that in effect alleviate the impact of stringent RoO. Although most regimes employing these provisions make them applicable to all members, some regimes implement them asymmetrically: for instance, to accommodate country-specific idiosyncrasies in production structures or to provide greater leniency to a developing member country when development levels differ drastically among the parties to the agreement. These provisions can be of great importance particularly to countries with a limited production base and/or in the absence of relatively cheap inputs and production processes in the PTA area. We discuss four types of such provisions in turn.

First, some regimes have adopted what are in many cases highly detailed product-specific provisions that allow for phasing in of the RoO. The MERCOSUR-Chile FTA provides a seven-year adjustment period for Paraguay to start applying the FTA's import content RoO of 40 percent in selected headings across a host of sectors such as food products, chemicals, plastics, textiles, apparel, footwear, base metals, and machinery. During the adjustment period, Paraguay applies a 60 percent import content rule. The MERCOSUR-Bolivia FTA allows Bolivia to export to MERCOSUR countries selected goods at 50 percent import content for the first five years, and others at 60 percent for the first three years, as opposed to the 40 percent import content requirement that will subsequently take effect. For its part, Paraguay is permitted to export to Bolivia at 60 percent import content for the first three years of the agreement.

---

[26] See, for instance, Suominen (2004) or Estevadeordal and Suominen (2006) for details.

The EU's extra-European agreements with Mexico and Chile also allow for some product-specific deviations from the Pan-Euro standard for a certain period of time.[27] In the case of the EU-Mexico FTA, these pertain to one whole HS chapter (knitted apparel) and to 25 headings (or subheadings) in chemicals, textiles, footwear, machinery, and vehicles and endure from two to six years prior to converging to the benchmark RoO. The RoO for footwear are more restrictive for the EU than in its other FTAs: the same RoO apply as in the EU's FTAs with Chile and South Africa up to a certain quota, beyond which the rest of the EU's exports to the Mexican market are regulated by much more stringent RoO. RoO phase-ins are fewer in the case of the EU-Chile FTA than in the EU's other FTAs, pertaining only to textiles and bicycles and only for the first three years of the agreement.

A second means of adding leniency to an agreement's RoO protocol are permanent deviations for a country or a set of countries from the RoO regime that would otherwise apply. For example, the RoO of the Andean Community agreement allow the less-developed members, Bolivia and Ecuador, to use nonoriginating components for up to 60 percent of the value of an originating final good, as opposed to the maximum 40 percent applicable to the other members. LAIA allows its less-developed partners to use nonoriginating components for up to 60 percent of the value of originating final goods, as opposed to the 50 percent criterion applying to the rest of the members. In COMESA, products of importance to economic development to the partners (selected headings in mineral products, chemicals, machinery, and optical instruments) enjoy a 25 percent RVC requirement, as opposed to the across-the-board 35 percent RVC requirement that otherwise applies.

Additionally, the EU-Mexico and EU-Chile FTAs allow for permanent deviations from the single-list Pan-Euro model. In these cases, the deviations are rather minor and apply only to selected industrial products (see Estevadeordal and Suominen, 2003). Nonetheless, they indicate that Mexico and Chile did achieve some favorable sectoral outcomes in the RoO bargaining.

---

[27] For a detailed treatment, see Estevadeordal and Suominen (2003).

Third, some RoO regimes have created innovative optional means of calculating value content to reduce the regimes' restrictiveness. In SADC, a more-developed member may allow a less-developed member to count processes as originating that are usually left outside the calculation of value content under the SADC agreement. Regimes modeled after NAFTA provide a number of optional ways for calculating RVC in vehicles when the producer uses predefined intermediate goods from Chapters 40 and 84, as well as for calculating the RVC for these intermediate goods.[28]

However, it is Singapore's FTAs that incorporate perhaps the most innovative and comprehensive mechanisms to add flexibility to the calculation of value content. These mechanisms are designed to help the many Singaporean industries that have extensive outsourcing ties, especially in Southeast Asia, to qualify for the preferential treatment provided by Singapore's FTA partners. The two key mechanisms that Singapore's FTAs employ for this purpose are outward processing, recognized in all of Singapore's FTAs, and the Integrated Sourcing Initiative, incorporated in the U.S.-Singapore FTA.

The concept of OP enables Singapore to outsource part of the manufacturing process, usually the lower-value-added or less labor-intensive activities, to neighboring countries, yet to count the value of Singaporean production done prior to the outsourcing activity as local, Singaporean content in meeting the RoO required by the export market. Figure 2.8 illustrates the process. Although the OP concept applies only to products whose origin is determined under a particular FTA by a value-added rule, it is credited with having encouraged outsourcing of labor-intensive and low-value processes and retaining higher-value activities in Singapore.

---

[28] The producer of a vehicle may average the calculation of RVC over the fiscal year for any one of the following categories: (1) the same model line of vehicles in the same class of vehicles produced in the same plant in the territory of a party; (2) the same class of motor vehicles produced in the same plant in the territory of a party; or (3) the same model line of motor vehicles produced in the territory of a party. Meanwhile, the producer can calculate the RVC of intermediate goods for vehicles by (1) averaging the calculation over any quarter or month or the fiscal year of the motor vehicle producer to whom the good is sold, if the good is sold as an aftermarket part; (2) calculating the average separately for any or all goods sold to one or more motor vehicle producers; or (3) calculating the average separately for those goods that are exported to the territory of the other party.

Figure 2.8 | Operation of Outward Processing in Singapore's FTAs

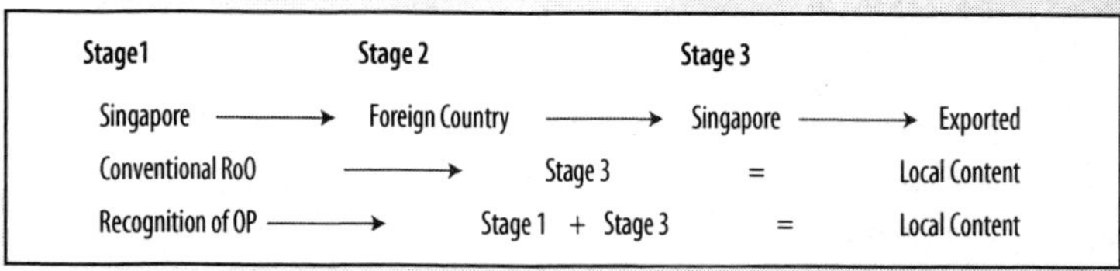

The ISI is designed to reflect the economic realities of globally distributed production linkages and to further encourage U.S. multinationals to take advantage of outsourcing opportunities in the ASEAN countries. It applies to nonsensitive, globalized sectors, such as information technologies. Under the ISI scheme, certain information technology components and medical devices are not subject to RoO when shipped from either of the FTA partners to the other.

The fourth mechanism by which some agreements increase the leniency of their RoO regimes is tariff preference levels (TPLs). TPLs allow goods that do not otherwise satisfy the RoO protocol for those goods to qualify, up to some prespecified annual quotas, for the preferential treatment afforded those goods under the PTA. Above these quota levels, nonoriginating goods become subject to the importer's MFN tariff. Most commonly applying to textiles and apparel, TPLs are employed particularly in NAFTA-model RoO regimes. They are generally extended by all agreement parties to all other agreement parties and are made available to producers on a first-come, first-served basis until the quota is exhausted.

NAFTA provides TPLs for such nonoriginating products as cotton and man-made fiber apparel, wool apparel, man-made fiber fabrics, and fiber-spun yarn. Depending on the product category, the TPLs reach up to 80 million square meters equivalent (SMEs) for Canadian and 45 million SMEs for Mexican exports to the U.S. market, and 12 million SMEs for selected U.S. exports to Mexico. The RoO regime in the most recent agreement signed by the United States, CAFTA, offers TPLs for only two of the Central American member countries, Costa Rica and Nicaragua, and phases them out quickly. In the case of Costa Rica, TPLs are set at 500,000

SMEs, limited to wool, and due to expire two years after the agreement enters into force. Nicaragua's TPLs start at 100 million SMEs and are phased out in equal annual cuts over the agreement's first five years.

Still other regimes employ what could be viewed as a modified form of TPLs, allocating quotas not fully free of RoO, but against some more lenient product-specific RoO. For instance, the SADC provides quotas under more lenient RoO for the textile and apparel exports of Malawi, Mozambique, Tanzania, and Zambia to the SACU region for a period of five years from the initiation of the SADC agreement.

Conclusion

This chapter has presented a novel descriptive and analytical mapping of preferential rules of origin around the world. We have (1) reviewed the types of RoO used around the world; (2) drawn comparisons of the structure of RoO across a host of PTAs; (3) presented methodologies for constructing generalizable measurements for the degree of restrictiveness and selectivity of product-specific RoO and the level of flexibility provided by the various regime-wide RoO; and (4) explored RoO trends over time.

An implicit lesson of this chapter is that restrictiveness of RoO cannot be understood without consideration of all RoO regime components, whether product-specific or regime-wide, much less the economic features of the integrating economies. We have also provided cursory evidence that RoO are to an important extent driven by political economy dynamics. The analytical tools developed here can be employed beyond existing contributions in order to evaluate the politics behind the definition of RoO as well as the economic effects of RoO—something the next four chapters endeavor to do. Chapter 7 strives to put forth constructive policy proposals for dealing with the maze of RoO and their potentially negative consequences.

More generally, we hope that this chapter inspires further efforts to disaggregate and dissect the various PTA disciplines. Such a task is central for developing a full understanding of the contractual diversity in the rapidly proliferating PTA universe, and, ultimately, for making recommendations for designing PTAs in ways that are conducive to unfettered global commerce.

Appendix 2.1 PTAs Considered in the Study

Pan-Euro
EU-Chile (EUCHL)
EU-Mexico (EUMEX)
EU-South Africa (EUZAF)
U.S.-Chile (CHLUSA)
NAFTA
U.S.-Colombia (USACOL)
U.S.-Panama (USAPAN)
U.S.-Peru (USAPER)
Argentina-Brazil-Peru (ARGBRAPE)
Paraguay-Peru (PRYPER)
Uruguay-Peru (URYPER)
Argentina-Colombia (ARGCOL)
Argentina-Ecuador (ARGECU)
Argentina-Venezuela (ARGVEN)
Brazil-Colombia (BRACOL)
Brazil-Ecuador (BRAECU)
Brazil-Venezuela (BRAVEN)
Paraguay-Colombia (PRYCOL)
Paraguay-Ecuador (PRYECU)
Paraguay-Venezuela (PRYVEN)
Uruguay-Colombia (URYCOL)
Uruguay-Ecuador (URYECU)
Uruguay-Venezuela (URYVEN)
CACM
CACM-Dominican Republic (CACM-DR)
CAFTA-Dominican Republic (CAFTA-DR)
Canada-Costa Rica (CANCRI)
Canada-Israel (CANISR)
Andean Community (ANDEAN C)
CARICOM
Chile-Canada (CHLCAN)
Chile-CACM (CHLCACM)
Chile-Mexico (CHLMEX)
Chile-Peru (CHLPER)
G3
MERCOSUR
MERCOSUR-Bolivia (MERCOSURBO)
MERCOSUR-Chile (MERCOSURCH)
Mexico-Bolivia (MEXBOL)
Mexico-Costa Rica (MEXCRI)
Mexico-Nicaragua (MEXNIC)
Mexico-Northern Triangle (MEXNT)
Mexico-Uruguay (MEXURY)
Chile-Colombia (CHLCOL)
Chile-Ecuador (CHLECU)
U.S.-Australia (USAAUS)
U.S.-Bahrain (USABAH)
U.S.-Israel (USAISR)
U.S.-Jordan (USAJOR)
U.S.-Korea (USAKOR)
U.S.-Morocco (USAMOR)
U.S.-Singapore (USASING)
U.S.-Oman (USAOMN)
ASEAN
ASEAN-China (ASEANCHN)

ASEAN-Korea (ASEANKOR)
Australia–New Zealand (ANZCERTA)
Australia-Singapore (AUSSING)
Australia-Thailand (AUSTHA)
Bangkok
Chile-China (CHLCHN)
Chile-Korea (CHLKOR)
COMESA
ECOWAS
Japan-Malaysia (JPNMYS)
Japan-Singapore (JPNSING)
Japan-Thailand (JPNTHA)
Mexico-Japan (MEXJAP)
P4
SADC
SAFTA
Thailand-New Zealand (THANZ)
Peru-Thailand (PERTHA)
GCC

Appendix 2.2 RoO Combinations around the World, by Regime

Table 2A-1 RoO Combinations around the World, by Regime

(percentages)	Andean Community	ANZCERTA	Argentina-Brazil-Peru	Argentina-Venezuela	Argentina-Colombia	Argentina-Ecuador	ASEAN	ASEAN-China	ASEAN-Korea	Australia-Singapore	Australia-Thailand	Bangkok	Brazil-Colombia	Brazil-Ecuador	Brazil-Venezuela
NC + TECH	2.0	0.0	18.1	12.0	14.0	14.6	16.0		8.2		0.1		17.1	17.6	12.1
NC + VC	1.4	0.1	11.1	13.3	13.9	13.6	79.4		76.3		0.0		14.1	14.2	14.2
NC + VC + TECH								100.0	0.1	100.0		100.0			
Wholly Obtained							0.0		0.5		0.2				
Subtotal	**3.3**	**0.1**	**29.2**	**25.2**	**27.8**	**28.3**	**95.4**	**100.0**	**85.1**	**100.0**	**0.4**	**100.0**	**31.2**	**31.8**	**26.3**
CI		0.0													
CI + TECH											0.0				
CI + VC															
CI + VC + TECH															
CI + ECTC															
CI + ECTC + TECH															
Subtotal	**0.0**	**0.0**	**0.0**	**0.0**	**0.0**	**0.0**	**0.0**	**0.0**	**0.0**	**0.0**	**0.0**	**0.0**	**0.0**	**0.0**	**0.0**

(continued on next page)

Table 2A-1 RoO Combinations around the World, by Regime *(continued)*

(percentages)	Andean Community	ANZCERTA	Argentina-Brazil-Peru	Argentina-Venezuela	Argentina-Colombia	Argentina-Ecuador	ASEAN	ASEAN-China	ASEAN-Korea	Australia-Singapore	Australia-Thailand	Bangkok	Brazil-Colombia	Brazil-Ecuador	Brazil-Venezuela
CS		25.1					1.9		1.1		22.4				
CS + TECH		0.3									0.2				
CS + VC		0.2									0.2				
CS + VC + TECH															
CS + ECTC		5.1									5.9				
CS + ECTC + TECH															
CS + ECTC + VC															
Subtotal	**0.0**	**30.7**	**0.0**	**0.0**	**0.0**	**0.0**	**1.9**	**0.0**	**1.1**	**0.0**	**28.8**	**0.0**	**0.0**	**0.0**	**0.0**
CH	96.7	31.8	59.8	65.6	68.6	68.3	2.0		2.4		29.5		65.2	64.9	64.6
CH + TECH		0.0	6.8						0.3		1.5				
CH + VC		6.8		5.7					0.1		4.1		0.2		5.7
CH + VC + TECH															
CH + ECTC		7.1		0.6	0.6	0.6	0.5		0.4		5.3		0.6	0.6	0.6

(continued on next page)

Table 2A-1 RoO Combinations around the World, by Regime *(continued)*

(percentages)	Andean Community	ANZCERTA	Argentina-Brazil-Peru	Argentina-Venezuela	Argentina-Colombia	Argentina-Ecuador	ASEAN	ASEAN-China	ASEAN-Korea	Australia-Singapore	Australia-Thailand	Bangkok	Brazil-Colombia	Brazil-Ecuador	Brazil-Venezuela
CH + ECTC + TECH															
CH + ECTC + VC		3.6									6.2				
Subtotal	**96.7**	**49.4**	**66.6**	**72.0**	**69.3**	**68.9**	**2.5**	**0.0**	**3.2**	**0.0**	**46.7**	**0.0**	**66.1**	**65.5**	**70.9**
CC		14.7	2.4	1.9	2.0	2.0	0.2		4.7		12.8		1.9	1.9	1.9
CC + TECH		2.0							4.7						
CC + VC		0.2		0.1	0.1	0.1			0.0		3.7		0.1	0.1	0.1
CC + VC + TECH		2.6									5.6				
CC + ECTC		0.2	1.8	0.8	0.8	0.7					2.0		0.7	0.7	0.8
CC + ECTC + TECH									1.1						
CC + ECTC + VC															
Subtotal	**0.0**	**19.7**	**4.3**	**2.8**	**2.9**	**2.8**	**0.2**	**0.0**	**10.5**	**0.0**	**24.1**	**0.0**	**2.7**	**2.7**	**2.8**
TOTAL	100.0	100.0	100.0	100.0	100.0	100.0	100.0	100.0	100.0	100.0	100.0	100.0	100.0	100.0	100.0

(continued on next page)

Table 2A-1 RoO Combinations around the World, by Regime *(continued)*

(percentages)	CACM	CACM-DR	CAFTA-DR	Canada-Costa Rica	CARICOM	Chile-CACM	Chile-Canada	Chile-China	Chile-Colombia	Chile-Ecuador	Chile-Korea	Chile-Mexico	Chile-Peru	Chile-U.S.	COMESA
NC + TECH	0.0	0.3	0.5		12.4	8.2	0.0		1.3	9.3		0.1	0.3		
NC + VC			0.6		25.9	0.1		88.0	0.2		0.6	0.6	0.6		100.0
NC + VC + TECH										0.0					
Wholly Obtained		11.4			5.6	1.7	0.0							0.0	
Subtotal	**0.0**	**11.6**	**1.1**	**0.0**	**43.9**	**10.0**	**0.0**	**88.0**	**1.5**	**9.4**	**0.6**	**0.6**	**0.9**	**0.0**	**100.0**
CI	0.2	0.1	0.1	5.0			1.0					0.4		0.0	
CI + TECH				0.1			0.0								
CI + VC				0.5											
CI + VC + TECH				0.0											
CI + ECTC			0.0	0.4			0.2					0.3			
CI + ECTC + TECH			0.1	0.0	0.1										
Subtotal	**0.2**	**0.1**	**0.2**	**6.2**	**0.1**	**0.0**	**1.2**	**0.0**	**0.0**	**0.0**	**0.0**	**0.8**	**0.0**	**0.0**	**0.0**
CS	30.2	13.7	19.9	13.6		19.1	10.3		0.3		1.6	3.0	0.0	15.8	
CS + TECH	0.9	0.4	0.2				0.1							0.2	

(continued on next page)

Table 2A-1 RoO Combinations around the World, by Regime *(continued)*

(percentages)	CACM	CACM-DR	CAFTA-DR	Canada-Costa Rica	CARICOM	Chile-CACM	Chile-Canada	Chile-China	Chile-Colombia	Chile-Ecuador	Chile-Korea	Chile-Mexico	Chile-Peru	Chile-U.S.	COMESA
CS + VC			0.2			0.0	0.1		0.1		2.0	0.8		0.3	
CS + VC + TECH				0.0											
CS + ECTC	0.2	0.6	6.1	1.0		0.5	4.4				0.3	2.3		6.3	
CS + ECTC + TECH							0.0							0.1	
CS + ECTC + VC							0.0				0.2			0.0	
Subtotal	**31.3**	**14.6**	**26.3**	**14.7**	**0.0**	**19.6**	**15.0**	**0.0**	**0.4**	**0.0**	**4.0**	**6.1**	**0.0**	**22.8**	**0.0**
CH	37.5	52.0	24.3	37.6	53.0	54.3	17.5	0.9	83.9	90.6	44.4	46.2	82.9	24.1	
CH + TECH	0.5	0.9	1.3	0.0	0.2	0.6	0.2					0.0		1.3	
CH + VC			1.2	2.8			3.4		0.0		4.6	0.3		2.0	
CH + VC + TECH				0.1											
CH + ECTC	6.7	6.7	8.7	10.1	1.5	0.3	18.5		0.7		10.8	16.0	5.8	11.2	
CH + ECTC + TECH							0.1							0.1	
CH + ECTC + VC			0.2				0.5		0.0		0.5	0.5		0.4	
Subtotal	**44.8**	**59.6**	**35.7**	**50.6**	**54.6**	**55.2**	**40.3**	**0.9**	**84.6**	**90.6**	**60.2**	**63.0**	**88.7**	**39.1**	**0.0**

(continued on next page)

Table 2A-1 RoO Combinations around the World, by Regime *(continued)*

(percentages)	CACM	CACM-DR	CAFTA-DR	Canada-Costa Rica	CARICOM	Chile-CACM	Chile-Canada	Chile-China	Chile-Colombia	Chile-Ecuador	Chile-Korea	Chile-Mexico	Chile-Peru	Chile-U.S.	COMESA
CC	21.1	6.3	22.3	16.8	1.4	15.2	28.3	11.2	11.7		22.9	28.2	1.9	23.0	
CC + TECH		0.0	0.5	0.1			0.1				0.0	0.0		0.8	
CC + VC			0.1						0.1		1.7	0.6		0.0	
CC + VC + TECH															
CC + ECTC	2.6	7.7	8.2	5.9			9.5		1.7		4.9	0.6	2.7	8.5	
CC + ECTC + TECH			5.7	5.8			5.6				5.7		5.8	5.9	
CC + ECTC + VC															
Subtotal	**23.7**	**14.1**	**36.7**	**28.6**	**1.4**	**15.2**	**43.5**	**11.2**	**13.5**	**0.0**	**35.2**	**29.5**	**10.4**	**38.1**	**0.0**
TOTAL	100.0	100.0	100.0	100.0	100.0	100.0	100.0	100.0	100.0	100.0	100.0	100.0	100.0	100.0	100.0

(continued on next page)

Table 2A-1 RoO Combinations around the World, by Regime *(continued)*

(percentages)	ECOWAS	EU-Chile	EU-Mexico	EU-South Africa	G3	GCC	Japan-Malaysia	Japan-Singapore	Japan-Thailand	MERCOSUR	MERCOSUR-Bolivia	MERCOSUR-Chile	Mexico-Bolivia	Mexico-Costa Rica	Mexico-Japan
NC + TECH		19.0	19.3	18.9	0.1		0.2	13.0	1.2	4.8	21.9	21.2		0.0	0.2
NC + VC		11.7	11.0	11.1	0.4		0.6		0.4	13.7	20.2	22.3	0.0	0.0	0.2
NC + VC + TECH		4.3	3.8	4.2		100.0									
Wholly Obtained		7.5	7.1	7.4				61.7							
Subtotal	**0.0**	**42.4**	**41.2**	**41.5**	**0.5**	**100.0**	**0.8**	**74.7**	**1.7**	**18.5**	**42.1**	**43.5**	**0.0**	**0.1**	**0.5**
CI		0.3	0.3	0.3	0.1								0.4		
CI + TECH		1.6	1.4	1.6											
CI + VC					0.5										
CI + VC + TECH															
CI + ECTC		1.0	0.6	1.0	0.3								0.3	0.0	0.0
CI + ECTC + TECH		0.3	0.4	0.3											
Subtotal	**0.0**	**3.3**	**2.7**	**3.2**	**0.9**	**0.0**	**0.0**	**0.0**	**0.0**	**0.0**	**0.0**	**0.0**	**0.7**	**0.0**	**0.0**
CS	100.0				1.7		50.2		19.1				2.9	2.9	8.5
CS + TECH					0.1									0.0	

(continued on next page)

Table 2A-1 RoO Combinations around the World, by Regime *(continued)*

(percentages)	ECOWAS	EU-Chile	EU-Mexico	EU-South Africa	G3	GCC	Japan-Malaysia	Japan-Singapore	Japan-Thailand	MERCOSUR	MERCOSUR-Bolivia	MERCOSUR-Chile	Mexico-Bolivia	Mexico-Costa Rica	Mexico-Japan
CS + VC					4.7		0.2						4.2	4.3	0.1
CS + VC + TECH															
CS + ECTC					1.5			0.0	0.1				2.0	1.7	2.0
CS + ECTC + TECH															
CS + ECTC + VC					0.2										0.0
Subtotal	**100.0**	**0.0**	**0.0**	**0.0**	**8.2**	**0.0**	**50.4**	**0.0**	**19.2**	**0.0**	**0.0**	**0.0**	**9.1**	**8.9**	**10.7**
CH		21.8	21.1	21.2	26.0		14.3	18.6	39.1	63.8	45.1	45.8	25.1	24.8	25.4
CH + TECH		14.0	13.7	14.8	0.1		0.2	0.2	0.1	9.5		0.0	0.0	0.0	0.1
CH + VC		13.0	12.4	13.3	2.2		0.4	0.0	0.2	8.1	12.7	10.7	2.7	2.8	3.2
CH + VC + TECH		0.3	0.4	0.5											
CH + ECTC		1.0	2.1	1.3	18.3		2.5	5.2	7.6				18.6	19.1	13.3
CH + ECTC + TECH		0.1	0.5	0.1			5.5		0.2				0.3	0.3	
CH + ECTC + VC			0.4		0.5			0.0					0.5	0.5	0.5
Subtotal	**0.0**	**50.2**	**50.6**	**51.2**	**47.1**	**0.0**	**23.0**	**24.0**	**47.2**	**81.5**	**57.9**	**56.5**	**47.2**	**47.5**	**42.5**

(continued on next page)

Table 2A-1 RoO Combinations around the World, by Regime *(continued)*

(percentages)	ECOWAS	EU-Chile	EU-Mexico	EU-South Africa	G3	GCC	Japan-Malaysia	Japan-Singapore	Japan-Thailand	MERCOSUR	MERCOSUR-Bolivia	MERCOSUR-Chile	Mexico-Bolivia	Mexico-Costa Rica	Mexico-Japan
CC		4.2	4.2	4.1	29.3		13.7		19.8				29.5	31.6	30.3
CC + TECH			1.3		0.0		8.0		5.2				0.0		0.1
CC + VC					0.2								0.4	0.3	
CC + VC + TECH															
CC + ECTC			0.0		8.0		3.7	1.3	5.8				7.2	5.7	10.0
CC + ECTC + TECH					5.9		0.4		1.1				5.7	5.9	5.9
CC + ECTC + VC													0.1		
Subtotal	**0.0**	**4.2**	**5.5**	**4.1**	**43.3**	**0.0**	**25.8**	**1.3**	**32.0**	**0.0**	**0.0**	**0.0**	**42.9**	**43.5**	**46.3**
TOTAL	100.0	100.0	100.0	100.0	100.0	100.0	100.0	100.0	100.0	100.0	100.0	100.0	100.0	100.0	100.0

(continued on next page)

Table 2A-1 RoO Combinations around the World, by Regime *(continued)*

(percentages)	Mexico-Northern Triangle	Mexico-Nicaragua	Mexico-Uruguay	NAFTA	P4	Pan-Euro	Paraguay-Colombia	Paraguay-Ecuador	Paraguay-Peru	Paraguay-Venezuela	Peru-Thailand	SADC	SAFTA	Thailand-New Zealand	Uruguay-Colombia
NC + TECH		0.0	0.1	0.4		18.8		8.4	5.5	0.5	0.6	15.2		3.9	0.5
NC + VC		0.0	0.2			11.1		0.0				23.8			
NC + VC + TECH						4.3						0.8			
Wholly Obtained				0.0		7.4					3.3	8.9			
Subtotal	**0.0**	**0.0**	**0.3**	**0.4**	**0.0**	**41.5**	**0.0**	**8.4**	**5.5**	**0.5**	**3.9**	**48.6**	**0.0**	**3.9**	**0.5**
CI	0.6	0.4	0.9	0.8		0.3						1.9		0.2	
CI + TECH				0.0		1.6					0.1				
CI + VC															
CI + VC + TECH															
CI + ECTC	0.4	0.3	0.3	0.4		1.1						0.5			
CI + ECTC + TECH						0.3									
Subtotal	**1.0**	**0.7**	**1.2**	**1.1**	**0.0**	**3.2**	**0.0**	**0.0**	**0.0**	**0.0**	**0.1**	**2.4**	**0.0**	**0.2**	**0.0**

(continued on next page)

Table 2A-1 RoO Combinations around the World, by Regime *(continued)*

(percentages)	Mexico-Northern Triangle	Mexico-Nicaragua	Mexico-Uruguay	NAFTA	P4	Pan-Euro	Paraguay-Colombia	Paraguay-Ecuador	Paraguay-Peru	Paraguay-Venezuela	Peru-Thailand	SADC	SAFTA	Thailand-New Zealand	Uruguay-Colombia
CS	9.1	2.8	7.4	9.4	20.3						25.5	0.8		24.8	
CS + TECH				0.1							0.3			0.0	
CS + VC	0.2	4.1	0.2	0.1	0.0						0.3		3.4		
CS + VC + TECH															
CS + ECTC	3.5	2.5	3.2	4.3	0.5						1.2			0.2	
CS + ECTC + TECH				0.0										0.0	
CS + ECTC + VC		0.2		0.0											
Subtotal	**12.8**	**9.6**	**10.7**	**14.0**	**20.8**	**0.0**	**0.0**	**0.0**	**0.0**	**0.0**	**27.3**	**0.8**	**3.4**	**25.0**	**0.0**
CH	23.6	24.6	40.6	18.0	44.8	21.2	99.6	89.5	93.6	99.2	36.2	44.5	96.6	40.8	97.2
CH + TECH	0.1	0.0	0.0	0.2		14.7					1.3	1.8		0.3	
CH + VC	0.8	2.7	0.1	3.7	4.2	13.3					0.8	0.1		1.6	
CH + VC + TECH						0.6						1.3			
CH + ECTC	17.8	19.1	16.0	18.4	1.4	1.3	0.0				8.1			0.2	0.6

(continued on next page)

Table 2A-1 ▌RoO Combinations around the World, by Regime *(continued)*

(percentages)	Mexico-Northern Triangle	Mexico-Nicaragua	Mexico-Uruguay	NAFTA	P4	Pan-Euro	Paraguay-Colombia	Paraguay-Ecuador	Paraguay-Peru	Paraguay-Venezuela	Peru-Thailand	SADC	SAFTA	Thailand-New Zealand	Uruguay-Colombia
CH + ECTC + TECH	0.1			0.4		0.1									
CH + ECTC + VC	0.3	0.5	0.5	0.6	4.2									5.4	
Subtotal	**42.7**	**46.9**	**57.3**	**41.2**	**54.5**	**51.2**	**99.6**	**89.5**	**93.6**	**99.2**	**46.4**	**47.7**	**96.6**	**48.2**	**97.8**
CC	28.8	29.8	24.7	28.0	16.7	4.1		1.8	0.1		21.2	0.5		13.3	0.6
CC + TECH		0.0	0.4	0.1							0.1			1.1	
CC + VC	0.0	0.3			2.4									3.3	
CC + VC + TECH					5.6									4.7	
CC + ECTC	9.2	6.8	5.4	9.6	0.1		0.4	0.2	0.7	0.3	1.1			0.2	1.0
CC + ECTC + TECH	5.7	5.6		5.6							0.0				
CC + ECTC + VC		0.1													
Subtotal	**43.6**	**42.7**	**30.5**	**43.3**	**24.7**	**4.1**	**0.4**	**2.1**	**0.8**	**0.3**	**22.4**	**0.5**	**0.0**	**22.6**	**1.6**
TOTAL	100.0	100.0	100.0	100.0	100.0	100.0	100.0	100.0	100.0	100.0	100.0	100.0	100.0	100.0	100.0

Note: CC= change at the level of chapter; CH= change at level of heading; CI= change at level of item; CS= change at level of subheading; ECTC= exception attached to a particular change in tariff classification; NC= no change in tariff classification required; TECH= technical requirement; VC= value content requirement.

Appendix 2.3 Methodologies for Measuring Restrictiveness of RoO

Restrictiveness Index by Estevadeordal (2000)

The observation rule yields a RoO restrictiveness index as follows:

$$
\begin{aligned}
y &= 1 \text{ if } y^* \leq \text{CI} \\
y &= 2 \text{ if CI} < y^* \leq \text{CS} \\
y &= 3 \text{ if CS} < y^* \leq \text{CS and VC} \\
y &= 4 \text{ if CS and VC} < y^* \leq \text{CH} \\
y &= 5 \text{ if CH} < y^* \leq \text{CH and VC} \\
y &= 6 \text{ if CH and VC} < y^* \leq \text{CC} \\
y &= 7 \text{ if CC} < y^* \leq \text{CC and TECH}
\end{aligned}
$$

where y^* is the potential level of restrictiveness of RoO (rather than the observed level of restrictiveness); CI is the level of restrictiveness imposed by a requirement of a change in tariff classification at the level of tariff item (8–10 HS digits), CS is the level of restrictiveness imposed by a requirement of a change at the level of subheading (6 digits), CH is the level of restrictiveness imposed by a requirement of a change at the level of heading (4 digits), and CC is the level of restrictiveness imposed by a requirement of a change at the level of chapter (2 digits); VC is the level of restrictiveness imposed by a value content criterion; and TECH is the level of restrictiveness imposed by a technical requirement.

Suominen (2004) makes three modifications to the observation rule in the case of RoO for which no CTC is specified in order to allow for coding of such RoO in the Pan-Euro, SADC, and other regimes in which not all RoO feature a CTC component. First, the level of restrictiveness of RoO based on the import content rule is equated to that imposed by a change in heading requirement (value 4) if the content requirement allows nonoriginating inputs up to a value of 50 percent of the ex-works price of the product. Value 5 is assigned when the share of permitted nonoriginating inputs is below 50 percent, as well as when the import content criterion is combined with a technical requirement. Second, RoO featuring an exception alone are assigned a value of 1 if the exception concerns a heading or a number of headings and a value of 2 if the exception concerns a chapter or a number of chapters. Third, RoO based on the wholly obtained criterion are assigned a value of 7.

Restrictiveness Index by Harris (2007)

Harris's restrictiveness index is based on a system in which points are added or subtracted from the restrictiveness score for a particular rule of origin based on different elements used in its definition. The change in classification points are based on the magnitude of the required change, as are exception points and addition points (Additions are like negative exceptions, in that they permit nonoriginating inputs that would otherwise be prohibited by the change in classification requirement). Value test points are based on the magnitude of the required value content, with adjustments that depend on the method used for calculating value. The point values were calibrated by observing the relative frequencies of alternative rule combinations in a sample of 13 PTAs in the Americas.

Restrictiveness Points

Change in classification points:

ΔI	+2
ΔS	+4
ΔH	+6
ΔC	+8

where

ΔI represents a required change at the HS item level
ΔS represents a required change at the HS subheading level
ΔH represents a required change at the HS heading level
ΔC represents a required change at the HS chapter level

Exception points:

exI	+4
> exI and ≤ exS	+5
> exS and ≤ exH	+6
> exH and ≤ exC	+7
> exC	+8

where

exI represents an exception at the HS item level
exS represents an exception at the HS subheading level
exH represents an exception at the HS heading level
exC represents an exception at the HS chapter level

Addition points:

addI	−5
> addI and ≤ addS	−6
> addS and ≤ addH	−7
> addH and < addC	−8
add without CC	+8

where

addI represents an addition at the HS item level
addS represents an addition at the HS subheading level
addH represents an addition at the HS heading level
addC represents an addition at the HS chapter level
add without CC represents an addition without a requirement for a change in classification

Value test points:

>0% and≤40%	+5
>40% and≤50%	+6
>50% and≤60%	+7
>60%	+8
Net cost	+1

where the percentages represent the value content requirement imposed by the rule

Technical requirement points:	+4
Alternative rule points:	−3
Wholly obtained points:	+16

References

Cadot, Olivier, Jaime de Melo, and Marcelo Olarreaga. 2001. "Can Duty Drawbacks Have a Protectionist Bias? Evidence from Mercosur." Working Paper No. 2523. Washington, DC: World Bank.

Cadot, Olivier, Antoni Estevadeordal, Akiko Suwa Eisenmann, and Thierry Verdier. 2006. *The Origin of Goods: Rules of Origin in Regional Trade Agreements.* Oxford: Oxford University Press.

Canada Gazette. 2003. "Regulations Amending the NAFTA Rule of Origin Regulations." *Canada Gazette,* January 1. Available at canadagazette.gc.ca/partII/2003/20030115/html/sor24-e.html.

Cornejo, Rafael, and Jeremy Harris. 2007. "Convergence in the Rules of Origin Spaghetti Bowl: A Methodological Proposal." IDB/INTAL Working Paper No. 34. Washington, DC: Inter-American Development Bank.

Driessen, Bart, and Folkert Graafsma. 1999. "The EC's Wonderland: An Overview of the Pan-European Harmonised Origin Protocols." *Journal of World Trade* 33(4):19–45.

Estevadeordal, Antoni. 2000. "Negotiating Preferential Market Access: The Case of the North American Free Trade Agreement." *Journal of World Trade* 34(1):141–66.

Estevadeordal, Antoni, Jeremy Harris, and Kati Suominen. 2007. "Multilateralizing Rules of Origin around the World." Paper presented at WTO/HEI/NCCR Trade/CEPR Conference "Multilateralizing Regionalism," September 10–12, Geneva.

Estevadeordal, Antoni, and Kati Suominen. 2003. "Rules of Origin in FTAs in Europe and in the Americas: Issues and Implications for the EU-Mercosur Inter-Regional Association Agreement." In Alfredo G. A. Valladão and Roberto Bouzas (eds.), *Market Access for Goods and Services in the EU-Mercosur Negotiations.* Paris: Chaire Mercosur de Sciences Po.

———. 2005. "What Are the Effects of Rules of Origin on Trade?" Unpublished.

———. 2006. "Mapping and Measuring Rules of Origin around the World." In Olivier Cadot, Antoni Estevadeordal, Akiko Suwa-Eisenmann, and Thierry Verdier (eds.), *The Origin of Goods: Rules of Origin in Regional Trade Agreements*. Oxford: Oxford University Press and London: Centre for Economic Policy Research.

Estevadeordal, Antoni, Kati Suominen, and Robert Teh (2008). *Handbook on Regional Trade Agreements*. Cambridge: Cambridge University Press.

Garay, L. J., and R. Cornejo. 2002. "Metodología para el análisis de regímenes de o rigen: aplicación en el caso de las Américas." INTAL-ITD-STA Documento de Trabajo 8. Washington, DC: Inter-American Development Bank.

Harris, Jeremy. 2007. "Measurement and Determination of Rules of Origin In Preferential Trade Agreements." Ph.D. Diss., University of Maryland, College Park.

Hirsch, Moshe. 2002. "International Trade Law, Political Economy and Rules of Origin: A Plea for a Reform of the WTO Regime on Rules of Origin." *Journal of World Trade* 36(2):171–89.

IDB (Inter-American Development Bank. 2002. *Beyond Borders: The New Regionalism in Latin America*. Economic and Social Progress in Latin America: 2002 Report. Washington, DC: IDB.

Joint Statement by Prime Minister Harper, President Bush and President Calderón, North American Leaders' Summit, Montebello, Quebec, Canada, 21 August, 2007. Available at http://www.epa.gov/hpv/pubs/general/statement-declaration-en.pdf

Portugal-Perez, A. 2006. "Disentangling the Determinants of Rules of Origin in North-South Preferential Trade Agreements. Evidence for NAFTA. Université de Genève. Unpublished.

Reyna, Jimmie V. 1995. *Passport to North American Trade: Rules of Origin and Customs Procedures under NAFTA*. Colorado Springs: Shepard's/McGraw Hill.

Suominen, Kati. 2003. "Selective Liberalization in Response to Globalization: Rules of Origin as Determinants of Market Access Provisions in PTAs." *Integration and Trade* 19(7):153–85.

———. 2004. "Rules of Origin in Global Commerce." Ph.D. diss., University of California, San Diego.

WTO (World Trade Organization. 2002a. "Rules of Origin Regimes in Regional Trade Agreements." Committee on Regional Trade Agreements (April 5).

———. 2002b. "Coverage, Liberalization Process and Transitional Provisions in Regional Trade Agreements." Committee on Regional Trade Agreements (5 April).

PART II
POLITICAL ECONOMY OF RULES OF ORIGIN

CHAPTER 3

Negotiating Preferential Market Access: The Case of the North American Free Trade Agreement*

Antoni Estevadeordal

In recent times there has been a large amount of literature related to the theoretical analysis of free trade agreements (FTAs).[1] Nevertheless, there has been as yet very little empirical research on the dynamics of how these agreements have been negotiated and implemented, their impact on the pattern of trade and investment flows, their positive or negative externalities with respect to the multilateral system, their effects on the productive and investment decisions in each of the parties involved, and more generally, issues regarding the political economy process behind the negotiating process. This chapter attempts to make a contribution with respect to the first question, that is the dynamics of negotiating preferential market access in FTAs. In particular, it offers a detailed analysis of one of the most important preferential agreements negotiated in the Americas in recent times, NAFTA. It also provides a new analytical framework for exploring the interdependence among various commercial policy instruments used in preferential market access negotiations.

The focus is on the role of two key instruments: the preferential tariff phaseout program and the accompanying rules of origin negotiated under NAFTA. This issue has been clearly stated by Mayer (1999): "Why

---

* This chapter is a slightly modified version of Estevadeordal (2000).

[1] See, for example, Bhagwati and Panagariya (1996).

this NAFTA? Why its long phase outs of protection for some products and immediate elimination for others, its exemptions, its rules of origin?" (111) and "The [NAFTA] negotiators faced essentially two categories of [market access] problems: How fast should the tariffs come down? And what counted as a 'North American' good?" (117). This chapter tries to document some of the links between those questions.

Economists have tended to view market access negotiations solely in terms of tariff (and nontariff) negotiations. From an analytical point of view, the role of RoO, that is the rules that are designed to determine the origin of products in international trade, has usually been restricted to a "secondary" or "supportive" function. As such, RoO were seen to assist in the application or implementation of other "primary" instruments. Preferential RoO help to determine when a particular good will be granted preferential tariff treatment. Nonpreferential RoO help to determine the application of a specific nonpreferential policy, such as whether a particular good will be subject to antidumping duties following an antidumping investigation. This chapter emphasizes the role of RoO in preferential trade agreements as an independent commercial policy instrument. In fact, the empirical results support the view that, in the case of NAFTA, RoO were used as an additional and distinctive commercial policy instrument with respect to the preferential tariff phaseout built into the agreement.

Negotiating Preferential Market Access in the Americas: The Timing of NAFTA Negotiations

Although this chapter focuses on the NAFTA negotiations between the United States and Mexico, it raises issues that can easily be extended to the analysis of other FTAs, in particular those agreements in the Americas which have been modeled after NAFTA. The most immediate precedent of NAFTA was the Canada-U.S. FTA, which was negotiated during the second half of the 1980s and entered into force in 1989. A year later, in August 1990, President Carlos Salinas of Mexico proposed to then–U.S. President George H. W. Bush the negotiation of an FTA between the United States and Mexico. In September 1990, Canada agreed to join the negotiations. The three-party negotiations were formally launched at a ministerial meeting in June 1991. The agreement was signed a little over a year later, in December 1992, and entered into force on 1 January 1994.[2] In this chapter any analysis of the Canadian involvement in the NAFTA negotiations is explicitly excluded, as most of the market access issues were not new but extensions of the previous agreement with the United States.

Since the mid-1980s there has been a growing interest in regional approaches to trade liberalization. Ethier (1998) has used NAFTA, and in particular the U.S.-Mexico negotiations, as the best example of this "new regionalism," which is characterized by the following stylized facts:

1. The agreement typically involves one or more smaller countries linking up with a large country.
2. The small countries have recently made, or are making, significant unilateral reforms.
3. Dramatic moves to free trade between countries are not featured. The degree of liberalization in the agreement is typically modest.
4. The liberalization achieved is primarily by the small countries, not by the large countries. The agreements are one-sided.
5. The agreements often involve "deep" integration, that is, they include provisions affecting other economic policies.
6. The agreements are regional in a geographical sense. The participants are neighbors.

In the Americas this "new" regionalism has been an important additional component to broad packages of trade reforms in the region. During this period most countries moved toward substantial market-oriented economic reforms that included, almost without exception, a profound unilateral trade liberalization. In addition, all of this has happened in the context of multilateral trade liberalization commitments around the world,

[2] See Mayer (1999) for a political economy analysis of the NAFTA negotiations and Tornell and Esquivel (1995) for a Mexican perspective on the NAFTA negotiations.

which culminated in the Uruguay Round Agreements in 1994 and the creation of the World Trade Organization in 1995.

It is important to emphasize the timing of the NAFTA negotiations in order to understand its impact on subsequent agreements in the region. NAFTA was implemented just a few months short of the signing of the Final Act of the Uruguay Round in Marrakesh. Moreover, during the same year, important advances were being made in the Southern Cone in preparation for the creation of MERCOSUR among Argentina, Brazil, Paraguay, and Uruguay to be launched on 1 January 1995. Later in the year, in December 1994, the most ambitious initiative for economic integration in the Americas was launched at the Miami Summit of the Americas under the name of the Free Trade Area of the Americas (FTAA). In addition, during the same time period, two key countries in the hemisphere were in the process of consolidating their positions as strategic trade hubs in the region.

In the same year that NAFTA was implemented, Mexico was able to secure three important agreements based on the NAFTA model: with Costa Rica in April, with Colombia and Venezuela (known as the G3 Agreement) in June, and with Bolivia in September. All three agreements were implemented at the beginning of 1995. For Chile, 1994 marked an acceleration of its efforts to reach a series of bilateral agreements in the hemisphere. This started with the agreement with Mexico (1991) and progressed through those with Venezuela (1992), Colombia (1993), and Ecuador (1994). What followed during this and subsequent years was the initiation of free trade talks with MERCOSUR countries and Canada and the deepening of Chile's agreement with Mexico. Although they have important differences, the agreements signed by Chile have also progressively become more similar to the NAFTA model.

Negotiating Preferential Market Access in NAFTA

There are two basic instruments when approaching market access negotiations under a free trade agreement. The first instrument is the preferential tariff program vis-à-vis the tariff structure applied to other nonmember parties on an MFN basis. The second instrument is the system of RoO governing the determination of whether or not a particular product is originating from a partner country so it can fully benefit from the preferential treatment. To date, we do not have detailed empirical studies analyzing the interdependence that exists between these two key commercial policy instruments when negotiating FTAs.

Preferential Tariffs

Market access in traditional preferential agreements, in particular among Latin American countries, used to be negotiated by means of a fixed preferential tariff below the MFN rates and, in many cases, only for a selected group of products or sectors. Unilateral and multilateral tariff reductions had the effect of progressively eroding preference margins initially agreed upon. To maintain those margins over time, countries needed to constantly renegotiate the agreements. Later on, preferential agreements were based on constant relative margins of preference through the negotiation of preferential tariff reductions as a percentage of the currently applied MFN rates. Most of the "new" FTAs have followed the NAFTA model in many respects, moving toward tariff phaseout programs that are relatively quick, automatic, and nearly universal. The tariff elimination process follows prespecified timetables ranging from immediate elimination up to phaseouts generally over a one-year period, with special phaseout periods for those products regarded as "sensitive." The negotiations usually start with an agreement on a base rate or base level from which phaseout schedules will be applied. Those base rates usually coincide with the MFN rates applied to third parties at the time of negotiations. This was the case, for instance, in NAFTA after initial proposals to use bound rates from the General Agreement on Tariffs and Trade (GATT) were rejected. In other cases, it has been necessary to take into account previous preferences negotiated under other agreements in order to establish the initial base rate. These rates can also be subject to negotiations with the aim of beginning the phaseout schedules from lower rates. In a second stage, parties must agree on specific tariff elimination programs or phaseout schedules to bring the initial base rates to zero within a defined time period.

In the case of NAFTA, each country's base rate was based on pre-NAFTA MFN applied tariff rates. Hence, the base tariff rates contained in each party's schedules are different. The average base rate for Mexico was 10 percent, while the average U.S. rate was about 4 percent.

The second component of the tariff negotiations is the staging categories, which identify the time frame over which parties agreed to phase out their respective tariffs. As each party negotiated the timeframe over which it would reduce its duties, the agreement includes different staging categories or phaseout programs for the same product in each party's respective schedule. Early in the negotiations the parties agreed to put goods into several categories depending on their sensitivity to import competition, reflecting the magnitude of the liberalization effect as well as the political weight of each sector.

The four main NAFTA staging categories specifying the number of equal-sized annual cuts until full liberalization were A (immediate); B (five stages); C (10 stages); and C+ (15 stages).[3] Additionally, the NAFTA schedules include other categories, such as D (continued to be duty free) plus some special categories, such as B+ (seven stages); B6 and BI (five stages with initial small reductions vis-à-vis large initial reductions); C10 (nine stages). At the time of implementation (1 January 1994), tariffs for about half of all import categories were eliminated immediately.

Most of the remaining tariffs were set to disappear within a period of five years. The few exceptions would be eliminated during periods of up to 15 years. The most drastic phaseout was carried out by Mexico, with initial cuts above 50 percent on average. The United States, which had started with low tariffs, implemented an almost immediate full tariff liberalization with the exception of specific sensitive sectors, such as food products and textiles, apparel, and footwear manufactures. The extent of the tariff liberalization can be measured by the number of years until full liberalization is achieved, as reported in Table 3.1.

[3] It is interesting to note that it was the United States that insisted on the C+ category. This embarrassed the U.S. Chief negotiator who later said, "It was as if we were the developing country" (quoted in Mayer 1999: 117).

Table 3.1 ▌Average Years to Liberalization in NAFTA

ISIC sectors	Mexico to United States	United States to Mexico	Mexico to Canada	Canada to Mexico
1. Agriculture	2.46	1.00	2.19	1.20
2. Forestry	2.57	0.55	2.57	0.12
5. Fishing	3.15	0.20	3.15	0.29
10. Coal	1.00	0.00	1.00	0.14
11. Petroleum	7.50	0.50	7.50	4.00
12. Uranium	1.00	0.00	1.00	0.00
13. Metal ores	1.50	0.38	1.50	0.00
14. Other mining	1.73	0.40	1.73	0.21
15. Food products	6.29	1.71	5.66	3.67
16. Tobacco	10.00	1.75	10.00	4.17
17. Textiles	5.35	4.71	7.51	6.84
18. Apparel	4.92	4.09	9.34	9.42
19. Leather and footwear	5.16	4.96	5.67	6.63
20. Wood	5.29	0.92	5.37	3.33
21. Paper	4.H7	0.56	4.88	3.27
22. Publishing and printing	2.44	0.50	2.44	1.65
23. Coke and petroleum	5.53	0.35	5.53	2.12
24. Chemicals	4.37	1.36	4.40	2.68
25. Rubber	7.16	1.35	7.20	6.86
26. Other non-metallic	4.09	1.88	3.74	1.68
27. Basic metals	6.58	5.13	6.58	5.50
28. Fabricated metals	5.78	1.29	5.82	5.06
29. Machinery and equipment	3.36	1.00	3.36	1.66
30. Office and computing	1.58	0.70	1.58	0.16
31. Electrical machinery	6.43	0.88	6.43	4.16
32. Radio, TV; communications	1.71	1.05	1.71	0.80
33. Medical, precision instruments	2.10	0.95	2.10	1.34
34. Motor vehicles	4.85	2.13	4.85	6.03
35. Other transport equipment	3.15	1.14	3.15	2.87
36. Furniture	3.43	1.03	3.65	3.87

Source: Author's calculation based on the official text of NAFTA.

Note: "ISIC Sectors" refers to two-digit sectors from the International Standard Industrial Classification (Revision 3), United Nations, New York, 1990.

Rules of Origin

Because of its discriminatory nature, a preferential agreement must distinguish "nonmember-originating" from "member-originating" products in order to determine which products are to be granted preferential access. The growth of international trade in goods that are not manufactured in a single country has made the issue of the rules for determining the "origin" of goods traded into one of the most important and complex areas of preferential market access negotiations. Although this has been an area well known to trade lawyers and customs specialists (see, for example, Vermulst, Waer, and Bourgeois, 1994) it has just recently caught the attention of economists.

The economic analysis of RoO has been relatively limited, in terms both of formal modeling and of empirical testing. It has been argued, from an analytical point of view, that the way in which RoO are defined and applied within modern preferential agreements plays an important role in determining the degree of protection they confer and the level of distortionary trade effects which they produce (see Hoekman, 1993).

One of the most convincing treatments of the potential "hidden" protectionism of RoO has been elaborated by Krishna and Krueger (1995), who argued that RoO can induce a switch in sourcing from low-cost nonregional to high-cost regional inputs in order for producers to take advantage of the preferential rates. Since the tariff applies to the transaction value of final goods whenever preferences are deep and RoO are restrictive, there is an incentive for regional producers to buy intermediate goods from regional sources. So by displacing low-cost intermediate goods from the rest of the world, restrictive rules of origin provide additional protection to regional producers of intermediate goods to the apparent detriment of downstream or final goods producers.

This apparent conflict could be explained in terms of the specific production relations that exist between component producers and users. If the linkages between the different parts of the production chain are very tight, it may be difficult for a foreign final goods producer to locate components within the region and remain competitive. In this way, RoO export "protection" for both the intermediate and final goods producers.

Moreover, outside producers of intermediate goods hurt by restrictive RoO may have an incentive to move production facilities into the lowest-cost country within the region, even though it is not the low-cost producer worldwide. This situation could potentially distort efficient investment decisions and hinder the liberalizing effects of an FTA.

As explained more fully in Chapter 2, conceptually, there are two basic criteria for determining origin. The criterion of "wholly obtained or produced," where only one country enters into consideration in attributing origin, and the criterion of "substantial transformation," where two or more countries have taken part in the production process. The first criterion applies mainly to commodities and related products which have been entirely grown, extracted from the soil or harvested within the country in question or manufactured there from any of these products. Such products acquire origin by virtue of the total absence of the use of any second-country components or materials. Even a minimal content of imported components will imply the product's losing its qualification of "wholly produced." Most countries have adopted the precise definition contained in the Kyoto Convention (Table 3.5) for this criterion.

The "substantial transformation" criterion is the second concept recognized by the Kyoto Convention as a basis on which origin of goods may be determined. The Kyoto Convention does not offer a single approach for defining substantial transformation. One of the goals underlying the NAFTA negotiations on RoO was to develop specific criteria to give more precision to this concept. There are at least three methods in NAFTA:

1. a change in tariff classification, requiring the product to change its tariff heading (CTH; chapter, CC; heading, CH; subheading, CS; or item, CI) under the Harmonized Commodity Description System (Harmonized System) in the originating country;
2. a domestic content or regional value content rule requiring a minimum percentage of local value added in the originating country (or setting the maximum percentage of value originating in nonmember countries); and

3. a technical requirement prescribing that the product must undergo specific manufacturing processing operations in the originating country.

These methods have been used with different degrees of precision under different FTAs. In the case of agreements negotiated in the Americas, we find at one extreme of this "continuum" traditional agreements where a general rule is being used across the board for all tariff items (e.g., under the traditional LAIA agreements the general rule of origin that applies across the board is based on a change in tariff classification at the heading level or, alternatively, a regional value added of at least 50 percent of the FOB export value). At the other extreme, we encounter the type of RoO negotiated under NAFTA, which incorporates a general rule plus additional specific rules negotiated at the product level (6-digit HS), combining in many different ways the three methods described above. An immediate precedent with a lower degree of specificity can be found in the FTA between the United States and Canada. RoO negotiated for the G3 agreement, the Mexican bilateral with Costa Rica and Bolivia and the recent Chilean bilateral with Mexico and Canada are also close to those in the NAFTA model. Meanwhile, rules introduced under MERCOSUR and the MERCOSUR bilateral with Chile and Bolivia, as well as the Central America Common Market RoO, can be considered intermediate models between the two extreme cases (see Garay and Estevadeordal, 1996).

The NAFTA RoO negotiations introduced a highly disaggregated methodology. Aside from the definition of a general rule that applies to all goods based on the "wholly produced or obtained" rule (Article 401; this rule applies mainly to natural goods, such as minerals, raw foodstuffs, and animals), NAFTA adopted specific rules at the product level (generally using a 6-digit HS level of disaggregation).

These specific rules were adopted to close loopholes that might allow third-country producers to obtain NAFTA duties by performing assembly, processing, or minimal production operations in the territory of one of the parties. Those rules are extremely comprehensive and detailed and are described in a 150-page annex using the product definition of the Harmonized System. The criteria used to define origin are based on changes in tariff classification (at the chapter, heading, subheading, or item level, with the possibility of including exceptions), regional value content, technical tests, or a combination of these three criteria.

During the negotiations,

> using the NAFTA rules of origin as a means of securing foreign investment was not a primary goal [of the United States]. Instead, the objectives were primarily aimed at preventing third country participation in the NAFTA preferential tariff benefits, and in providing a system of enforcement... The main concern was that the rules not result in a flood of low cost imports into the US market... Like the United States, Mexico was concerned about the effect that the NAFTA would have on its domestic industries. This concern was heightened by the fact that, with the exception of a few industrial giants, e.g. VITRO and CEMEX, Mexican companies had little experience in trading abroad. More importantly, because of restrictions on sales in the Mexican market, Mexican companies had yet to experience competition in the Mexican market by foreign firms. Thus, Mexico was particularly concerned that a reduction of duties would result in a flow of foreign low-cost goods, a circumstance it resolved to prevent through strict rules of origin.
>
> Indeed, immediately upon entry into force, Mexico experienced a huge surge in imports of Chinese products, which Mexico addressed by, among other things, instituting the largest (in terms of tariff items covered) antidumping investigation ever filed and by establishing new certificates of origin requirements for imports of non-preferential merchandise. (Reyna, 1995: 36–37, 41)

The structure of the NAFTA RoO is presented in Table 3.2. The table illustrates the degree of specificity used in the making of the RoO in NAFTA, in particular, for the most sensitive sectors, such as autos,

Table 3.2 Structure of Rules of Origin in NAFTA (All Products and Manufacturing Sectors) (percentage of tariff items in each category)

		All products	Food	Textiles	Wood	Paper	Chemicals	Non-metallic mineral products	Basic metal industries	Fabricated metal products and machinery equipment	Other manufacturing industries
Rules of	CC	27.0	81.7	5.6	8.6	64.1	4.8	56.5	35.4	7.4	43.2
origin	CC/E	5.8	6.9	31.8	1.4		1.9				
based on	CC/E/Tech	5.7	33.4	33.4							
change in	CC or CH/E/RVC	1.3					2.2		5.5	2.6	8.9
chapter	CC or CH/E/RVC	1.1			22.9						11.2
	CC/E or CS/E/RVC	11.2					56.6				
	Subtotal	**52.1**	**88.6**	**70.8**	**32.9**	**64.1**	**65.5**	**56.5**	**40.9**	**10.0**	**63.3**
Rules of	CH	7.9	1.9		61.4	5.2	1.5	5.2	4.5	17.6	20.7
origin	CH/E	14.2	5.0	25.8	5.7	30.1	6.4	31.8	53.0	9.2	13.6
based on	CH/RVC	3.1		1.9			12			4.1	1.8
change in	CH or RVC									1.4	
heading	CH or CH/RVC										
	CH or CS/RVC	6.9								1.7	
	CH or CS/E/RVC		1.3				4.8			27.4	
	CH/E or CH/RVC										
	CH/E or CH/E/RVC	1.9								7.1	

(continued on next page)

Table 3.2 Structure of Rules of Origin in NAFTA (All Products and Manufacturing Sectors) *(continued)*
(percentage of tariff items in each category)

		All products	Food	Textiles	Wood	Paper	Chemicals	Non-metallic mineral products	Basic metal industries	Fabricated metal products and machinery equipment	Other manufacturing industries
	CH/E or CS/E/RVC						1.7				
	CH/E or CI/RVC									1.3	
	CH/E or CI/E/RVC									1.1	
	Subtotal	**34.0**	**8.2**	**27.7**	**67.1**	**35.3**	**26.4**	**37.0**	**57.7**	**70.9**	**36.1**
Rules of origin based on change in subheading	CS	1.3		1.3	4.4			1.3		4.4	
	CS/E		3.8	5.8				3.8		5.8	
	CS or CS/RVC		2.4				2.4				
	Subtotal	1.3		2.4	5.1	10.2	2.4	5.1		10.2	
	Total	**87.4**	**96.8**	**98.5**	**100.0**	**99.4**	**94.3**	**98.6**	**98.4**	**91.1**	**99.4**

Source: Author's calculations based on the official text of NAFTA.

Note: Only percentages above 1% of the total are reported. The following abbreviations are used (see text): CC: change in chapter; CH: change in heading; CS: change in subheading; CI: change in item; E: change in tariff classification including, exceptions; TECH: other technical requirements; RVC: regional value content component.

electronics, and textiles. For these important sectors, the challenge of establishing RoO that restricted the preferential benefits of the agreement to the NAFTA parties without cutting off foreign investment and the availability of foreign materials and components was extraordinary. In the end, the negotiators had to adopt very special rules tailored to the problems of each specific sector. For example, in the case of the textiles and apparel sector, roughly two-thirds of the products are governed by a rule requiring a change in chapter or heading, excluding specific headings (CC/E or CH/E, respectively). In fact, for most products the rules do not permit a change in tariff classification from a heading that includes coarse or fine wool, cotton, hair, and natural or man-made fibers, the so-called yarn forward rule by which in order to qualify as originating, a textile or apparel good must be produced entirely, from the yarn-spinning stage forward, in a NAFTA territory.

For the other third of textiles and apparel products, NAFTA rules require a change in tariff classification and that the goods be "both cut, sewn or otherwise assembled in North America" (CH/E/TECH). In the case of the automotive sector, the main challenge was the need to establish an RVC rule acceptable to the three parties and to improve the methods for calculating and verifying RVC under the rule.[4] Table 3.2 shows that almost 50 percent of the products under the category "fabricated metal products, machinery and equipment" incorporate an RVC requirement. Similarly, electronic products were also subject to complex RoO negotiations. Generally, those products were subject to three types of rules: (1) a change in tariff classification; (2) a change in tariff classification combined with an RVC requirement; and (3) a rule that either requires or prohibits the incorporation of specific parts, assemblies, or subassemblies.

To conclude this section, the interdependence of the two instruments under consideration will be intuitively explored before a more statistical approach is attempted. Table 3.3 looks at the NAFTA tariff phaseout program from the point of view of the speed of the tariff liberalization process,

---

[4] See Mayer (1999) for a political economy analysis of the NAFTA RoO negotiations in the automotive sector.

that is, the number of years that it takes for each party to undertake the full elimination of its tariffs on a bilateral basis with other FTA partners. For example, on average Mexico eliminates its tariffs applied to the United States in about five years, while the United States takes around one-and-a-half years to complete full tariff liberalization vis-à-vis Mexico.

Table 3.3 looks at a simple relationship between the NAFTA phaseout program and the most relevant structural patterns of RoO in the agreement. If RoO are ordered by an ad hoc level of restrictiveness (see full discussion later in the chapter), we find some degree of correlation between the two instruments. Slow liberalization is associated with higher restrictiveness in terms of origin requirements.

From a "narrow" interpretation of the role of RoO as "supporting" instruments in the application of a particular policy (in a general sense, this could apply to either preferential or nonpreferential policies), this correlation would suggest that high levels of protection (slow liberalization) are associated with stringent rules that hypothetically support the tariff protection. However, when RoO are viewed as distinctive policy instruments to target the input composition of final products, their interaction with the tariff instrument could have a positive or negative correlation. The correlation in Table 3.3 would suggest a complementarity function, but a more formal statistical approach is needed to establish this relationship.

Table 3.3 ▌ Years to Liberalization and Rules of Origin in NAFTA

	Years to liberalization			
Rules of origin criteria	Mexico to United States	United States to Mexico	Mexico to Canada	Canada to Mexico
CI	1.75	1.00	1.75	2.50
CS	2.65	1.21	2.65	1.41
CS&RVC	2.28	0.52	2.28	1.11
CH	4.90	2.28	5.11	4.56
CH&RVC	4.71	1.68	4.79	4.36
CC	4.34	1.72	4.47	6.46
CC&TECH	5.23	4.40	9.61	9.44

Source: Author's calculations based on the official text of NAFTA.

Note: See Table 3.2 for a description of the abbreviations used to classify RoO.

An Empirical Specification

This section explores the degree of interdependence between the two key instruments in preferential market access negotiations, that is the preferential tariff phaseout and the RoO, using an ad hoc econometric model. There are several difficulties with this approach.

First, the suggested specification of the model structure is identified "from the ground up," based on insights on how preferential market access negotiations take place in the real world, rather than formalized in a theoretical model based on behavioral assumptions of the economic parties involved in those types of negotiations.[5]

Second, one of the endogenous variables cannot be observed directly; that is, the real level of restrictiveness implied by the RoO is not "observable."

Third, the NAFTA negotiations were a "game" played by three parties in which those parties agreed to negotiate one of the instruments (preferential tariffs) bilaterally, and the other instrument (RoO) jointly, thereby complicating any interaction analysis. From this perspective, a full model of the negotiating dynamics would have to consider the point of view of all parties simultaneously. In this chapter, the analysis is restricted to the interactions between Mexico and the United States in the negotiations.

The noninclusion of the Canadian strategy can be justified on several grounds. Most importantly, Canada joined the NAFTA negotiations in order to preserve some of the gains achieved under the Canada-U.S. FTA. While maintaining the bilateral preferential tariff structure with the United States negotiated under the previous FTA, Canada negotiated new RoO with the United States and Mexico.

This section introduces an econometric specification where one of the endogenous variables is an "ordered categorical variable" (an index of restrictiveness of RoO) and the other is a regular "continuous variable"

---

[5] It would be possible to justify an econometric specification such as the one used in this chapter based on contributions from some recent theory literature modeling negotiation dynamics.

(the "speed" of preferential liberalization or the number of years to full intra-area liberalization).[6] A number of trade-related variables are used as independent (and instrumental) variables, that is, the levels of intra-industry trade, the import and export ratios, the MFN tariff differentials to third parties, the initial preferential margin, and finally, the other party's offers of tariff liberalization.

To carry out this exercise, I use a nontraditional simultaneous structure where, in the first equation, the "latent values" (that is the real unobserved values) of the endogenous categorical variable—RoO—depend on some exogenous variables. Remember that this is the variable that is determined jointly by the parties participating in the negotiations. Therefore, the explanatory variables to be included must represent structural factors that determine how the parties jointly agree on a common set of RoO under the agreement. In turn, in the second equation, the continuous endogenous variable—preferential tariff phaseouts—is assumed to be a function not of the actual observed values of the categorical variable (RoO), but of their real or "latent" intensity indices, as well as an additional set of other explanatory factors. As this variable is country specific, I estimate equations for each of the parties participating in the negotiations (Mexico and the United States).

The proposed modeling feature is appropriate in this case as the categories associated with the data for the endogenous categorical variable are an artifact of the way the codification of the RoO was conducted (see detailed description on how RoO data were constructed later in the chapter). The model can be represented with the following equations (alternative specifications are discussed in Appendix 3.1):

$$y_1{}^* = \beta_1{}'X_1 + \nu_1, \tag{3.1}$$

$$y_{2i}{}^* = \gamma_{2i} y_1{}^* + \beta_{2i}{}'X_{2i} + \nu_{2i}, \tag{3.2}$$

[6] The approach taken in this chapter follows a tradition of empirical research on explaining tariff negotiations. A good survey of the literature with an empirical application to the NAFTA tariff negotiations is Kowalczyk and Davis (1998).

where the latent variable y_1* is the *latent* level of restrictiveness of RoO, y_2* is a continuous variable measuring the number of years to liberalization, and X_1 and X_2 are vectors of the explanatory variables independently distributed from the error terms v_1 and v_2. These v_1 and v_2 are supposed to be jointly normally distributed with mean zero and a positive definite variance matrix $\Sigma = [\sigma]$. The subindex *i* is included as a reference to the separate country-specific equations to be estimated.[7]

In this model, the influence on the depth or speed of preferential tariff liberalization is attributed to the real or latent indices of restrictiveness imposed by the RoO rather than to the observed level of restrictiveness of the RoO. The codification of the RoO data simply acts as a constraint on the information available to the analyst. Most RoO are designed on the basis of some very specific sector analysis (generally this information is provided directly by the private sector) of their effects in the medium to long term, as such rules are not generally phased out over time in these types of agreements. Then, independent of the degree of liberalization negotiated for a particular product, the rule will still be operative after the market has been fully opened to all FTA members.

Therefore, the rule has to be designed, to a certain degree, independently of the preferential liberalization program granted to each specific product. However, information on the degree of restrictiveness of the RoO is usually part of the "information set" used by the tariff negotiator. The presence of a very restrictive rule of origin could be used as an additional protective measure in a slow liberalization program or a compensatory mechanism in a faster liberalization schedule. Under this specification, the underlying reduced form can be easily derived explicitly in terms of the latent variable, and the estimation admits a two-stage procedure as in Amemiya (1978, 1979) and Nelson and Olson (1978).

---

[7] Note that the full model requires a simultaneous estimation of $(i + 1)$ equations. The first equation is a RoO equation to explain the joint negotiation of a common RoO regime on the basis of several structural variables. Second, *i* country-specific equations, where each phaseout of preferential tariffs from country *i* to country *j* is explained in terms of some country-specific factors, as well as the common RoO variable. Because of the econometric complexities of the estimation procedure of $(i + 1)$ equations, where one of the endogenous variables is a categorical variable, this estimation approach will be attempted in future work rather than in this chapter.

Data

This section briefly describes issues regarding data construction. Our data set focuses on information regarding the NAFTA negotiations between Mexico and the United States. The database is constructed at the 6-digit level of the Harmonized System. At this level of product disaggregation the following variables are constructed.

First, the degree or speed of preferential tariff liberalization is measured by the number of years to achieve zero intra-agreement tariffs. This variable is given by NAFTA's phaseout schedule. According to the structure of the liberalization program, each product line at the 8-digit (or in some cases at the 10-digit) HS level is associated with a specific phaseout program. When these data are averaged out at the 6-digit level, we get a continuous variable for the number of years to liberalization.

Second, I construct an index of the level of restrictiveness of the NAFTA rules of origin to be used as the observability rule for the ordered categorical variable in the first equation of the model. NAFTA's rules of origin were negotiated at the product level (mostly at the 6-digit tariff line level) and were defined using the three methods described in the "Rules of Origin" section, that is, a change in tariff heading (CTH), a regional value content (RVC) or a technical (TECH) requirement. The first component can be specified as requiring a change at the chapter level (CC, 2-digit HS), heading level (CH, 4-digit HS), subheading level (CS, 6-digit HS), or item level (CI, greater than 6-digit HS), with the possibility of including specific exceptions. The three methods can also be combined under the same rule of origin, for example, a change in subheading plus a specific regional value content. Moreover, there are many cases where the agreement defines alternative RoO for the same product.

To obtain this restrictiveness index, I first codify each rule or set of rules according to which of these different criteria are employed.[8] Then, a qualitatively ordered index is constructed under the following assumptions. First, a change in tariff classification at the chapter level tends to be more stringent than one at the heading level, a change at the heading

[8] This methodology was developed in Garay and Estevadeordal (1996).

level more stringent than one at the subheading level, and so on. Second, a regional content requirement adds more restrictiveness to a given rule, as does a technical requirement. For each pair (or sometimes trio) of alternative rules being applied to the same product, I select the one with the higher restrictiveness index. Finally, I construct the categorical variable RoO (y_1*) assigning to each 6-digit HS product category an ordered numerical value according to the following rule:[9]

$$
\begin{aligned}
y &= 1 \text{ if } y^* \leq \text{CI}, \\
y &= 2 \text{ if CI} < y^* \leq \text{CS}, \\
y &= 3 \text{ if CS} < y^* \leq \text{CS\&RVC}, \\
y &= 4 \text{ if CS\&RVC} < y^* \leq \text{CH}, \\
y &= 5 \text{ if CH} < y^* \leq \text{CH\&RVC}, \\
y &= 6 \text{ if CH\&RVC} < y^* \leq \text{CC}, \\
y &= 7 \text{ if CC} < y^* \leq \text{CC\&TECH}.
\end{aligned}
$$

Third, several explanatory (and instrumental) variables are considered. To measure the depth of tariff liberalization, I construct a measure of the initial preferential margin between parties *i* and *j* as the relative margin between the respective MFN rate applied to third countries and the initial preferential rate applied to the FTA partner. The variable is defined as follows:

$$
\begin{aligned}
\textit{PRE-MAR}_{ij} = \; & [\{(1 + \textit{MFN}_i \textit{Tariffs})/ \\
& (1 + \textit{PREFERENTIAL}_{ij} \textit{Tariffs} \text{ in 1*year})\} - 1] \times 100.
\end{aligned}
$$

To account for trade deflection effects, I compute a measure of the absolute value of the spread between each party's MFN rates and third-country rates as follows:

$$
\textit{MFN-DIF}_{ij} = |[\{(1 + \textit{MFN}_i)/(1 + \textit{MFN}_j)\} - 1] \times 100|.
$$

---

[9] The benchmark levels of restrictiveness (1 to 7) have been chosen on the basis of the most frequent combinations of the RoO in NAFTA.

Finally, I compute several trade-based measures using average data for the pre-NAFTA period (1990–92) to be included as additional independent factors in our econometric estimation. In particular, I compute Grubel-Lloyd intra-industry indices as well as import and export ratios. Appendix Tables 3A.1–3A.3 report the average values of those variables at 3-digit level of disaggregation using the International Standard Industry Classification (ISIC).

Regression Analysis

The proposed structural specification of equations (3.1) and (3.2) can be estimated using the following variables:

$$RoO\text{-}RI = f_1(MFN\text{-}DIF, IIT\text{-}ME\text{-}US, IIT\text{-}ME\text{-}RoW, IIT\text{-}US\text{-}RoW), \tag{3.1}$$

$$YE\text{-}ME\text{-}US = f_2(RoO\text{-}RI, YE\text{-}US\text{-}ME, PRE\text{-}MAR\text{-}ME, IMP\text{-}RAT\text{-}ME, EXP\text{-}RAT\text{-}ME), \tag{3.2a}$$

$$YE\text{-}US\text{-}ME = f_3(RoO\text{-}RI, YE\text{-}ME\text{-}US, PRE\text{-}MAR\text{-}US, IMP\text{-}RAT\text{-}US, EXP\text{-}RAT\text{-}US), \tag{3.2b}$$

where

RoO-RI = rules of origin restrictiveness index;
MFN-DIF = most-favored nation tariff differential between Mexico and United States;
IIT-ME-US = intra-industry trade between Mexico and United States (1990–92);
IIT-ME-RoW = intra-industry trade between Mexico and the rest of the world (1990–92);
IIT-US-RoW = intra-industry trade between the United States and the rest of the world (1990–92);
YE-ME-US = years to liberalization of Mexico to the United States under NAFTA;
YE-US-ME = years to liberalization of the United States to Mexico under NAFTA;

PRE-MAR-ME = initial preferential margin of Mexico vis-à-vis the United States;
PRE-MAR-US = initial preferential margin of the United States vis-à-vis Mexico;
IMP-RAT-ME = Mexican imports from the United States relative to Mexico's total trade (1990–92);
EXP-RAT-ME = Mexican exports to the United States relative to Mexico's total trade (1990–92);
IMP-RAT-US = United States imports from Mexico relative to total U.S. trade (1990–92); and
EXP-RAT-US = United States exports to Mexico relative to total U.S. trade (1990–92).

Following the methodological discussion outlined at the beginning of this section, the estimation proceeds in two stages. First, I estimate equation (3.1) using an ordered probit regression of the categorical variable *RoO-RI* using instrumental variables. This dependent variable is constructed under a specific "observability rule" described in the previous section. This estimation allows me to obtain the predicted values for the index of restrictiveness of RoO as a continuous indicator, which in turn is used to estimate sequentially equations (3.2a) and (3.2b) using standard ordinary least-squares (OLS) procedures.[10] The results of the ordered probit and OLS estimations are reported in Tables 3.4 and 3.5, respectively.

In Table 3.4, I report the results of the ordered probit estimation of the RoO equation (3.1). The overall results confirm that the structure of trade barriers to members and nonmembers as well as other structural trade-related variables are important factors in explaining the level of

[10] See note 7 on the econometric approach of this chapter. I do not attempt to estimate simultaneously equations (3.2a) and (3.2b) jointly with (3.1), the reason being that in order to use the two-stage estimation procedure as in Amemiya (1978, 1979) and Nelson and Olson (1978), it is preferable to consider two separate models: the Mexican model, represented by equations (3.1) and (3.2a), and the U.S. model, represented by equations (3.1) and (3.2b).

Table 3.4 ▌NAFTA Rules of Origin, Ordered Probit Estimation

		Dependent variable: rules of origin restrictiveness index (*RoO-RI*) Equation [3.1]			
MFN Tariff Differential		1.57	2.05	1.55	2.07
(*MFN-DIF*)		(5.12)	(5.83)	(5.05)	(5.90)
Intra-industry trade Mexico-U.S.		0.17	0.16	0.18	0.17
(*IIT-ME-US*)		(2.37)	(2.26)	(2.51)	(2.40)
Intra-industry trade Mexico-RoW		1.28	1.27	1.27	1.27
(*IIT-ME-RoW*)		(20.72)	(20.54)	(20.59)	(20.37)
Intra-industry trade U.S.-RoW		−1.63	−1.64	−1.61	−1.62
(*IIT-US-RoW*)		(−22.85)	(−22.93)	(−22.43)	(−22.51)
Preferential margin Mexico-U.S.			−0.91		−1.03
(*PRE-MAR-ME-US*)			(−2.89)		(−3.27)
Preferential margin U.S.-Mexico			0.83		0.84
(*PRE-MAR-US-ME*)		(1.51)		(1.52)	
Mexico import ratio with U.S.				−0.21	−0.22
(*IMP-RAT-ME*)				(−4.01)	(4.26)
U.S. import ratio with Mexico				−0.4	−0.4
(*IMP-RAT-US*)				(−1.79)	(−1.81)
	chi2	936.55	945.5	954.65	965.8
	Prob> chi2	(0.000)	(0.000)	(0.000)	(0.000)
	Obs.	5,005	5,005	5,005	5,005

Note: z-statistics in parentheses.

restrictiveness built into the common RoO regime. First, I obtain very significant results in favor of the hypothesis about the role of RoO in preventing "trade deflection." The higher the absolute spread between Mexican and U.S. tariffs to third parties (*MFN-DIF*), the higher is the restrictiveness built into the RoO. As Mexican MFN tariffs prior to NAFTA were higher than U.S. MFN tariffs for most products, the positive and significant coefficient of *MFN-DIF* may reflect the fact that some Mexican and U.S. producers tried to prevent cheap competing imports of inputs from third parties from being shipped through the United States into Mexico, where they could then be used as intermediate inputs in the production of final goods in Mexico to be re-exported to the United States.

An additional interpretation, not mutually exclusive, is that high levels of RoO restrictiveness are associated with high initial protection rates. As the U.S. rates are, for the most part, low and relatively uniform, *MFN-DIF* acts as a proxy for the initial Mexican base rates, which I do not introduce independently in the equation to avoid a multicolinearity problem.[11]

The intra-industry variables are introduced as proxies for the degree of intra-industry linkage between the two economies. I introduce three potential measures of the linkages between the economies: intra-area linkages and individual party linkage vis-à-vis the rest of the world (*IIT-ME-US*, *IIT-ME-RoE*, and *IIT-US-RoW*).[12] All the variables are found to be statistically significant. In the first case, that is, the intra-industry trade variable between Mexico and the United States, the coefficient is positive. This can be interpreted as the incentive to preserve existing intra-industry complementarity between Mexico and the United States through higher levels of restrictiveness.

At the same time, the data show a strong positive correlation between *RoO-RI* and *IIT-ME-RoW*. Higher levels of intra-industry trade between Mexico and the rest of the world for a particular sector may indicate a higher potential for outsourcing by Mexican producers that can hinder regional interests in becoming the primary source for inputs in industries in that sector. In the case of the index of intra-industry trade between the United States and the rest of the world, the coefficient is significant and negative.

As is the case with the previous indicator, many different forces may be at work behind these correlations, and the net effect depends upon the relative strength of such forces. In this case, a plausible explanation may be the fact that U.S. sectors with higher intra-industry linkages with

---

[11] The correlation between restrictiveness and tariff protection appears in the data when a measure of national tariff rates is introduced into the equation. This relationship between RoO and protection through tariffs also appears when the second equation of the model is estimated.

[12] The correlation among intra-industry indices is very low: 0.17 between *IIT-ME-US* and *IIT-ME-RoW*; -0.03 between *IIT-ME-US* and *IIT-US-RoW*; and 0.08 between *IIT-ME-RoW* and *IIT-US-RoW*.

non–NAFTA members may want to preserve their sources of foreign outsourcing while at the same time keeping their presence in a larger preferential market. Also, in the case of the United States, high levels of intra-industry trade with the rest of the world in a given sector may indicate that producers in the sector are competitive and will eventually lobby for fast access to FTA partner markets. These are not, in any way, the only explanations; rather, they signal potential mechanisms in the complex operation of this commercial instrument that targets primarily intermediate and input goods trade. A more-disaggregated analysis is needed to capture some sector-specific explanations. Nevertheless, the first key finding of this chapter is clear: the structure of the RoO is highly correlated with the MFN tariff differential as well as with different measures of industry linkages existing between FTA members and nonmember countries.

Equation (3.2) is estimated separately for each country using standard OLS techniques. Table 3.5 reports the results for Mexico's preferential liberalization program in respect to the United States and vice versa. The results can be summarized as follows. First, the degree of restrictiveness of the RoO (*RoO-RI*) is an important factor in explaining the policy formation of the central instrument in preferential tariff negotiations, that is, the depth or speed of tariff liberalization among FTA members.

The estimates in Table 3.5 show that the degree of reciprocal liberalization between Mexico and the United States (*YE-ME-US* and *YE-US-ME*) is positively and significantly correlated with the RoO restrictiveness index (*RoO-RI*). This is the second key result of the chapter: origin matters when the preferential liberalization scheme is determined. RoO, when considered across the entire tariff universe, act as an additional instrument to preferential tariff liberalization.

Products that are under a slow liberalization program carry more restrictive rules of origin. This is a strong result that views RoO as an independent endogenous instrument in FTA tariff negotiations with a "complementary" role in the design of a discriminatory tariff policy. A more sophisticated interpretation of this result is the existence of a "substitution" postliberalization effect. Once tariffs have been completely phased out, origin requirements will remain, thereby implying that the degree of

Table 3.5 ▌ Preferential Tariff Liberalization in NAFTA, OLS Estimation

	Dependent Variable			
	Years to liberalization of Mexico to the U.S. (*YE-ME-US*) Equation [3.2a]		Years to liberalization of U.S. to Mexico (*YE-US-ME*) Equation [3.2b]	
Intercept	7.75	7.03	2.56	1.42
	(74.03)	(61.45)	(43.89)	(19.25)
Rules of origin restrictiveness index	0.61	0.43	1.04	0.83
(*RoO-RI*)	(8.67)	(6.14)	(14.12)	(11.80)
Years to liberalization to partner				
(a: *YE-US-ME*)		0.19		0.23
(b: *YE-ME-US*)		(14.40)		(23.51)
Preferential margin				
(a: *PRE-MAR-ME-US*)	−0.45	−0.43	−0.1	−0.08
(b: *PRE-MAR-US-ME*)	(−7.11)	(−6.57)	(−8.65)	(−7.28)
Import ratio				
(a: *IMP-RAT-ME*)	0.56	0.68	−0.29	−0.21
(b: *IMP-RAT-US*)	(4.15)	(5.11)	(−0.58)	(−0.44)
Export Ratio				
(a: *EXP-RAT-ME*)	0.81	0.9	1.45	0.45
(b: *EXP-RAT-US*)	(4.84)	(5.43)	(3.49)	(1.15)
R^2	0.51	0.53	0.1	0.15
R^2 Adj.	0.51	0.53	0.1	0.15
Obs.	5,005	5,005	5,005	5,005

Note: *t*-statistics in parentheses

"protection" attached to the rules will remain in place: products that are relatively more protected (slow liberalization, high initial tariffs) will still be subject to more restrictive rules.

The other key explanatory variables in these equations are the initial levels of the preferential margins. Both variables enter into the equations with negative and significant signs. For example, consider the case of the Mexico equation. One would expect that higher margins of preference for Mexico vis-à-vis the United States are good proxies for sectors with higher protectionist interests, that is, sectors seeking slow liberalization programs. However, higher margins of preference may well indicate sectors that are already relatively open to the United States vis-à-vis a third party, and therefore further degrees of liberalization may be expected. In addition, lower margins of preference, given the higher tariffs of Mexico, indicate sectors protected from outside parties as well as from the United States. One could then expect that efforts will be made to keep barriers high for those sectors (slow liberalization).

Finally, the import and export ratios both have a positive and significant impact on the degree of liberalization, except in the case of the U.S. import ratio, where the coefficient is not significant. The import ratio effect may capture some well-known empirical results of the endogenous protection literature. In response to increased import competition, domestic interests intensify their lobbying activity for protection; that is, higher import ratios lead to demands for slow liberalization.[13]

However, some models à la Grossman and Helpman (1994) predict a negative relation, arguing that the higher the import demand, the higher the cost for the government to introduce a tariff distortion in that sector. Maggi and Rodriguez (1998) develop a model in which the government uses trade distortionary instruments (quotas, voluntary export restrictions, etc.) other than tariffs, predicting that the protection level increases with import penetration in sectors that are protected with tariffs and in sectors that are protected with quantitative restrictions. An interesting line of research would be to try to extend this type of result in a model à la Ju and Krishna (1998) with RoO. The results in this section are still preliminary, waiting for a more-disaggregated sector analysis to capture different negotiating dynamics when specific sectors are analyzed.

Conclusion

This chapter has used statistical methods to explain the interaction between two key market access instruments used in FTA negotiations. In particular, it has examined the policy design of the preferential tariff

[13] Note that our variable is a proxy for import penetration instead of an imports/domestic consumption measure.

phaseouts and the rules of origin structure under the NAFTA negotiations between Mexico and the United States. The first result of the chapter is that RoO are instruments against trade deflection. The greater the difference between Mexican and U.S. MFN tariffs, the higher the incentives for trade deflection and, therefore, the higher the degree of restrictiveness imposed by RoO. Moreover, proxy variables for industry linkages between the two economies play an important and significant role as fundamental explanatory factors of the structure of RoO. The simultaneous structure of the model also shows that the degree of preferential tariff liberalization between the NAFTA partners is highly and significantly correlated with the degree of restrictiveness of RoO. Sectors with higher RoO are also the ones with longer phaseout periods for tariff liberalization. In other words, borrowing the language of the endogenous protection literature, one could conclude that the same forces that push for tariff protection also push for more restrictive RoO. I interpret this result as evidence that in FTA negotiations, RoO and preferential tariffs are both primary policy instruments for market access negotiations.

Appendix 3.1

As I have not started with a fully developed theoretical model and my main interest is to conduct a thorough data analysis, it is important to be explicit about other alternative approaches to the particular econometric specification used in this chapter. First, we can consider the following alternative model as presented in the chapter:

Model A:

$$y_1{}^* = \beta_1{}'X_1 + v_1, \tag{3.1a}$$

$$y_{2i}{}^* = \gamma_{2i} y_1{}^* + \beta_{2i}{}'X_{2i} + v_{2i}, \tag{3.2a}$$

This specification would implicitly assume that the observability rule used to construct the RoO variable (see "Data") also acts as a constraint on the tariff negotiator's choice set as well as on the analyst. That is, the model would imply that the tariff negotiator would only be using the "simple" codification of RoO in her negotiating strategy for preferential tariff liberalization. This may be true in some cases. However, the original model is preferable for several reasons. First, the actual information made available to the negotiators, mostly through private sector inputs in this type of negotiations on RoO, is much more sophisticated and complete than the simplified codes used here for computational purposes. Second, this alternative specification would have some nontrivial estimation problems (see Blundell and Smith, 1994).

There is another alternative specification that considers the continuous endogenous variable (preferential tariff phaseout programs negotiated by each party) as entering as an explanatory variable in the RoO equation. From a game-theoretical point of view, this is a plausible alternative to modeling a negotiating process where years of liberalization and rules of origin are negotiation outcomes that are jointly determined. The model could be written as follows:

Model B

$$y_1^* = \gamma_{1i}' Y_{2i}^* + \beta_1' X_1 + \nu_1, \tag{3.1b}$$

$$y_{2i}^* = \gamma_{2i}' y_1^* + \beta_{2i}' X_{2i} + \nu_{2i}, \tag{3.2b}$$

where Y_{2i}^* is the vector of years to liberalization for each country. However, as argued earlier in the chapter, this is a somewhat less-appealing model on economic grounds. Moreover, from an econometric point of view, while the system represented by equations (3.1b) and (3.2b) could in principle be estimated using standard maximum-likelihood methods, the resulting likelihood function is extremely nonlinear and thus difficult to maximize using standard methods. This joint estimation feature will be explored in future research.

Table 3A.1 ▌Preferential Margin between Mexico and the United States

	Mexico to United States		United States to Mexico	
ISIC sectors	Mean	Standard deviation	Mean	Standard deviation
1. Agriculture	8.69	7.38	1.02	3.01
2. Forestry	9.06	4.48	0.54	1.27
5. Fishing	12.99	7.45	0.24	0.83
10. Coal	10.00	0.00	0.00	0.00
11. Petroleum	1.39	0.93	0.00	0.00
12. Uranium	10.00	0.00	0.00	0.00
13. Metal ores	8.30	3.04	0.00	0.00
14. Other mining	9.16	3.60	1.09	2.25
15. Food products	6.67	6.84	2.14	3.37
16. Tobacco	3.67	7.15	0.00	0.00
17. Textiles	5.46	4.80	2.76	3.89
18. Apparel	8.23	6.41	4.16	5.08
19. Leather and footwear	7.65	6.19	3.16	2.33
20. Wood	8.25	6.01	2.55	2.56
21. Paper	5.39	3.52	1.84	1.85
22 Publishing and printing	8.63	6.86	1.33	1.89
23. Coke and petroleum	3.68	3.02	0.81	1.83
24. Chemicals	6.93	4.10	2.96	3.17
25. Rubber	5.32	4.09	3.36	1.80
26. Other non-metallic	9.60	5.74	3.75	3.04
27. Basic metals	4.36	3.94	2.08	2.84
28. Fabricated metals	7.28	5.14	3.42	2.44
29. Machinery and equipment	9.03	4.65	2.85	1.57
30. Office and computing	12.93	6.58	2.61	1.53
31. Electrical machinery	5.54	3.41	3.48	1.74
32. Radio, TV, communications	10.83	4.99	4.14	2.73
33. Medical, precision instruments	11.03	4.24	3.57	2.61
34. Motor vehicles	7.97	6.15	2.34	1.54
35. Other transport equipment	9.61	5.04	3.87	4.72
36. Furniture	11.27	6.22	3.91	3.08

Source: Author's calculations based on the official text of NAFTA.
Note: "ISIC sectors" refer to 2-digit sectors from the International Standard Industrial Classification (Revision 3), United Nations, New York 1990.

Table 3A.2 Most-Favored Nation Tariff Differential between Mexico and the United States

ISIC Sectors	Mean	Standard deviation	Minimum	Maximum	Mean of *MFN-DIF*
1. Agriculture	9.32	9.02	−38.27	30.00	10.66
2. Forestry	10.11	3.16	0.00	20.00	10.11
5. Fishing	17.66	5.38	−2.91	20.00	17.80
10. Coal	10.00	0.00	10.00	10.00	10.00
11. Petroleum	7.50	5.00	0.00	10.00	7.50
12. Uranium	10.00	0.00	10.00	10.00	10.00
13. Metal ores	9.19	2.40	0.00	10.00	9.19
14. Other mining	8.82	3.14	−0.90	15.00	8.84
15. Food products	9.99	9.03	−19.23	30.00	11.76
16. Tobacco	41.67	12.91	25.00	50.00	41.67
17. Textiles	5.21	5.41	−7.69	20.00	6.13
18. Apparel	9.26	6.53	−12.28	20.00	9.96
19. Leather and footwear	6.01	6.98	−20.29	17.65	7.94
20. Wood	13.57	2.91	5.50	20.00	13.57
21. Paper	7.33	2.63	−0.99	15.38	7.34
22. Publishing and printing	9.16	6.24	−0.99	20.00	9.23
23. Coke and petroleum	7.52	3.80	−2.91	10.00	7.81
24. Chemicals	7.42	4.60	−11.50	20.00	7.94
25. Rubber	11.35	3.46	3.77	20.00	11.35
26. Other non-metallic	10.49	4.38	−4.24	20.00	10.58
27. Basic metals	6.02	4.04	−9.09	20.00	6.36
28. Fabricated metals	11.86	4.77	−11.50	20.00	11.97
29. Machinery and equipment	10.01	4.15	−1.96	20.00	10.04
30. Office and computing	11.60	5.82	0.99	20.00	11.60
31. Electrical machinery	9.81	3.59	95.00	18.81	9.81
32. Radio, TV, communications	7.77	5.63	−11.30	17.65	8.44
33. Medical, precision instruments	9.02	4.97	−4.55	20.00	9.06
34. Motor vehicles	10.40	5.90	−5.98	17.65	11.06
35. Other transport equipment	8.50	6.22	−6.78	20.00	9.65
36. Furniture	12.38	4.69	−3.85	20.00	12.47

Source: Author's calculations based on the official text of NAFTA.

Note: All statistics refer to the simple difference between the respective MFN rates, except for the Mean of the *MFN-DIF* variable, computed as explained in the text. "ISIC sectors" refers to 2-digit sectors from the International Standard Industrial Classification (Revision 3), United Nations, New York, 1990.

Table 3A.3 Intra-Industry Trade between Mexico, the United States, and the Rest of the World (average Grubel-Lloyd Index at 3-digit Level for 1990–92)

ISIC sectors	Mexico – United States	Mexico – Rest of the World	United States – Rest of the World
1. Agriculture	0.84	0.74	0.59
2. Forestry	0.99	0.92	0.25
5. Fishing	0.13	0.79	0.64
10. Coal	0.03	0.03	0.18
11. Petroleum	0.02	0.00	0.02
12. Uranium	0.00	0.00	0.01
13. Metal ores	0.43	0.45	0.86
14. Other mining	0.58	0.92	0.45
15. Food products	0.73	0.49	0.81
16. Tobacco	0.89	0.21	0.07
17. textiles	0.67	0.68	0.68
18. Apparel	0.67	0.25	0.18
19. Leather and footwear	0.67	0.67	0.28
20. Wood	0.87	0.40	0.70
21. Paper	0.28	0.26	0.82
22. Publishing and printing	0.64	0.65	0.65
23. Coke and petroleum	0.51	0.55	0.65
24. Chemicals	0.54	0.78	0.79
25. Rubber	0.45	0.33	0.80
26. Other non-metallic	0.68	0.68	0.69
27. Basic metals	0.75	0.58	0.62
28. Fabricated metals	0.67	0.40	0.66
29. Machinery and equipment	0.46	0.17	0.89
30. Office and computing	0.87	0.98	0.93
31. Electrical machinery	0.84	0.38	0.87
32. Radio, TV, communications	0.70	0.13	0.63
33. Medical, precision instruments	0.76	0.16	0.55
34. Motor vehicles	0.41	0.38	0.65
35. Other transport equipment	0.24	0.43	0.57
36. Furniture	0.89	0.54	0.35

References

Amemiya, T. 1978. "The Estimation of a Simultaneous Equation Generalized Probit Model." *Econometrica* 46:1191–1205.

Amemiya, T. 1979. "The Estimation of a Simultaneous Equation Tobit Model." *International Economic Review* 20:169–81.

Bhagwati, J., and A. Panagariya. 1996. "Preferential Trading Areas and Multilateralism: Strangers, Friends or Foes?" In J. Bhagwati and A. Panagariya (eds.), *The Economics of Preferential Trade Agreements.* Washington, DC: AEI Press.

Blundell, R., and R. Smith. 1994. "Coherency and Estimation in Simultaneous Models with Censored or Qualitative Dependent Variables." *Journal of Econometrics* 64:355–73.

Estevadeordal, A. 2000. "Negotiating Preferential Market Access: the Case of the North American Free Trade Agreement." *Journal of World Trade* 34(1):141–66.

Ethier, W. J. 1998. "The New Regionalism." *Economic Journal* 108:1149–61.

Garay, L. J., and A. Estevadeordal. 1996. "Protection, Preferential Tariff Elimination and Rules of Origin in the Americas." *Integration and Trade* 1:2–25.

Grossman, G., and E. Helpman. 1994. "Protection for Sale." *American Economic Review* 84:833–50.

Hoekman, B. 1993. "Rules of Origin for Goods and Services—Conceptual Issues and Economic Considerations." *Journal of World Trade* 27(4): 81–99.

Ju, J., and K. Krishna. 1998. "Firm Behavior and Market Access in Free Trade Area with Rules of Origin." NBER Working Paper No. 6857, Cambridge, MA: National Bureau of Economic Research.

Kowalczyk, C., and D. Davis. 1998. "Tariff Phase-Outs: Theory and Evidence from GATT and NAFTA." In J. Frankel (ed.), *Regionalization in the World Economy.* Chicago: Chicago University Press.

Krishna, K., and A. O. Krueger. 1995. "Implementing Free Trade Areas: Rules of Origin and Hidden Protection." In A. Deardorff, J. Levinsohn, and R. Stern (eds.), *New Directions in Trade Theory.* Ann Arbor: University of Michigan Press.

Maggi, G., and A. Rodriguez. 1998. "Import Penetration and the Politics of Trade Protection." NBER Working Paper No. 6711. Cambridge, MA: National Bureau of Economic Research.

Mayer, F. W. 1999. *Interpreting NAFTA*. New York: Columbia University Press.

Nelson, F., and L. Olson. 1978. "Specification and Estimation of a Simultaneous Equation Model with Limited Dependent Variables." *International Economic Review* 19:695–705.

Reyna, J. 1995. *Passport to North American Trade*. Colorado Springs, CO: Shepard's/McGraw-Hill.

Tornell, A., and G. Esquivel. 1995. "The Political Economy of Mexico's Entry to NAFTA." NBER Working Paper No. 5322. Cambridge, MA: National Bureau of Economic Research.

Vermulst, E., P. Waer, and J. Bourgeois (eds.). 1994. *Rules of Origin in International Trade: A Comparative Study* Ann Arbor: University of Michigan Press.

CHAPTER 4

Selective Liberalization in Response to Globalization: Rules of Origin as Determinants of Market Access Provisions in PTAs*

Kati Suominen

The latest wave of globalization—defined here as the increase in cross-border trade and capital flows—has been accompanied by a spectacular proliferation of preferential trading arrangements around the world. The encouraging movement toward regional and global liberalization is, however, hardly neutral to domestic politics. Trade has distributional consequences; trade liberalization entails that some actors lose while others gain.

It is the politics of trade that are at the heart of this chapter. I endeavor to show that both the formation and the format of PTAs result from the provision of differentiated obligations to actors with divergent preferences over trade policy outcomes. PTAs absent of sectoral selectivity are politically untenable: an agreement constructed to strike a balance between opposing interests and offering side payments to the losers is an agreement that (1) solves the political dilemmas facing governments seeking to court a range of interests and (2) has hopes of becoming ratified, and, indeed, self-enforcing.

* Versions of this chapter have appeared in *Integration & Trade* 7(19)(July–December 2003) and in Andreas Langenohl and Kirsten Westphal, eds.,*Conflicts in a Transnational World: Lessons from Nations and States in Transformation* (Frankfurt: Peter Lang, 2006). The chapter is also a shortened version of an essay in the author's Ph.D. dissertation (Suominen, 2004).

I illustrate these claims by focusing on two market access regulations central to any PTA, preferential tariff phaseout schedules and exclusions. My main contention is that rules of origin, another crucial market access instrument in PTAs, play a central, independent role in arbitrating cross-sectoral variation in the length of phaseouts and sectoral frequency of exclusions in PTAs.

I make a three-step argument. First, RoO have properties that allow governments to use them as substitutes for exclusions of sensitive products from coverage in the PTA with which the RoO are associated. RoO, in other words, enable governments to incorporate sensitive products into the PTA's coverage and subject them to preferential tariff liberalization schedules, rather than excluding these products and leaving them covered by the most-favored nation tariff. Substituting for exclusions, RoO make PTA formation politically possible.

However, and second, I argue that even the most restrictive RoO carry uncertainties that render them an *imperfect substitute* for exclusions, compelling sectors with stringent RoO to lobby for prolonged preferential tariff liberalization schedules. Sectors with loose RoO are marked by fast liberalization because of the absence of political economy pressure for long phaseouts. Third, exclusions—which can be conceptualized as infinite or unlaunched phaseouts—fall on sectors where (1) the pre-PTA tariff is so high that even RoO of maximum restrictiveness fall well short of substituting for the tariff and (2) RoO are unable to help upstream producers to capture markets for intermediate goods in downstream sectors.[1] I provide empirical evidence of the relationship between the restrictiveness of RoO on the one hand, and the length of tariff phaseouts and the occurrence of exclusions, on the other, through an econometric analysis of the EU-Mexico Free Trade Agreement, which entered into force in July 2000.

This study seeks to go beyond the prior theoretical studies on PTA formation by arguing that RoO arbitrate not only the decision whether

[1] Simply put, I use the level of restrictiveness of RoO to derive the preferences of different economic actors over preferential liberalization and to provide cues about the intensity of actors' preferences and lobbying weight in the negotiation of phaseout schedules.

to continue PTA talks or to fold them, but also the outcome of the next phase of PTA building, where the choice is either to exclude sensitive sectors from the PTA's coverage or to incorporate them in the PTA under prolonged tariff phaseouts—a distinction not previously made in the literature. I accomplish this by (1) contrasting the protection provided by RoO to that provided by exclusions and (2) allowing for a continuum of possible policy instruments selected to govern a sector in a PTA, instead of conceiving these instruments as dichotomous—either exclusion or immediate liberalization—as is done in most prior studies on preferential trading.

The first section of this chapter elaborates on the dependent variables, the length of preferential tariff phaseout, and the frequency of exclusions in the EU-Mexico FTA. The second section lays out the argument and the hypotheses and briefly discusses their relationship to existing studies. In the third section, I provide an overview of the structure of the key independent variable, the RoO of the EU-Mexico FTA. The fourth section puts forth the empirical specification and discusses the results. The fifth section concludes the chapter.

The Dependent Variable: Sectoral Tariff Phaseouts

There is great variation in the length of phaseouts—the speed of preferential tariff lowering from the base rate duty to a zero duty—and in the frequency of excluded products, both across economic sectors in a given PTA, and across different PTAs. In the EU-Mexico FTA, the EU agreed to eliminate its duties on Mexican industrial goods either immediately upon the agreement's entry into force (category A) or three years into the agreement, after three equal-sized annual tariff cuts (category B). For its part, Mexico established four different categories of tariff lowering for EU goods: immediate liberalization (category A) or liberalization after three, five, or seven years of phaseouts (categories B, B+, and C, respectively). For agricultural products, the schedules are more complex. Both parties pledged to cut tariffs immediately in some sectors (category 1), while phasing in duty-free treatment over three (category 2), eight (category 3), nine (category 4a), or ten (category 4) years in others. However, not all goods were subjected to tariff phaseouts. The access of numerous Mexican agricultural goods to the EU market became governed by a system of tariff quotas, and a number of agricultural goods—such as grains, meat, potatoes, some fruit, sugar, and milk derivatives—were excluded from the agreement's coverage altogether.[2]

Table 4.1 displays the average length of tariff phaseouts and the share of excluded tariff items by section of the Harmonized System in the EU-Mexico FTA. The calculations for phaseouts in the agricultural sectors (sections 1–4) include only products governed by tariffs, rather than also products covered by a tariff quota or a mixed tariff. Over the range of product categories, the EU's dismantling schedules average 1.7 years; Mexican phaseouts are longer, averaging nearly 4 years.[3] The sectoral distribution of long phaseout programs is different in the two countries: the EU's liberalization is slowest in raw and processed agricultural products, textiles and apparel, and arms and ammunition, whereas Mexico's longest phaseouts fall on processed agricultural products, plastics, base metals, textiles and apparel, footwear, and stone and glass.[4] Exclusions are concentrated in sectors where both parties have some of the slowest tariff phaseout schedules, namely, the raw material, agricultural, and food-processing sectors.

The EU-Mexico FTA is hardly sui generis: most PTAs forged around the world include similar sectoral variation in their phaseout programs. It is the task of this chapter to develop a deductive argument that helps account for the sources of such variation.

---

[2] The parties agreed to revise the market access provisions of these products in 2003. Notably, the EU gained immediate market access to Mexico for such exports as certain vegetables, fruits and fruit juices, tobacco, cheese, beer, liquors, spirits (vodka, cognac, certain whisky, gin), cut flowers, and olive oil. Trade in quality wines was liberalized in 2003.

[3] The average values of all sectors for phaseouts and exclusions at the bottom of the table are calculated from the values by section; calculations at the 6- or 8-digit level alter these figures slightly. For instance, the EU's total average percentage of exclusions rises to nearly 8 percent when calculations are made at the 8-digit level.

[4] To be sure, the table disguises intrasectoral variation in phaseouts given that the tariff-lowering schedules were negotiated at the level of tariff item, or at the 8-digit level of the HS.

Table 4.1 Average Tariff Phaseouts and Share of Exclusions in the EU-Mexico FTA by HS Section

Section	EU to Mexico (years)	Mexico to the EU (years)	Exclusions by EU (%)	Exclusions by Mexico (%)
1. Live animals	5.4	3.6	35.4	44.6
2. Vegetable products	3.9	2.6	25.6	14.7
3. Fats and oils	4.7	7.6	2.3	33.9
4. Food, beverages, and tobacco	6.5	4.0	36.2	37.2
5. Mineral products	0.0	1.4	0.0	0.0
6. Chemicals	0.7	3.5	1.6	17.9
7. Plastics	0.8	5.9	0.0	0.0
8. Leather goods	0.4	4.3	0.0	0.0
9. Wood products	0.9	3.9	0.0	0.0
10. Pulp and paper	0.0	4.6	0.0	0.0
11. Textiles and apparel	2.8	4.7	0.0	0.0
12. Footwear	1.6	4.7	0.0	0.0
13. Stone and glass	0.6	4.7	0.0	0.0
14. Jewelry	0.0	2.5	0.0	0.0
15. Base metals	1.1	5.8	0.0	0.0
16. Machinery and electrical equipment	0.3	4.3	0.0	0.0
17. Transportation equipment	1.0	3.3	0.0	0.0
18. Optics	0.2	2.4	0.0	0.0
19. Arms and ammunition	2.7	0.0	0.0	0.0
20. Works of art, miscellaneous	0.4	3.5	0.0	0.0
Average	*1.7*	*3.9*	*5.1*	*7.4*

Sources: Author's calculations on the basis of the FTA text; Estevadeordal and Suominen (2003).

Argument: RoO as the Source of Prolonged Phaseouts

Why do tariff phaseouts vary drastically across economic sectors in PTAs? And why are so few exclusions observed—why do governments in most PTAs subject the vast majority of economic sectors to some liberalization process despite the ostensive political risks of inflicting losses on domestic protectionist interests? Finally, why do exclusions fall on sectors they do? This chapter strives to answer these questions by exploring the operation of rules of origin. The first part of this section discusses the functions and properties of RoO. The second part lays out the explanatory framework that links RoO to PTA formation in general and to prolonged tariff phase-outs in particular and puts forth the hypotheses.

Functions and Properties of RoO

As noted in previous chapters, there are two types of rules of origin, non-preferential and preferential.[5] Preferential RoO, the focus of this study, define the intra-PTA inputs and/or processes that must be included in a final product in order for the product to be regarded as originating in the PTA area—and thus to qualify for PTA-conferred preferential treatment by the importing PTA partner. In essence, RoO entail a minimum cost share of the value of the final product that must arise within the PTA.

The economic justification for preferential RoO is to curb trade deflection—to avoid transshipment of products from non–PTA members through a low-tariff PTA partner to a high-tariff one. As such, RoO are an inherent feature of FTAs where the member states' external tariffs diverge and/or where the members wish to retain their individual tariff policies vis-à-vis the rest of the world (ROW). RoO would be unnecessary in a customs union (CU) with a common external tariff (CET) that covered the whole tariff universe. However, in practice, RoO are widely used in CUs, either as a transitory tool in the process of moving toward the CET or as a more permanent means of covering product categories where reaching agreement on a CET is difficult, for instance, because of large tariff differentials between the member countries. RoO are a feature of virtually all PTAs around the world and hardly inconsequential given that more than a third of global commerce takes place within PTAs.[6]

---

[5] Nonpreferential RoO are used to distinguish foreign from domestic products in establishing antidumping and countervailing duties, safeguard measures, origin-marking requirements, and/or discriminatory quantitative restrictions or tariff quotas, as well as in the context of government procurement.

[6] When unilateral preferential schemes such as the Generalized System of Preferences are accounted for, no less than 60 percent of world trade is estimated to be conducted on a preferential basis. Importantly, the unilateral preferential programs carry many of the same disciplines as PTAs.

Importantly here, as an effective means to deter transshipment, RoO can tempt economic interests to strive to use them beyond the efforts to avert trade deflection.[7] Often negotiated at up to the 8- or 10-digit level of disaggregation, RoO, like the tariff, make a superbly targetable instrument. Moreover, that RoO are generally defined in highly technical terms rather than assigned a numerical value entails that they can be tailored for each individual product differently and that they are not nearly as immediately quantifiable and comparable across products as the tariff is.

Indeed, RoO are widely considered a trade policy instrument that can work to offset the benefits of tariff liberalization.[8] Most prominently, RoO can be employed to favor intra-PTA industry linkages over those between the PTA and ROW and, as such, to indirectly protect PTA-based input producers vis-à-vis their extra-PTA rivals (Krueger, 1993; Krishna and Krueger, 1995). Stringent RoO can compel intra-PTA firms with low-cost extra-PTA supply sources to turn to higher-cost inputs produced within the PTA in order to obtain preferential treatment for their final products, particularly in sectors where the preferential margin—the difference between the importer's MFN tariff and preferential tariff—is wide. As such, RoO are akin to a tariff on the intermediate product levied by the importing country (Falvey and Reed, 2000; Lloyd, 2001a) and can be used by one PTA member to secure its PTA partners' input markets for the exports of its own intermediate products (Krueger, 1993; Krishna and Krueger, 1995).

If RoO introduce a price wedge in the intermediate market, they could be expected to engender opposition by downstream producers intent

[7] Indeed, that governments forgo negotiating simple regional value-added rules and, rather, engage in prolonged, contentious bargaining over highly complex and different types of RoO suggests that RoO play a role beyond resolving the trade deflection problem.

[8] Analysts' interest in RoO has surged over the past few years. See Krueger (1993); Krishna and Krueger (1995); Jensen-Moran (1996); Garay and Estevadeordal (1996); Stephenson (1997); Scollay (1997); Ju and Krishna (1998); Appiah (1999); Falvey and Reed (2000); Estevadeordal (2000); Duttagupta (2000); Duttagupta and Panagariya (2003); Lloyd (1997, 2001a, 2001b); Rodriguez (2001); Augier and Gasiorek (2002); Brenton and Manchin (2002); Cadot et al. (2002); Flatters (2002); Garay and Cornejo (2002); Hirsch (2002); Krishna (2002); Estevadeordal and Miller (2002); Estevadeordal and Suominen (2003); Suominen (2004); and contributions in Cadot, Estevadeordal, and Suwa-Eisenmann (2006).

on retaining their extra-PTA low-cost supply sources while still qualifying for the PTA-conferred preferential treatment. However, the scholarly literature offers two theoretical reasons why downstream producers may accept or even favor stringent RoO.

First, RoO may simply be the price that downstream producers have to pay for the PTA: despite risking costly trade diversion, restrictive RoO can help placate protectionist sectors so as to render PTA formation politically feasible (Duttagupta, 2000).

Second, downstream producers can draw contingent benefits from stringent RoO and, as such, be willing to shoulder the heightened production costs. For instance, should the linkages between different stages of production in the industry be tight, extra-PTA final goods producers would likely be hard pressed to locate appropriate components within the PTA and remain competitive vis-à-vis the intra-PTA producers in the PTA market. Even if extra-PTA firms were to locate in the PTA market via what I term tariff-jumping-like "RoO jumping," discrimination would continue until the regional sourcing met the RoO requirements (Graham and Wilkie, 1998). RoO can thus be used to meet the political economy goal of extending protection to both intra-PTA input and final goods producers. In an econometric study of the determinants of the restrictiveness of the RoO in NAFTA, Estevadeordal (2000) shows that the same political economy factors that drive tariff protection also drive RoO.

In sum, RoO are to help avert trade deflection—to pre-empt free-riding by ROW producers on PTA-conferred preferential treatment. However, when set at stringent levels, RoO have two properties that render them effective at shielding sensitive sectors from the liberalizing effects of a PTA, and even for converting protectionist producers into supporters of PTA formation. One, RoO can be employed for protectionist purposes to insulate, much like prohibitive transportation costs, a protectionist industry from the impact of trade deflection that a RoO-less PTA (or PTA with very loose RoO) would entail.[9] Two, stringent RoO in

[9] If Foreign were able to satisfy only a fraction of import demand in Home, Home's producer prices could remain relatively unchanged post-PTA, diminishing opposition to PTA formation in Home, yet augmenting the demand for PTA formation in Foreign given that producer prices in Home would remain at above-world levels.

downstream industries will compel downstream producers that seek to qualify for PTA-conferred preferences to obtain their inputs from within the PTA area, which provides Home's input producers with captive markets downstream and, thus, opportunities for extracting rents that would be unavailable in the absence of the PTA.[10]

Explanation

How do RoO relate to PTA formation and tariff phaseout programs? There are two possible answers: (1) governments may use RoO as tools to accentuate the softening impact of prolonged phaseouts on protectionist sectors, in which case RoO will complement preferential tariffs, or (2) they may employ RoO to mollify protectionist sectors when pursuing fast liberalization, in which case RoO serve as substitutes to preferential tariffs (Estevadeordal, 2000). I argue that these two possibilities need not be mutually exclusive when examined against the option of excluding a sector from the PTA's coverage altogether and leaving it covered by the existing MFN tariff. Rather, I suggest that governments use RoO to placate sectors opposed to any form of preferential liberalization, fast or slow, in order to avoid excluding sectors from the PTA's coverage altogether. As I show, it is viewing RoO in this light that allows establishment of the microfoundations for the relationship between RoO and preferential tariff lowering—that restrictive RoO will be conducive to long phaseouts, and loose RoO to short phaseouts.

The following elaborates on the implications of this notion. The argument is based on six assumptions. One, governments opt for the combination of trade policy instruments that yields the highest net gain in the form of tariff revenues (which can be usefully redistributed to special interests or the public) and campaign contributions by industry lobbies. Two, each country has a mix of more- and less-protected industries, so that tariff revenue is positive and some industries feature a higher MFN

[10] RoO, in other words, can overcompensate protectionist upstream producers for the damage done by trade liberalization as a result of performing functions—capturing markets—that render them superior to the no-PTA option in these producers' utility functions.

tariff than others. Three, campaign contributions and lobbying in general are always costly. Four, there are no transfers from one partner to another. Five, although PTA members will apply a common protocol of rules of origin (read from the same list), they will have their own lists of sectoral exclusions and tariff-lowering schedules (read from different lists), as is usually the case in PTAs. Six, RoO are set domestically in Home and thus exogenous to the bargaining over the PTA; this assumption, as I shall discuss, is particularly appropriate in a study of the EU's RoO regimes.

RoO as Imperfect Substitute for the Tariff

By adopting the RoO instrument, governments can (1) reduce the political costs that full liberalization would entail for sectors opposed to being included in the PTA and (2) court proliberalization lobbies by counteracting the prospect of escalation of sectoral exclusions—mutual defections by the PTA-forming governments—that would render the PTA meaningless to its demandeurs.[11] That sectors jeopardized by PTA formation can be more easily bought off to be included in the PTA through the use of the

[11] Note also that the Home government should prefer PTA formation to exclusions: with downstream producers having incentives to export to high-priced Foreign, demand in final goods in Home will be met through imports, which increases tariff revenue to the Home government. The argument behind the potential for the escalation of exclusions is as follows. Consider the extreme case of a RoO-less FTA with an immediate tariff phaseout: it would be highly liberalizing, as third-country goods would flow into the FTA market through the lowest-tariff country. Unlike in a customs union with a CET, each member state in a PTA (an FTA or an incomplete customs union) maintains its own external tariff; as a result of the PTA, the lowest-tariff country for a given import product would obtain all tariff revenue for the PTA's imports of that product. In the absence of trade deflection, producer surplus in Home could remain at ex ante levels if Foreign was able to satisfy only a small fraction of Home's demand. Under all other circumstances, producer surplus in Home would fall (Grossman and Helpman, 1995). However, I posit that when trade deflection is present, the failure of Foreign to satisfy the Home market would be made up by transshipment—in which case producer surplus in Home would unequivocally fall below pre-PTA levels. Thus, although Home's protectionist sectors would balk at the PTA in the absence of trade deflection when their profits risk being undercut, they will certainly do so when trade deflection is allowed. Home government would also lack incentives to form the PTA should the overall transshipment patterns favor Foreign, causing Home to suffer a net loss in tariff revenue.

RoO instrument is all the more plausible given that RoO are preset and endogenous to the preferences of these very sectors.[12]

These notions suggest that once the PTA is fully free of duty, the most restrictive RoO will be in sectors with the highest preferential margin (i.e., in the presence of a zero preferential tariff and a high MFN tariff), so that the level of restrictiveness of a PTA member's RoO will mirror the height of its MFN tariff. However, I argue that although RoO and the MFN tariff are offsetting instruments, there are a number of reasons why RoO cannot be expected to measure up to the tariff's restrictiveness. Although RoO, much like exclusions, can deter the entry of products from ROW post-PTA to free-ride on PTA-wide free trade, RoO, unlike exclusions, will not be able to do so as long as the potential exporters (1) meet the RoO requirements at lower costs than they would incur when paying the MFN tariff to the Home market *and* (2) produce sufficiently to reduce producer prices in the Home market. However, whether this will happen cannot be known perfectly ex ante. At a minimum, then, the choice of RoO inherently carries uncertainty concerning the subsequent trade and price effects.

Moreover, Foreign exporters have incentives to cheat, or to seek to circumvent the high compliance costs of RoO; thus, there is uncertainty

---

The specter of third-country products penetrating the PTA market via the low-tariff Foreign—ROW's free-riding on the PTA-provided preferential treatment—could thus be expected to lead Home's protectionist sectors to call for (1) not launching PTA talks at all or (2) excluding their products from the PTA's coverage. Of the two options, the latter is more feasible to the Home government intent on courting the demandeurs of the PTA, first and foremost, assuming constant returns to scale, export-competing sectors, and actors with relation-specific investments—high sunk costs—in the PTA area. However, once Home and Foreign opt for a PTA with exclusions rather than not negotiating at all, they are left with a problem. In this scenario, each government will either fully liberalize or fully exclude any given sector, as partial liberalization would in the presence of transshipment be unequivocally inferior to full exclusion and/or no PTA formation to the protectionist sectors. However, should the petitions for exclusions escalate on both sides precisely in sectors where gains from trade would exist—where Home and Foreign could improve the lot of their exporters—they can torpedo the rationales for PTA formation and revert the bargaining governments to status quo ante. In short, the specter of rampant transshipment engenders rampant exclusions, precluding PTA formation.

[12] See Suominen (2004) for the derived preferences of economic actors over the stringency of RoO.

as to how binding the RoO will be. Even the most rigorous origin certification requirements for compliance with RoO in Foreign and verification mechanisms in customs in Home cannot be expected to be fully reliable. RoO will be fully binding only in the presence of a perfect alignment between RoO mandated by the PTA and RoO implemented by Foreign exporters and Home customs.[13]

Paradoxically, it is RoO that are set prior to the decision to negotiate a PTA with a particular partner—RoO that are pre-established, as they are in the EU, for instance, in order to reduce uncertainty among Home's producers about the structure of RoO in Home's future PTAs—that are particularly prone to engendering ex ante uncertainty. Note that when RoO are preset, they are not tailored specifically to counter inflows from the new partner in question, but rather, forged at a prior date.

Preset RoO have two implications. First, they mean that protectionist sectors lack perfect information about the protection a given RoO can provide vis-à-vis each new PTA partner—that is, whether and how much RoO might leak in comparison to the MFN tariff that currently governs trade between Home and the potential PTA partner. Second, upstream producers expecting to capture markets through stringent RoO downstream upon the new PTA's entry into force are uncertain about the extent of derived demand emanating from export-competing downstream producers for originating components, as such demand is in good part a function of the overall import demand in the new PTA partner country. Thus, although the preset format provides for certainty regarding the structure of RoO, it also imposes a straitjacket RoO regime that engenders uncertainty about the effects of the very structure of RoO when applied vis-à-vis partners with divergent economic features.[14]

---

[13] PTAs vary in their certification requirements. Some, such as NAFTA, require certification by the exporter only. Others require certification to be made not by the exporter, but at the request of the exporter by a governmental agency or an entity to which the government has delegated the authority to issue certifications. Still others, such as the EU's FTAs, require certification to be made first by the exporter and then by the governmental or delegated body. See Chapter 2.

[14] The intuition that RoO cannot be expected with full certainty to be a perfect substitute for the tariff also has empirical grounds and follows (albeit in a circular manner) from the argument above: if RoO were a perfect substitute or a complement to the MFN tariff,

Restrictiveness of RoO, Length of Tariff Phaseouts, and Frequency of Exclusions

It is the expected imperfection of the RoO instrument that this chapter turns on. Anticipating RoO to be an imperfect substitute for exclusion or at a minimum not knowing the exact effects of RoO vis-à-vis a new PTA partner, Home's protectionist producers will have incentives to lobby to perpetuate protection through prolonged tariff phaseouts in their government's phaseout schedule. It is in sectors where producers would prefer RoO to be as perfect as tariffs in barring import penetration—where the relevance of RoO as trade policy instrument is high—that the very imperfections in RoO lead to lobbying for long phaseouts. In other words, whereas the difference between protection provided by the MFN tariff and protection provided by RoO may be equally wide across sectors, the damage inflicted on a sector by this difference grows with the prior tariff the sector enjoys. Thus, the level of restrictiveness of RoO drives the length of tariff phaseouts.

The argument is best illustrated by considering the preferences of Home's upstream and downstream producers with restrictive and loose RoO. There are four sectoral outcomes.

---

they would have the same effect as exclusions and render PTA formation moot by ex ante frustrating Foreign exporters' efforts to access Home's market. No PTAs would be formed, as Foreign would be unlikely to expend negotiation resources much less ratify a PTA where Home had either excluded all sectors where Foreign could gain market access or imposed a rule of origin that was able to block increases in trade flows like an exclusion. Yet, PTAs—and PTAs that are not rife with exclusions and that are neither CUs nor de facto CUs—are observed. Moreover, PTAs in general have been found to boost trade among their members even in their early years, when preferential tariffs are still positive; if trade did not increase at all, RoO would be the likeliest culprit and as protectionist as the pre-PTA tariff between the partners. If trade declined, RoO would be a complement to, not a substitute for, the tariff. Furthermore, if a PTA was launched regardless of Foreign's opposition and RoO were a perfect substitute for the MFN tariff, Home's producers would not ever have to issue petitions for exclusion from the PTA, much less obtain them. Yet, virtually no PTA is fully devoid of exclusions. Conversely, if RoO did not help shield against incoming trade flows, there would be no incentive to lobby for them much less adopt them in PTAs. Yet, virtually all PTAs have RoO. Thus, even the most restrictive of RoO can be viewed as lying—or at least expected by actors involved in building a PTA to lie—somewhere between full liberalization and full exclusion.

First, in upstream sectors, protectionist upstream producers that can be expected to have obtained restrictive RoO ex ante and be concerned about the leakiness of RoO have incentives to lobby for long phaseouts in these upstream sectors. That they have obtained stringent RoO evince their lobbying weight; furthermore, rents arising from the protection provided by RoO (as well as by captive markets downstream) could be expected to have boosted the lobbying strength of these producers.

In contrast and second, export-competing upstream producers will likely have invested little in pursuing stringent RoO. These producers also have few incentives to lobby for long phaseouts in their (upstream) sectors.

Third, in import-competing downstream sectors, RoO will likely be set at very stringent levels. Downstream producers require protection provided by restrictive RoO, while their domestic upstream providers have no incentives to oppose a restrictive RoO. The more import-competing upstream producers are, the likelier they are to join forces with the downstream sector to lobby for restrictive RoO. However, that RoO are only an imperfect substitute for the tariff should provide powerful incentives to both protectionist up- and downstream producers to lobby for long phaseouts.[15]

Fourth, in globally export-competing downstream sectors with downstream producers procuring inputs globally, downstream producers can be expected to have lobbied for RoO of maximum looseness in order to retain their supply links in ROW. However, their upstream providers can be expected to have called for RoO whose restrictiveness rises the more import-competing the upstream provider. The restrictiveness of RoO is thus plausibly located between the preferences of these two sets of actors.

However, when downstream is globally export-competing and hence not subject to import penetration, *tariff* protection to hedge against the leakiness of RoO for both up- and downstream producers is inconsequen-

[15] Importantly, even if Home's upstream producers lobbied for quick phaseouts in their domestic market in downstream sectors where they expect Foreign producers to start using their inputs and exporting the final good Home, they would likely be faced with adamant opposition to quick tariff lowering by Home's import-competing downstream producers.

tial, and neither has incentives to lobby for long phaseouts. Downstream producers do not need protection, and upstream producers, even if protectionist, will not be faced with the transshipment of final goods containing cheap third-country parts given that downstream is export-competing. Thus, sectors with RoO of loose to medium levels of restrictiveness can be expected to feature relatively quick tariff liberalization.

The stylized predicted lobbying incentives and outcomes for phaseouts in Home can be depicted as follows:

Restrictiveness of Preset RoO

Location in Production Chain	Restrictive	Loose
Upstream	Upstream lobbies for long phaseouts Outcome: long phaseouts	Upstream lacks incentives to lobby for long phaseouts Outcome: no or short phaseouts
Downstream	Downstream lobbies for long phaseouts Upstream lobbies for long phaseouts Outcome: long phaseouts	Downstream lacks incentives to lobby for long phaseouts Upstream lacks incentives to lobby when downstream is globally competitive Outcome: no or short to medium-length phaseouts

In sum, once negotiations over tariff phaseouts are launched, sectors that have in ex ante bargaining obtained the most stringent RoO—import-competing upstream and downstream sectors—also have the greatest incentives to lobby for long phaseouts *because of* RoO's inability to substitute for the tariff.[16] Meanwhile, the imperfection of RoO as a

[16] To be sure, the argument here does not allow for a protectionist producer to have failed in the past to lobby for and obtain RoO whose restrictiveness is aligned with the producer's need for protection. In such cases, producers with loose RoO could be expected to lobby for long phaseouts. However, the argument here also implies that they may not necessarily succeed in the lobbying game given precisely their inability to secure restrictive RoO in the past and hence their subsequent failure to profit from RoO. The argument also assumes that stringent RoO require an investment in lobbying; governments, in other words, are expected to set the RoO at low levels in the absence of lobbying.

substitute for the tariff is inconsequential to sectors that are globally export-competing—and where the preset rule of origin is likely loose to begin with.

Note that exclusions, if still employed, would under this argument fall on sectors where RoO of maximum stringency are not only unable to substitute for MFN tariffs, but also unable to capture markets because of the absence of processing—first and foremost in raw materials, where possibilities for capturing downstream markets do not exist and where the partner country's meeting even the wholly obtained criterion is relatively automatic.[17] Meanwhile, the impact of RoO on the phaseouts of Foreign, the taker of RoO, is ambiguous given that RoO are a function of political economy variables in Home alone: there is a theoretical disconnect between RoO and preferential tariff phaseouts in the taker country, with phaseouts being driven by variables other than RoO.

Hypotheses

The argument yields two testable hypotheses:

H1: *The more stringent the RoO, the likelier a prolonged phaseout by the PTA partner whose RoO are employed in the PTA, ceteris paribus.*

H2: *Sectors where RoO fall well short of substituting for MFN tariffs and fail to provide captive markets despite being stringent—sectors where MFN tariffs are particularly high and RoO highly stringent—will be excluded from the PTA by the partner whose RoO are employed in the PTA, ceteris paribus.*

---

[17] For instance, if Home produces wheat at higher cost than Foreign, a PTA would lead to Foreign wheat entering Home; by virtue of producing wheat domestically, Foreign meets even the most stringent, wholly obtained RoO, while Home's wheat producers obtain no benefit from the stringent RoO in the very sector of wheat because of the absence of captive market prospects. To be sure, they might benefit from stringent RoO in (downstream) food-processing industries, where they can capture markets for inputs (wheat), and hence prefer to operate via RoO, not exclusions. Exclusions should thus occur in raw materials sectors with a high MFN tariff—and hence likely with a rule of origin that is ex ante set at very high levels.

Relationship to Existing Explanations

This study has four immediate potential contributions. First, the explanation proposed here is to my knowledge the first effort to show why and when long phaseouts are chosen over exclusions in PTAs. Duttagupta and Panagariya (2003) and Grossman and Helpman (1995) both examine circumstances where PTA formation becomes politically tenable; however, both view RoO as the arbitrator between the dichotomous outcome of PTA formation versus no PTA formation (or exclusion versus no exclusion), and neither indicates when exclusions rather than long phaseouts result. Furthermore, Duttagupta (2000) and Duttagupta and Panagariya (2003), which argue that RoO can make sectors previously opposed to the establishment of a PTA disposed to it, (1) assume that the introduction of RoO will be accompanied by full and immediate preferential tariff liberalization and (2) present the introduction of RoO as a one-shot game that essentially ends in PTA formation once RoO are chosen. This chapter shows that RoO not only shape the decision as to whether to continue or terminate PTA talks, but also arbitrate the outcomes of the next phase of PTA building, where the choice is between exclusions and prolonged phaseouts—a distinction not previously made in the literature.

Second, I develop a novel, deductive argument for the relationship between the sectoral restrictiveness of RoO and the length of preferential tariff liberalization programs by countering the existing literature's tacit assumption that RoO and tariffs are perfect substitutes.

Third, I build on the methodology of the handful of existing studies on preferential tariff liberalization, particularly Estevadeordal (2000) and Kowalczyk and Davis (1998), in three ways. One, I modify the groundbreaking index for the restrictiveness of RoO developed by Estevadeordal (2000) in a study on NAFTA to account for the idiosyncrasies of the types of RoO employed by the EU. Yet the index here is fully compatible with that of Estevadeordal. Two, this chapter is the first to incorporate both the MFN tariff and the restrictiveness of RoO as independent variables in preferential tariff liberalization. Three, this study pioneers in examining the robustness of the RoO variable through industry fixed effects.

Fourth, on a broader level, this chapter provides a fresh explanation for the drive *away from* exclusions that is evident in today's PTAs. With the lowering of tariffs and transportation and communications costs around the world, sourcing abroad in low-cost locations has become an increasingly viable option to firms—and, indeed, a must for cutting costs in the face of tightening global competition.[18] This growing propensity toward fragmentation of production, however, presents a threat to high-cost domestic input providers. This chapter implies that these suppliers see an opportunity in PTAs to reduce the incentives for final goods producers to shift to sourcing from lower-cost suppliers abroad. Rather than settling for barriers—exclusions—in PTAs, inefficient input suppliers opt for RoO in order to hang on to a market share that will keep them afloat in the face of globalization. It would thus not be a coincidence that the restrictiveness of preferential RoO around the world has tended to increase over time.[19]

Independent Variable: The Structure and Restrictiveness of EU RoO

This section draws cross-RoO comparisons through an index grounded on the plausible restrictiveness of a given type of RoO. Estevadeordal (2000) constructs a categorical index ranging from 1 (least restrictive) to 7 (most restrictive) on the basis of NAFTA RoO. Although this chapter builds on Estevadeordal's index, some modifications are made to the index's observation rule (specified in Appendix 4.1) to account for the structure of EU RoO—in particular, the instances where the CTC component is not used.

---

[18] See, for example, Venables (1999) and Bond (2001). McLaren (2000) shows how the entry of independent suppliers into a market can reduce the incentives for vertical integration; this implies that trade liberalization and declining transportation costs can also undercut incentives for maintaining prior sourcing ties in the market should up- and downstream firms be separate from each other and the new entrants produce supplies at low costs.

[19] See Suominen (2004), Estevadeordal and Miller (2002), and Garay and Cornejo (2002).

Table 4.2 ▌Restrictiveness of RoO in the EU-Mexico FTA, by Section

HS section	RoO restrictiveness
1. Live animals	6.98
2. Vegetable products	6.57
3. Fats and oils	4.65
4. Food, beverages, and tobacco	4.98
5. Mineral products	3.53
6. Chemicals	3.90
7. Plastics	4.95
8. Leather goods	3.31
9. Wood products	2.89
10. Pulp and paper	4.57
11. Textiles and apparel	6.06
12. Footwear	4.11
13. Stone and glass	3.70
14. Jewelry	3.65
15. Base metals	4.20
16. Machinery and electrical equipment	4.79
17. Transportation equipment	4.62
18. Optics	4.96
19. Arms and ammunition	4.00
20. Works of art, miscellaneous	4.15
Average	***4.53***

Source: Author's calculations.

Table 4.2 illustrates the restrictiveness of RoO at the sectoral level in the EU-Mexico FTA. The RoO are nearly identical to the EU's standard, Pan-Euro RoO regime, which was unilaterally established at a prior date by the EU.[20] As such, the EU-Mexico RoO regime can be considered genuinely exogenous to the FTA bargain.

[20] The EU-Mexico RoO regime deviates from the Pan-Euro model only in regard to some dozen products (at the 4-digit level). The Pan-Euro system stems from the European Commission's drive to harmonize the EU's existing and future preferential RoO regimes in order to facilitate the operations of EU exporters dealing on multiple trade fronts and to pave the way for the EU's Eastern European FTA partners in particular to draw greater

The data reveal important variation in the degree of restrictiveness across economic sectors. Agricultural products are governed largely by the wholly obtained and change in chapter rules, and textiles and apparel are covered by change in chapter or technical requirements and also by the NAFTA-like yarn forward RoO, whereby clothing must have gone through a change in tariff classification from yarn to thread, from thread to cloth, and from cloth to clothing.[21] Meanwhile, sectors with lower restrictiveness values, such as leather, jewelry, and stone and glass, are predominated by change in heading or stand-alone import content RoO that impose a ceiling on nonoriginating components of 40–50 percent of the ex-works price of the final product. In between fall sectors such as machinery and optics, which often combine an import content rule with an exception, and transport equipment, which is governed by change in heading plus import content RoO.

The box-and-whisker plots in Figure 4.1 provide a more-nuanced look at the sectoral restrictiveness of the RoO. The plots essentially reveal the standard deviation in the restrictiveness values within sectors as calculated at the 6-digit level. The figure shows that the restrictiveness values of RoO are nearly uniform within Sections 13–21. This does not necessarily indicate the absence of intrasectoral variation in the *type* of RoO, only that regardless of their type, RoO within these sectors obtain the same restrictiveness values. There is much greater intrasectoral variation in restrictiveness values in Sections 1–12, with foodstuffs (Section 4), textiles (Section 11), and footwear (Section 12) featuring a wide range of restrictiveness values.

---

benefits from EU-provided preferential treatment via diagonal cumulation—which would be precluded by a lack of compatibility between the various RoO regimes. The European Commission's Regulation 46 of January 1999 reiterates the harmonized protocols, outlining the so-called single-list RoO. For further details on the Pan-Euro system and the EU's extra-European FTAs with Mexico, Chile, and South Africa, see Estevadeordal and Suominen (2003) and Suominen (2004).

[21] Thus, clothing manufactured in the FTA area from cloth woven there but using nonoriginating yarn will not qualify for preferential treatment.

Figure 4.1 | Dispersion of Restrictiveness of RoO Values in the EU-Mexico FTA, by Section

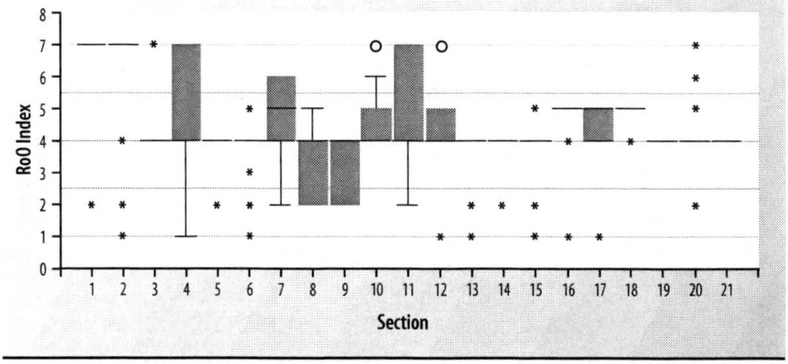

Source: Author's calculations based on the EU-Mexico RoO protocol.

Note: Box plots represent so-called interquartile ranges (IQRs). The lines in the middle of the boxes represent the median (50th percentile) of the data. The box extends from the 25th percentile to the 75th percentile, or through the IQR. The whiskers emerging from the boxes extend to the lower and upper adjacent values.The upper adjacent value is defined as the largest data point less than or equal to x(.75) + 1.5 IQR. The lower adjacent value is defined as the smallest data point greater than or equal to x(.25) + 1.5 IQR. Observed points more extreme than the adjacent values are individually plotted (outliers and extreme values are marked using x and o symbols).

Connecting RoO and Phaseouts: Empirical Specification

While isolating RoO has yielded important insights into their plausible trade effects, the actual market access afforded by and, hence, the trade effects of PTAs are inherently a function of *both* RoO and the extent of preferential tariff liberalization. This is particularly relevant in the case of the EU. That the EU is applying a uniform RoO regime across its PTA partners yet follows somewhat distinct tariff liberalization schedules across those partners begs for an analysis of the relationship between RoO and tariff preferences.

How are RoO and phaseouts connected? Table 4.3 serves as a starting point. It reports average phaseout years by values of the RoO index. Although longer phaseout values do appear to be somewhat correlated with the restrictiveness of RoO in the EU case, the data are excessively aggregate to permit any firm conclusions to be drawn.

Figure 4.2 links the EU's sectoral phaseouts with the restrictiveness of RoO, providing a somewhat clearer indication that the two variables fluctuate together.

Table 4.3 EU-Mexico FTA Phaseouts by the RoO Index Values (years)

Restrictiveness of RoO	Liberalization: EU to Mexico	Liberalization: Mexico to EU
1	1.48	5.35
2	0.66	4.30
3	0.00	8.00
4	0.96	4.20
5	0.56	4.03
6	0.91	5.71
7	3.80	4.62

Source: Author's calculations.

Figure 4.2 Phaseouts and Restrictiveness of RoO by Section in the EU-Mexico FTA

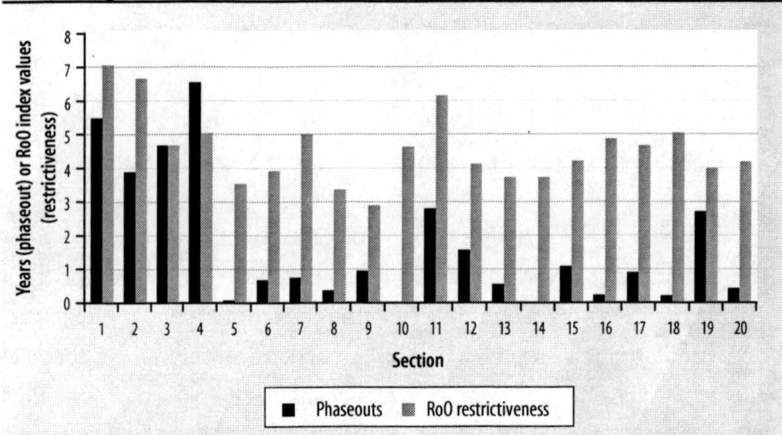

Source: Author's calculations.

Testing for RoO and Phaseouts

Aggregation at the sectoral level is excessively crude to establish a clear connection between the length of tariff phaseouts and the restrictiveness of RoO. I construct a more disaggregate and rigorous specification that evaluates the relationship between the two variables by estimating the following equation at the 6-digit level:

$$POUT\text{-}EU_i = b_0 + b_1 RoO\text{-}RI_i + b_2 PRE\text{-}MAR\text{-}EU_i + b_3 IMP\text{-}RAT\text{-}EU_i + b_4 EXP\text{-}RAT\text{-}EU_i + b_5 IIT\text{-}EU\text{-}MEX_i + b_6 IIT\text{-}EU\text{-}ROW_i + b_7 P\text{-}OUT\text{-}MEX_i + b_8 F_{(4k)i}, \quad (4.1)$$

where

- $POUT\text{-}EU_i$ stands for years to liberalization under the FTA in tariff line i;
- $RoO\text{-}RI_i$ is the restrictiveness of the FTA's RoO;
- $PRE\text{-}MAR\text{-}EU_i$ is the absolute preferential margin (the difference between the EU's MFN tariff and the preferential tariff to Mexico in the first year of the agreement);
- $IMP\text{-}RAT\text{-}EU_i$ stands for the import ratio (the ratio of imports from Mexico to the EU's total trade) in 1998;
- $EXP\text{-}RAT\text{-}EU_i$ is the export ratio (the ratio of exports to Mexico to the EU's total trade) in 1998;
- $IIT\text{-}EU\text{-}MEX_i$ *and* $IIT\text{-}EU\text{-}ROW_i$ are Grubel-Lloyd indices of intra-industry trade of the EU with Mexico and the EU with ROW in 1998, respectively;
- $POUT\text{-}MEX_i$ is the Mexican phaseout schedule; and
- $F_{(4k)i}$ is the fixed effect per 4-digit industry, as represented by (4*k*).

I subsequently replace the $PRE\text{-}MAR\text{-}EU_i$ variable with $EU\text{-}MFN_i$, which is the EU's MFN tariff for 1998.

Data on phaseouts are obtained from the FTA text at the 8-digit level and aggregated to the 6-digit level by taking simple averages. The variable for the restrictiveness of RoO is constructed at the 6-digit level of disaggregation on the basis of the RoO protocol. MFN tariffs are obtained from the United Nations Conference on Trade and Development's Trade Analysis and Information System (UNCTAD-TRAINS) at the 8-digit level and aggregated to the 6-digit level by taking simple averages. Import data are also from UNCTAD-TRAINS at the 6-digit level, and export data are obtained from SourceOECD.

The expectation is that ceteris paribus, sectors with restrictive RoO will be marked by long phaseouts. As for the control variables, first, high preferential margins can be expected to be proxies for sectors where the MFN tariff is also high—sectors that would lobby for long phaseouts. Second, the endogenous tariff literature suggests that high import ratios will lead to resistance to tariff liberalization, whereas high export ratios will indicate sectors that would lobby for fast market opening. Third, sectors where the EU has intra-industry trade with Mexico can be expected to lobby for quick bilateral liberalization, whereas sectors with high levels of intra-industry trade with the rest of the world will likely indicate competitive, open sectors that will also lobby for fast access to the Mexican market.[22] Fourth, quick tariff liberalization by Mexico may be reciprocated by the EU.[23] Fifth, the MFN tariff can be expected to be positively related to the length of phaseouts.[24] Including industry fixed effects at the 4-digit level of the ISIC Revision 3 classification allows assessment of the robustness of the policy variables, RoO, and MFN tariff.[25]

The results are reported in Table 4.4. They are as expected. First, columns I–IV show that the restrictiveness of rules of origin plays an im-

[22] The correlation among intra-industry indices is very low (0.12).

[23] Kowalczyk and Davis (1998) find that Mexico's tariff phaseouts were positively and significantly influenced by U.S. tariff phaseouts in NAFTA, which indicates reciprocity in the phaseout negotiations; however, U.S. phaseouts were unaffected by those of Mexico. Estevadeordal (2000), meanwhile, finds a positive and significant relationship both between Mexico's phaseouts and U.S. phaseouts and vice versa.

[24] To be sure, the MFN tariff and the RoO index arguably risk being correlated; the pairwise correlation is 0.44. However, regressing the independent variables on the RoO index yields an R-squared of 0.20, which is still well below the 0.37 in the equation with phaseouts as dependent variable. Moreover, given that the RoO instrument has roots going far deeper than the 1998 MFN tariff, including the two variables in the same equation is analytically justifiable. The preferential margin variable is dropped because of its likely correlation with the MFN tariff (pairwise correlation is 0.47, while reaching only 0.11 between RoO and preferential margins).

[25] Fixed effects are employed to capture any industry-specific effects on phaseout schedules. Thus, they essentially help control for industry variables such as industry concentration and labor unionization, which can plausibly affect the lobbying dynamics for phaseouts. Data on industry variables are not available at levels of disaggregation as high as for phaseout schedules (negotiated generally at the 8-digit level of the Harmonized System) and RoO (negotiated anywhere between 4 and 10 digits); aggregating these variables further up would result in important loss of nuance—as would aggregating them at the EU level.

Table 4.4 ▌ Restrictiveness of Rules of Origin and Preferential Tariff Liberalization by the EU in the EU-Mexico FTA: OLS Estimation

	Dependent variable: Years to liberalization, EU to Mexico								
Independent variables	**I**	**II**	**III**	**IV**	**V**	**VI**	**VII**	**VIII**	**IX**
Rules of origin restrictiveness index (*RoO-RI*)	0.70 (31.34)** 0.02	0.67 (30.27)** 0.02	0.68 (30.36)** 0.02	0.70 (29.98)** 0.02	0.38 (16.95)** 0.02		0.38 (17.03)** 0.02	0.15 (6.01)** 0.03	0.15 (6.03)** 0.03
Preferential margin, EU to Mexico (*PRE-MAR-EU*)		8.70 (6.87)** 1.27	9.24 (7.30)** 1.27	9.12 (6.63)** 1.37					
Import ratio, EU from Mexico (*IMP-RAT-EU*)		−0.67 (0.62) 1.08	−0.64 (0.59) 1.08	−1.42 (1.10) 1.29	−1.18 (1.04) 1.14	−0.84 (0.72) 1.17	−1.19 (1.05) 1.14	−1.15 (1.39) 0.83	−1.16 (1.39) 0.83
Export ratio, EU to Mexico (*EXP-RAT-EU*)		−0.49 (5.58)** 0.09	−0.50 (5.74)** 0.09	−0.53 (5.55)** 0.10	−0.60 (7.26)** 0.08	−0.66 (7.67)** 0.09	−0.55 (6.67)** 0.08	−0.07 (1.01) 0.07	−0.07 (0.96) 0.07
Intra-industry trade, EU-Mexico (*IIT-EU-MEX*)			−0.76 (5.35)** 0.14	−0.76 (5.10)** 0.15	−0.74 (5.71)** 0.13	−0.69 (5.13)** 0.13	−0.71 (5.46)** 0.13	−0.08 (0.83) 0.1	−0.08 (0.81) 0.1
Intra-industry trade, EU-ROW (*IIT-EU-ROW*)			0.01 (0.14) 0.10	0.10 (0.95) 0.10	0.10 (0.95) 0.10	0.09 (0.95) 0.09	0.01 (0.16) 0.09	0.01 (0.20) 0.07	0.01 (0.22) 0.07

(continued on next page)

Table 4.4 Restrictiveness of Rules of Origin and Preferential Tariff Liberalization by the EU in the EU-Mexico FTA: OLS Estimation *(continued)*

	Dependent variable: Years to liberalization, EU to Mexico								
Independent variables	**I**	**II**	**III**	**IV**	**V**	**VI**	**VII**	**VIII**	**IX**
EU MFN tariff, 1998					0.23	0.28	0.23	0.14	0.14
(*EU-MFN*)					(35.28)**	(46.26)**	(35.71)**	(19.59)**	(19.61)**
					0.01	0.01	0.01	0.01	0.01
Years to liberalization,				−0.03		−0.05	−0.05		−0.01
Mexico to EU				(3.08)**		(5.22)**	(5.46)**		(1.04)
(*POUT-MEX*)				0.01		0.01	0.01		0.01
Industry fixed effects	No	No	No	No	No	No	No	Yes	Yes
Constant	−1.92	−1.79	−1.74	−1.74	−1.05	0.76	−0.89	0.14	0.17
	(17.48)**	(14.80)**	(14.09)**	(12.90)**	(8.96)**	(10.16)**	(7.38)**	(1.09)	(1.28)
	0.11	0.12	0.12	0.14	0.12	0.08	0.12	0.13	0.13
Observations	4,932	4,929	4,929	4,156	4,110	4,110	4,110	4,058	4,058
Adjusted R-squared	0.17	0.18	0.18	0.21	0.39	0.35	0.39	0.68	0.68

Note: Absolute value of t-statistics in parentheses. Standard errors below t-statistics.

* significant at 5 percent level; ** significant at 1 percent level.

portant role in the definition of the EU's preferential liberalization scheme. The more restrictive the RoO, the greater the political economy pressure for long phaseouts; loose RoO indicate competitive sectors for which protection is less important.[26] Second, the initial level of the preferential margins enters into the EU phaseouts with positive and significant sign. This indicates that higher margins are proxies for sectors with protectionist interests—sectors with high MFN tariff and thus those pursuing slow phaseout schedules.

Third, the export ratio for the EU is negative and significant, suggesting that EU industries exporting to Mexico have few incentives to lobby for slow phaseouts. The import ratio, meanwhile, is not a significant predictor of phaseouts.[27] Fourth, high levels of intra-industry trade with both Mexico and ROW indicate EU sectors that would have incentives for pursuing fast liberalization with Mexico and that have important international trade links, and thus could be expected to be least protectionist. Fifth, the fourth column, which includes the role of reciprocity by Mexico in EU phaseouts, indicates that slow EU phaseouts are negatively affected by Mexican phaseouts. This may indicate not lack of reciprocity, but simply that Mexico's phaseouts are fast in sectors where the EU's phaseouts are slow and vice versa, as could be plausible in North-South integration.[28]

Columns V–VII include the MFN tariff, which enters the equation highly significant and positive and does pull the coefficient of the RoO variable down by nearly 50 percent. However, the RoO index remains robust. The results of the fixed-effects model are reported in columns VIII and IX. They convey that even after industry-specific effects are controlled for, RoO provide important explanatory power. To be sure, their coefficients

---

[26] Breaking the categorical *RoO-RI* variable into dummies shows that *RoO-RI* is not fully linear. Values of 1 and 2 of the index emerge as entailing relatively similar phaseouts as value 4, which likely captures the effects of the coding of a stand-alone TECH rule. It can be highly restrictive but is here assigned an index value of 1.

[27] This may capture a result by Trefler (1993), namely, that sectors where the imports are low to begin with are the most protected. Grossman and Helpman (1994) predict a negative relationship between imports and liberalization on the grounds that the higher the import demand, the greater the cost for the government to introduce a tariff distortion.

[28] Since EU and Mexican phaseouts can be seen as endogenous to one another, a complete understanding of the operation of reciprocity would entail a two-stage model.

are notably lower than in the prior specifications. Industry fixed effects do appear to sap out the explanatory value of the trade-related control variables, however.[29]

The second estimation is on a variant of (4.1) in which I replace the RoO index with a vector of dummies for the different types of RoO. Let R = (*CC, CH, CS, ECTC, VC, TECH, SOFTCC/CH*), where

CC = 1 when the rule of origin requires a change in tariff chapter;
CH = 1 when the rule of origin requires a change in tariff heading;
CS = 1 when the rule of origin requires a change in tariff subheading;
ECTC = 1 when the rule of origin adds an exception;
VC = 1 when the rule of origin requires a minimum intra-PTA share of the total value of the product;
TECH = 1 when the rule of origin requires that the product incorporate certain inputs or undergo certain processes; and
SOFTCC/CH = 1 when the rule of origin, despite requiring a change in heading or chapter, allows for the use of inputs from the same heading or chapter up to a certain share of the price of the final product.

The estimation is as follows:

$$\begin{aligned} POUT\text{-}EU_i = {} & b_0 + b_1 R_i + b_2 EU\text{-}MFN_i + b_3 IMP\text{-}RAT\text{-}EU_i + \\ & b_4 EXP\text{-}RAT\text{-}EU_i + b_5 IIT\text{-}EU\text{-}MEX_i + \\ & b_6 IIT\text{-}EU\text{-}ROW_i + b_7 POUT\text{-}MEX_i + b_8 F_{(4k)i}. \end{aligned} \tag{4.2}$$

The expectation is that the higher the level of difficulty of meeting the RoO requirements (such as that involved in changing the tariff chapter of the final product as opposed to that involved in changing its subhead-

---

[29] Importantly here, as expected, the theoretical disconnect between the restrictiveness of RoO and the phaseout schedules of the EU's partners is also an empirical one. In the same regression on Mexican tariff phaseouts (not shown here), the impact of RoO is much less pronounced than in the EU case and not significant throughout the estimations. See Suominen (2004).

ing), the more restrictive the RoO, and hence the longer the phaseout in sectors with such a demanding type of RoO.

Results in Table 4.5 indicate that as expected, sectors featuring change in chapter are more likely to obtain long phaseouts than those based on the change in heading component, and sectors with a change in heading component are more likely to obtain long phaseouts than sectors governed by the change in subheading component.[30] Sectors with perhaps the most demanding of RoO, wholly obtained and TECH, are also particularly likely candidates for prolonged phaseouts. The MFN tariff and industry fixed effects in column IV cause the most subtle facets and least potent of RoO—exceptions, soft RoO, and change in subheading—to lose their explanatory power. However, the wholly obtained and most CTC variables, VC, and TECH all have the correct signs and are significant.

Testing for Exclusions, RoO, and Tariffs

The second hypothesis—that exclusions from the PTA become more likely in situations where even the most-stringent rule of origin falls well short of living up to the protection provided by the tariff—is tested in a simple way by creating a dummy variable for sectoral exclusions and measuring it against the proposed RoO for the sector and the MFN tariff in the sector. I estimate the following probit equation at the 8-digit level of disaggregation:

$$EXCL_i = b_0 + b_1 RoO\text{-}RI_i + b_2 EU\text{-}MFN_i, \qquad (4.3)$$

where

> $EXCL_i$ is a dummy variable taking value 1 if a particular sector is excluded from the PTA and 0 otherwise;
> $RoO\text{-}RI_i$ is the RoO restrictiveness index; and
> $EU\text{-}MFN_i$ is the EU's 1998 MFN tariff.

[30] Standard errors, left out here in the interest of space, are very small for each of the RoO components, ranging from 0.08 for soft RoO to 0.18 for CS.

Table 4.5 Type of Rules of Origin and Preferential Tariff Liberalization by the EU in the EU-Mexico FTA: OLS Estimation

	Dependent variable: Years to liberalization, EU Mexico (*POUT-EU*)			
Independent variables	**I**	**II**	**III**	**IV**
Rules of origin restrictiveness index (*RoO-RI*)	0.39 (17.03)**			
EU MFN tariff, 1998 (*EU-MFN*)	0.23 (35.71)**		0.21 (35.15)**	0.15 (20.25)**
Import ratio, EU from Mexico (*IMP-RAT-EU*)	−1.19 (1.05)	−2.87 (2.56)*	−2.49 (2.54)*	−1.31 (1.59)
Export ratio, EU to Mexico (*EXP-RAT-EU*)	−0.55 (6.67)**	−0.06 (0.74)	−0.13 (1.76)	−0.06 (0.91)
Intra-industry trade, EU-Mexico (*IIT-EU-MEX*)	−0.71 (5.46)**	−0.18 (1.37)	−0.30 (2.62)**	−0.07 (0.73)
Intra-industry trade, EU-ROW (*IIT-EU-ROW*)	0.01 (0.16)	0.08 (0.91)	0.06 (0.78)	0.03 (0.47)
Years to liberalization, Mexico to EU (*POUT-MEX*)	−0.05 (5.46)**	−0.02 (1.96)*	−0.02 (3.02)**	−0.01 (1.12)
Wholly obtained (WO)		5.36 (36.61)**	4.28 (32.39)**	1.47 (7.52)**
Change in chapter (CC)		1.11 (8.90)**	0.08 (0.67)	0.44 (3.36)**
Change in heading (CH)		0.3 (3.26)**	0.29 (3.58)**	0.31 (3.36)**
Change in subheading (CS)		0.14 (0.80)	0.31 (1.95)	0.22 (1.29)
Exception to change in tariff classification (ECTC)		0.56 (5.21)**	0.4 (4.17)**	0.08 (0.64)
Value content (VC)		0.16 (1.91)	0.16 (2.24)*	0.42 (4.64)**
Technical requirement (TECH)		1.58 (17.17)**	1.08 (13.20)**	1.05 (8.46)**
Soft RoO		−0.23 (2.56)*	−0.49 (6.17)**	−0.13 (1.17)
Industry fixed effects	No	No	No	Yes
Constant	−0.89 (7.38)**	0.39 (3.32)**	−0.08 (0.77)	1.16 (1.29)
Observations	4,110	4,110	4,110	4,058
Adjusted R-squared	0.39	0.41	0.55	0.69

Note: Absolute value of t-statistics in parentheses.
* significant at 5 percent level; ** significant at 1 percent level.

Table 4.6a ▌EU RoO, MFN Tariffs, and Exclusions

	Dependent variable: Exclusion by EU from the EU-Mexico FTA		
Independent variables	**I**	**II**	**III**
Rules of origin restrictiveness index (*RoO-RI*)	0.21 (16.31)** 0.01		0.04 (2.39)* 0.02
EU MFN Tariff, 1998 (*EU-MFN*)		0.08 (41.07)** 0.002	0.08 (39.54)** 0.002
Constant	−2.44 (34.60)** 0.07	−2.60 (57.47)** 0.05	−2.78 (31.89)** 0.09
Observations	9,937	9,937	9,937
Pseudo *R*-squared	0.047	0.381	0.38

Note: Absolute value of *t*-statistics in parentheses.
* significant at 5 percent level; ** significant at 1 percent level.

The MFN tariff is here operationalized in two ways. One, I assign an arbitrary tariff value of 30 percent to items whose entry the EU regulated by means of a specific rate (usually expressed as euro per unit of quantity, such as kilograms or liters) or a mixed tariff (which combines an ad valorem tariff and a specific rate tariff quota). Two, I convert the MFN tariff variable into a "peak tariff" dummy that takes values of 1 when the MFN tariff is a peak tariff (above 15 percent) and 0 when it is below 15 percent.[31]

The estimation results are reported in Tables 4.6a and 4.6b. As expected, the higher the RoO restrictiveness value and the MFN tariff in a sector, the likelier the sector will be excluded from the PTA. This suggests that exclusions are chosen precisely in sectors where the rule of origin, despite its stringency, is far from an adequate substitute for the MFN tariff. Once the tariff is phased out, the rule will provide inadequate protection, its stringency notwithstanding.

---

[31] The correlation between the independent variables is 0.34 in the first operationalization, declining to 0.24 in the second. Both of the tariff variables are highly positively correlated with a dummy that indicates sectors producing agricultural products and minerals (or Sections 1–24 of the Harmonized System); the correlation is 0.75 in the first case and 0.78 in the second.

Table 4.6b | RoO, Tariff Peaks, and Exclusions

	Dependent variable: Exclusion by EU from the EU-Mexico PTA		
Independent variables	**I**	**II**	**III**
Rules of origin Restrictiveness index (*RoO-RI*)	0.21 (16.31)** 0.01		0.06 (3.64)** 0.02
EU MFN Tariff, 1998 (*EU-MFN*)		1.98 (41.85)** 0.05	1.93 (39.54)** 0.05
Constant	−2.44 (34.60)** 0.07	−2.20 (59.87)** 0.04	−2.47 (29.69)** 0.08
Observations	9,937	9,937	9,937
Pseudo *R*-squared	0.047	0.378	0.38

Note: Absolute value of *z*-statistics in parentheses. Standard errors below *z*-statistics.
* significant at 5 percent level; ** significant at 1 percent level.

Conclusion

Domestic politics instills selectivity in international agreements. This is particularly the case in the realm of trade, where globalization has accentuated the costs and benefits of economic openness to divergent domestic economic actors. As a result, governments are compelled to devise contracts of differentiated obligations—agreements that curtail the costs of openness to actors jeopardized by free trade, while amplifying the benefits of openness to actors thriving on the unfettered flow of goods.

I have sought to substantiate this argument through an exploration of the structure and interplay of two crucial market access instruments in any PTA, tariff phaseouts and rules of origin. My main finding is that RoO play an independent role in arbitrating the speed of preferential tariff liberalization. Producers with the most-demanding RoO lobby for the longest tariff phaseouts. They do so because the RoO instrument is but an imperfect substitute for the exclusion instrument—but they also accept the PTA because of the captive market prospects the RoO embedded in it offer, and importantly, because the very RoO are endogenous to their preferences to begin with. Meanwhile, in sectors where RoO are highly restrictive yet fail to provide captive market advantages, producers call for exclusions from the PTA's coverage.

The policy implication of the argument is clear: stringent RoO plus long phaseouts are the price economic agents and governments seeking integration will need to pay not only for PTA formation, but for foregoing manifold exclusions and building a meaningful PTA—a PTA that covers as large a share of the tariff universe as possible.

The assumptions on which this chapter is based are particularly appropriate for the study of the EU's RoO regimes, where RoO can be considered a unilateral instrument that is truly exogenous to the PTA bargain, including to the parties' tariff-lowering schedules. However, the argument is also immediately applicable to unilateral preferential schemes such as the Generalized System of Preferences, where the preference-extending country can be considered the setter of rules. Moreover, the argument will likely grow more generalizable given that many prolific PTA bargainers, such as the United States and Mexico, have been and are building PTAs that, except for slight product-specific adjustments, carry a RoO protocol based on an ex ante defined blueprint. Moreover, my effort to show how the *incentives* to lobby for restrictive RoO translate into incentives to lobby for long phaseouts in particular is broadly generalizable.

The welfare effects of FTAs with RoO vis-à-vis CUs, RoO-less FTAs, or the no-PTA option are beyond the scope of this chapter. Some might argue that by benefiting and entrenching input producers, FTAs with stringent RoO result in political constellations that will work ever more fiercely to hamper future moves toward the optimal trade policy outcome of multilateral trade liberalization—which, after all, would eliminate the impact and relevance of preferential RoO altogether. This, however, seems overly pessimistic. FTAs can well acquire a liberalizing momentum, fostering export interests and propelling them to demand further openness possibly precisely in order to free themselves from the constraints of stringent RoO.

References

Appiah, Alex Jameson. 1999. "Applied General Equilibrium Model of North American Integration with Rules of Origin." Ph.D. diss., Simon Fraser University, Vancouver, British Columbia, Canada.

Augier, Patricia, and Michael Gasiorek. 2002. "The EU and the Southern Mediterranean: The Impact of Rules of Origin." Unpublished.

Bond, Eric W. 2001. "Commercial Policy in a 'Fragmented' World." *American Economic Review* 91(2):358–62.

Brenton, Paul, and Miriam Manchin. 2002. "Making EU Trade Agreements Work: The Role of Rules of Origin." CEPS Working Document No. 183. Brussels: Centre for European Policy Studies.

Cadot, Olivier, Jaime de Melo, Antoni Estevadeordal, Akiko Suwa-Eisenmann, and Bolormaa Tumurchudur. 2002. "Assessing the Effect of NAFTA's Rules of Origin." Unpublished.

Cadot, Olivier, Antoni Estevadeordal, and Akiko Suwa-Eisenmann. 2006. "Rules of Origin as Export Subsidies." In Olivier Cadot, Antoni Estevadeordal, Akiko Suwa-Eisenmann, and Thierry Verdier (eds.), *The Origin of Goods: Rules of Origin in Regional Trade Agreements.* Oxford: Oxford University Press.

Duttagupta, Rupa. 2000. "Intermediate Inputs and Rules of Origin: Implications for Welfare and Viability of Free Trade Agreements." Ph.D. diss., University of Maryland, College Park.

Duttagupta, Rupa, and Arvind Panagariya. 2003. "Free Trade Areas and Rules of Origin: Economics and Politics." IMF Working Paper 03/229. Washington, DC: International Monetary Fund.

Estevadeordal, Antoni. 2000. "Negotiating Preferential Market Access: The Case of the North American Free Trade Agreement." *Journal of World Trade* 34(1):141–66.

Estevadeordal, Antoni, and Eric Miller. 2002. "Rules of Origin and the Pattern of Trade between the U.S. and Canada." Washington, DC: Integration, Trade and Hemispheric Issues Division, Inter-American Development Bank.

Estevadeordal, Antoni, and Kati Suominen. 2003. "Rules of Origin in FTAs in Europe and in the Americas: Issues and Implications for the

EU-Mercosur Inter-Regional Association Agreement." In Alfrredo G. A. Valladão and Roberto Bouzas (eds.), *Market Access for Goods and Services in the EU-Mercosur Negotiations*. Paris: Chaire Mercosur de Sciences Po.

Falvey, Rod, and Geoff Reed. 2000. "Rules of Origin as Commercial Policy Instruments." Research Paper No. 2000/18. Nottingham, U.K.: Centre for Research on Globalization and Labor Markets, University of Nottingham.

Flatters, Frank. 2002. "SADC Rules of Origin: Undermining Regional Free Trade." Paper presented at the Trade and Industrial Policy Strategies (TIPS) Forum, September 9–11, Johannesburg.

Garay, Luis Jorge, and Rafael Cornejo. 2002. "Metodología para el análisis de regímenes de origen: aplicación en el caso de las Américas." INTAL-ITD-STA Documento de Trabajo 8. Washington, DC: Inter-American Development Bank.

Garay, Luis Jorge, and Antoni Estevadeordal. 1996. "Protection, Preferential Tariff Elimination and Rules of Origin in the Americas." *Integration and Trade* 1:2–25.

Graham, Edward M., and Christopher Wilkie. 1998. "Regional Economic Agreements and Multinational Firms: The Investment Provisions of the NAFTA." In Hafiz Mirza (ed.), *Global Competitive Strategies in the New World Economy.* Cheltenham, U.K.: Elgar.

Grossman, Gene M., and Elhanan Helpman. 1994. "Protection for Sale." *American Economic Review* 84:833–50.

———. 1995. "The Politics of Free-Trade Agreements." *American Economic Review* 85:667–90.

Hirsch, Moshe. 2002. "International Trade Law, Political Economy and Rules of Origin: A Plea for a Reform of the WTO Regime on Rules of Origin." *Journal of World Trade* 36(2):171–89.

Jensen-Moran, Jeri. 1996. "Trade Battles as Investment Wars: The Coming Rules of Origin Debate." *Washington Quarterly* 19(1):239–53.

Ju, Jiandong, and Kala Krishna. 1998. "Firm Behavior and Market Access in a Free Trade Area with Rules of Origin." NBER Working Paper No. 6857. Cambridge, MA: National Bureau of Economic Research.

Kowalczyk, Carsten, and Donald Davis. 1998. "Tariff Phase-Outs: Theory and Evidence from GATT and NAFTA." In Jeffrey Frankel (ed.), *The Regionalization of the World Economy*. Chicago: University of Chicago Press.

Krishna, Kala. 2002. "Understanding Rules of Origin." Unpublished.

Krishna, Kala, and Anne O. Krueger. 1995. "Implementing Free Trade Areas: Rules of Origin and Hidden Protection." In Alan Deardorff, James Levinsohn, and Robert Stern (eds.), *New Directions in Trade Theory.* Ann Arbor: University of Michigan Press.

Krueger, Anne O. 1993. "Free Trade Agreements as Protectionist Devices: Rules of Origin." NBER Working Paper No. 4352. Cambridge, MA: National Bureau of Economic Research.

Lloyd, Peter J. 1997. "Towards a Framework of Trade and Competition Policy." *Asia-Pacific Economic Review* 3(2):1–13.

———. 2001a. "Rules of Origin and Fragmentation of Trade." In Leonard K. Cheng and Henryk Kierzkowski (eds.), *Global Production and Trade in East Asia*. Boston: Kluwer Academic .

———. 2001b. "Country of Origin in the Global Economy." Paper presented at the 14th General Meeting of the Pacific Economic Cooperation Council (PECC XIV), Hong Kong, November 28–30.

McLaren, John. 2000. "Globalization and Vertical Structure." *American Economic Review* 90(4).

Rodriguez, Peter. 2001. "Rules of Origin with Multistage Production." *World Economy* 24(1):210–20.

Scollay, Robert. 1997. "Preferential Rules of Origin, Regional Trading Arrangements and APEC." *Asia-Pacific Economic Review* 3(2):28–36.

Stephenson, Sherry. 1997. "The Economic Impact of Rules of Origin in the Asia-Pacific Region." *Asia-Pacific Economic Review* 3(2):14–27.

Suominen, Kati. 2004. *Rules of Origin in Global Commerce*. Ph.D. diss., University of California, San Diego.

Trefler, Daniel. 1993. "Trade Liberalization and the Theory of Endogenous Protection: An Econometric Study of U.S. Import Policy." *Journal of Political Economy* 101(1):138–60.

Venables, Anthony J. 1999. "Fragmentation and Multinational Production." *European Economic Review* 43(4–6):935–45.

Appendix 4.1

Estevadeordal's (2000) observation rule yields a RoO restrictiveness index as follows:

$$
\begin{aligned}
y &= 1 \text{ if } y^* \leq \text{CI} \\
y &= 2 \text{ if CI} < y^* \leq \text{CS} \\
y &= 3 \text{ if CS} < y^* \leq \text{CS and VC} \\
y &= 4 \text{ if CS and VC} < y^* \leq \text{CH} \\
y &= 5 \text{ if CH} < y^* \leq \text{CH and VC} \\
y &= 6 \text{ if CH and VC} < y^* \leq \text{CC} \\
y &= 7 \text{ if CC} < y^* \leq \text{CC and TECH}
\end{aligned}
$$

where y^* is the potential level of restrictiveness of RoO (rather than the observed level of restrictiveness); CI is the level of restrictiveness imposed by a requirement of a change in tariff classification at the level of tariff item (8–10 HS digits), CS is the level of restrictiveness imposed by a requirement of a change at the level of subheading (6 digits), CH is the level of restrictiveness imposed by a requirement of a change at the level of heading (4 digits), and CC is the level of restrictiveness imposed by a requirement of a change at the level of chapter (2 digits); VC is the level of restrictiveness imposed by a value content criterion; and TECH is the level of restrictiveness imposed by a technical requirement.

I make a number of modifications to the observation rule in the case of RoO for which no CTC is specified in order to allow for coding of such RoO in the Pan-Euro, SADC, and other regimes in which not all RoO feature a CTC component. First, the level of restrictiveness of RoO based on the import content rule is equated to that imposed by a change in heading requirement (value 4) if the content requirement allows nonoriginating inputs up to a value of 50 percent of the ex-works price of the product. Value 5 is assigned when the share of permitted nonoriginating inputs is below 50 percent, as well as when the import content criterion is combined with a technical requirement. Second, RoO featuring an exception alone are assigned a value of 1 if the exception concerns a heading or a number of headings and a value of 2 if the exception concerns a chapter or a number of chapters. Third, RoO based on the wholly obtained criterion are assigned a value of 7.

The observation rule is admittedly somewhat crude for accounting for the subtleties of the EU RoO, as it does not account for the "soft" CTC criterion used by the EU. However, it does allow for comparison of the EU and NAFTA RoO regimes.

PART III
ECONOMIC EFFECTS OF RULES OF ORIGIN

CHAPTER 5

What Are the Trade Effects of Rules of Origin?*

Antoni Estevadeordal and Kati Suominen

The purpose of this chapter is to inform policymaking about the trade effects of RoO and ways to neutralize distortions created by RoO. We employ a modified gravity model to assess the impact of RoO on both aggregate trade and trade in intermediate goods in five major economic sectors—chemicals, machinery, textiles, television and radio transmitters, and vehicles. Our sample covers 155 countries and nearly 100 PTAs around the world for 1981–2001.

This chapter makes four contributions. First, it goes beyond the conventional use of a dummy variable to capture the economic effects of PTAs.[1] Reducing PTAs to a dichotomous variable overlooks the important cross-PTA variation in the various trade disciplines governing preferential trade—such as standards, safeguards, and rules governing government procurement and investment. This, in turn, severely undercuts the credibility and usefulness of the arguments of both those who view PTAs as discriminatory instruments that obstruct global trade liberalization and those who regard PTAs as conducive to multilateral opening. By setting out to disaggregate PTAs into their component parts, this chapter inserts fresh rigor and nuance into the intensifying policy debate on the implications of preferential agreements for the multilateral trading system.

* This is a modified version of a chapter in Suominen (2004).

[1] See, for instance, the widely cited studies of Bayomi and Eichengreen (1995) and Frankel (1997). For work that differentiates among PTAs, see Estevadeordal and Robertson (2002) and Ghosh and Yamarik (2004).

Second, this chapter presents both the first global and over-time assessment of RoO's trade effects and the first examination of RoO's effects on aggregate trade and trade in intermediate goods. The few empirical studies that have operationalized RoO have focused on a single regime, that of NAFTA, finding that restrictive RoO dampen PTAs' trade-creating potential (Appiah, 1999; Cadot et al., 2002; Estevadeordal and Miller, 2002).

In contrast, by considering all major PTAs in a span of two decades, this chapter is able to establish whether stringent product-specific RoO in general undermine the benefits of liberalization among PTA partners, as well as whether the effects of RoO vary over time. The approach here is also able to capture the effects of general, regime-wide RoO, which are inherently omitted in single-regime studies. And by examining intermediate trade, we help close the gap in the understanding of the trade-diverting potential of RoO. As such, this chapter clarifies the propensity of RoO to breach Article XXIV of the General Agreement on Tariffs and Trade, which requires PTAs to eliminate all regulations that restrict commerce between the member states and also precludes the formation of PTAs that raise barriers vis-à-vis third parties.[2]

Third, although RoO are one of the most crucial determinants, if not the most crucial determinant, of trade in intermediates and locational decisions of investors, empirical studies on the fragmentation of production have yet to incorporate RoO.[3] This chapter opens avenues for incorporating RoO into the scholarship on the geography of production.

---

[2] Restrictive RoO are widely feared to result in misallocation of resources and undermine global welfare. Compounding these concerns is that RoO may encourage what we term "RoO-jumping" investment, investment diversion to the PTA area that is made in order to circumvent the RoO, yet that results in a misallocation of resources to a globally inefficient location of production. See Chapter 6 for further details.

[3] With the lowering of tariffs and transportation and communications costs around the world, sourcing has become an increasingly viable option to firms—and a must for cutting costs in the face of tightening global competition. See, for example, Fujita, Krugman, and Venables (1999). McLaren (2000) shows how the entry of independent suppliers into a market can reduce the incentives for vertical integration; this implies that trade liberalization and declining transportation costs can also undercut incentives to maintain prior sourcing ties in the market should up- and downstream firms be separate from each other and the new entrant produce supplies at low costs.

Fourth, the empirical exercises in this chapter add to the small pool of gravity model applications available at the sectoral level.[4] The vast majority of gravity models are geared to explaining aggregate flows of trade, rather than to allowing income elasticities and distance to vary by product. Meanwhile, the usefulness of most existing sectoral approaches is limited given that they simply regress sectoral flows on the same variables as aggregate trade flows, rather than generating sector-specific independent variables.[5] One of the most prominent strands of the disaggregated studies, and one we draw on, is focused on estimating a proxy for standards—essentially, technical barriers to trade—and hence does put forth a sectoral independent variable (Moenius, 1999, 2000; Wilson and Otsuki, 2001; Maskus, Wilson, and Otsuki, 2000). Indeed, our study paves the way to exploring the combined impact of technical barriers and RoO on trade.

The empirical results of this chapter are fourfold. First, restrictive RoO and high degrees of sectoral selectivity in RoO discourage aggregate trade flows. Second, regime-wide RoO—RoO that apply similarly to all sectors in a given PTA yet vary across PTAs—allow flexibility in the application of product-specific RoO and thus facilitate trade. As such, various regime-wide RoO provisions can counteract restrictive product-specific RoO's negative effects on trade. Third, at the sectoral level, both restrictive RoO and selectivity in RoO in final goods encourage trade in intermediate goods and can thus entail trade diversion in inputs. Fourth, exporters and producers learn over time to comply with stringent product-specific

---

[4] Bergstrand (1989) derives a gravity equation for a multi-industry world that allows for intra-industry trade. Vittas and Mauro (1997) estimate a gravity model on data for trade between OECD countries for five sensitive products and for aggregate trade. Brenton and Di Mauro (1998) focus on central and eastern European exports of sensitive products to the EU market in a panel of 45–47 source countries using 1995 data. Schumacher and Trubswetter (2000) explore aggregate and sectoral CEEC exports to the EU. Bertolini and Montanari (2002) also examine CEEC-EU trade at the aggregate level and in agriculture, food and beverages, and manufacturing. Leejour, de Mooji, and Nahuis (2001) employ the gravity model for estimating the effects of eastward enlargement of Europe. Dihel and Walkenhorst (2002) study trade between Germany, on the one hand, and the EU and non-EU countries, on the other, via a gravity model in eight sectors.

[5] The large standard errors in these studies have led analysts to argue that disaggregate flows might be best explored through specifications other than a gravity model. See Brenton and Di Mauro (1998).

RoO and to take greater advantage of permissive regime-wide provisions: "RoO learning" gradually reduces "RoO interference."

The first section of this chapter discusses the potential effects of RoO on trade. The second section puts forth the gravity application for examining RoO and presents the empirical specification and the results. The third section concludes the chapter.

Trade Effects of RoO: A Gravity Application

What are the effects of RoO on trade? A RoO-less PTA could be expected to result in dramatic changes in trade patterns due to the rise in transshipment through the member with the lowest tariff. The PTA would be highly liberalizing, given that the lowest tariff would apply to each import category. However, RoO can decrease in particular intermediate goods imports to the PTA area from ROW by increasing the incentives for intra-PTA sourcing among producers that strive to qualify for PTA-conferred preferential treatment. Intra-PTA trade can subsequently be expected to rise.[6] However, note that in the long run stringent RoO can moderate such an increase in trade flows by increasing the demand for intra-PTA inputs and thus raising their price, which, in turn, will increase costs for the intra-PTA final goods producers, decreasing final goods production and lowering downstream producers' derived demand for intra-PTA inputs. As such, RoO can gradually work to undercut intra-PTA trade in both inputs and final goods (Ju and Krishna, 1998).[7]

---

[6] Theoretical studies establish that RoO can divert trade in intermediate goods to the PTA area (Ju and Krishna, 1998; Duttagupta and Panagariya, 2001).

[7] To be sure, PTA formation per se can entail a shift to intra-PTA inputs from lower-cost ROW supplies as a result of the drop in intra-PTA tariffs, along the lines of the Vinerian (1950) trade diversion–trade creation argument. However, this standard notion of trade diversion would, in a RoO-less world, require assuming the absence of trade deflection and/or the existence of relatively similar MFN tariff regimes among the PTA partners (or members of a customs union, as in Viner), as otherwise transshipment would counteract the trade-diverting impact of the PTA. However, there is a crucial difference between RoO- and PTA-induced trade diversion: RoO can induce a turn to intra-PTA inputs *even when* the price of the lowest-cost ROW inputs is lower than that of the intra-PTA ones. This is because intra-PTA downstream producers must use a RoO-defined share of intra-

However, theoretical efforts to capture RoO's trade effects—first and foremost Ju and Krishna (1998) and Duttagupta and Panagariya (2001)—are hard pressed to derive the ultimate trade effects of RoO. This is owing largely to the inherent interaction of the intermediate and final goods markets. Moreover, at least two types of external shocks can affect trade flows. First, a higher return on inputs in the PTA area can attract investment into intermediate goods industries, which, in turn, can crowd out the market for inputs, reduce their price, and thus allow intra-PTA commerce to flourish. Second, the phasing out of preferential tariffs by any PTA member can accentuate the lure of shipping from or through the other members to that member under preferential terms. This will subsequently reduce RoO's interference in trade, as exporters will have greater incentives to comply with (or, alternatively, cheat and circumvent) the RoO.

Three theoretical results do seem relatively clear. First, restrictive RoO depress intra-PTA final goods trade below the levels that would be generated by a RoO-less PTA or a PTA with very loose RoO. This is due to (1) the increase in production costs imposed by RoO and (2) RoO's undermining the possibilities for transshipment. In other words, intra-PTA final goods producers would, in a RoO-less PTA, enjoy a cost advantage to themselves in a PTA with RoO; two like pairs of countries would thus, in the presence of stringent RoO, witness less growth in bilateral trade in final goods as a result of a PTA than if RoO were loose or absent. Second, at least in the short run, intra-PTA trade in intermediate goods would likely increase more in the presence of stringent RoO downstream than if RoO were loose or absent. Third, PTA-ROW commerce would likely be greater in the presence of a RoO-less PTA or a PTA with very loose RoO than in the face of a PTA with highly restrictive RoO.[8]

PTA inputs in their final goods when seeking to qualify for preferential treatment, regardless of the cost of the inputs. RoO, in other words, entail a minimum cost share that has to arise within the PTA. That RoO accentuate the prospects for trade diversion entails (1) an extension of protection to uncompetitive intra-PTA input producers and (2) "exporting protection" to the input suppliers in one PTA partner to the borders of another (Krueger, 1993; Krishna and Krueger, 1995).

[8] See Ju and Krishna (1998) for some disclaimers to this notion that pertain to the interaction of intermediate and final goods markets.

The purpose of this section is to provide clarity in regard to the trade effects of RoO. We seek to accomplish this by employing a modified gravity model to assess the trade effects of (1) product-specific RoO of different degrees of restrictiveness and selectivity; and (2) the flexibility instilled in RoO regimes by different types of regime-wide RoO provisions. That is, we put the RoO and Facil indices presented in Chapter 2 to work. We examine two types of trade flows: aggregate imports, and imports in intermediate goods in the chemical, machinery, textile, television and radio transmitters, and vehicle sectors. The sample covers 155 countries and nearly 100 PTAs for the years 1981–2001 for aggregate trade and 1988–2001 for trade in intermediates.[9] The following subsections discuss the gravity application for RoO and its potential contributions and present the empirical specifications and results.

RoO and the Gravity Model

The gravity model has been used widely to predict bilateral trade flows between countries. In its barest form, it posits that, with size controlled for, trade between two regions increases as bilateral trade barriers, relative to the average barrier to trade that the regions have with all their partners, decrease. Initially specified by Tinbergen (1962), Pöyhönen (1963), and Linnemann (1966), the model proved empirically robust yet became discredited for lacking theoretical underpinnings. More recent scholars, such as Anderson (1979), Bergstrand (1985, 1989, 1990), Helpman and Krugman (1985), and Deardorff (1997), have developed theoretical foundations for the gravity equation. Indeed, the Heckscher-Ohlin, Ricardo-Viner, and increasing returns to scale (IRS) models of trade have all been found to generate predictions consistent with the gravity model.[10] This study presents a novel way of capturing the effect of RoO on trade by employing a modified gravity model that accounts for the structure of RoO governing preferential economic relations between countries.

---

[9] For the list of countries, see Appendix 5.4. For the list of PTAs, see Appendix 5.5.

[10] The approaches have usually kept the constant elasticity of substitution preference structure.

Testing the Impact of RoO: Aggregate Trade

This subsection presents the empirical specification for exploring the impact of RoO on aggregate trade flows between countries. The dependent variable is imports by partner for 155 countries (listed in Appendix 5.4) for 1981–2001. The import data (imports CIF) are drawn from the International Monetary Fund's Direction of Trade Statistics and deflated with the U.S. consumer price index. The GDP and GDP per capita variables are expressed in constant 1995 dollars and based on the World Bank's World Development Indicators. The bilateral distance variable is based on calculations by Centre d'études prospectives et d'informations internationales (CEPII). The other dyadic variables are to a large extent constructed by the authors. The RoO regime variables are from Suominen (2004) and are based on the RoO protocols of the various PTAs considered in this study.[11] The restrictiveness index is based on Estevadeordal (2000) and is detailed in Chapter 2, with 1 being least restrictive and 7 most restrictive. Coding methods for both product-specific and regime-wide RoO are detailed in Chapter 1; the method of including them in the gravity data set is detailed in Appendix 5.1. Appendix 5.3 presents the descriptive statistics.

Empirical Specification

We estimate the following basic gravity equation using OLS:

$$\begin{aligned} \ln\left(V_{ij}\right) = {} & \beta_0 + \beta_1 \ln\left(GDP_i\right) + \beta_2 \ln\left(GDP_j\right) + \beta_3 \ln\left(GDPPC_i\right), \\ & + \beta_4 \ln\left(GDPPC_j\right) + \beta_5 \ln\left(DIST_{ij}\right) + \beta_6\left(BORDER_{ij}\right) \\ & + \beta_7\left(COMLANG_{ij}\right) + \beta_8\left(COL_{ij}\right) + \beta_9\left(COMCOL_{ij}\right) \\ & + \beta_{10}\left(PTA_{ij}\right) + \beta_{11} \ln\left(RoO\text{-}RI_{ij}\right) + \beta_{12}\left(FACIL_{ij}\right) + \varepsilon \end{aligned} \tag{5.1}$$

[11] Rather than employing the trade-weighted *RoO-RI*, we use the *RoO-RI* variable based on the observation rule in order to avoid endogeneity problems.

where

V_{ij} is the value of imports to country *i* from country *j*;
GDP_i is the exporter's GDP;
GDP_j is the importer's GDP;
$GDPPC_i$ is the exporter's GDP per capita ratio;
$GDPPC_j$ is the importer's GDP per capita ratio;
$DIST_{ij}$ is the distance between the capitals of the two countries and serves as a proxy for transportation costs;[12]
$BORDER_{ij}$ is a dummy that takes value 1 if countries *i* and *j* share a land border and 0 otherwise;
$COMLANG_{ij}$ is a dummy for cultural affinities that takes value 1 when the two countries speak the same language and 0 otherwise;
COL_{ij} is a dummy that takes value 1 when one country has been colonized by the other and 0 otherwise;
$COMCOL_{ij}$ is a dummy that takes value 1 when the two countries have been colonized by the same colonial power and 0 otherwise;
PTA_{ij} is a dummy that takes value 1 when two countries belong to the same PTA and 0 otherwise;
$RoO\text{-}RI_{ij}$ is the average of the restrictiveness values of the RoO (as measured at the 6-digit level of disaggregation) of the PTA regulating trade between the two countries and can take values anywhere between 1 and 7;
$FACIL_{ij}$ is the facilitation index of the PTA regulating trade between the two countries and can take values anywhere between 1 and 5; and
ε is a normally distributed error term.

[12] Another useful control variable would be a "distance from major economic centers"-variable; according to Soloaga and Winters (2001), after distance between *i* and *j* is controlled for, the farther country *i* is from all its trading partners, the greater its imports will be from country *j*—for example, Australia and New Zealand will likely trade with each other more, as a result of their being far apart from any other trading partners, than two other countries separated by the same distance (such as Poland and Spain) because the latter pair of countries have many trading partners nearby. We currently lack, for all of the 155 countries in the sample, the distance data required to construct such a variable.

All regressions include year, importer, and exporter dummies in order to control for any effects peculiar to a certain time or country beyond the variables included in the model. The importer and exporter dummies also serve as a proxy for the multilateral resistance term applied by Anderson and van Wincoop (2001), where trade between countries *i* and *j* depends on barriers to trade both between the two countries and between either of them and the rest of the world.[13]

The *GDP* and *GDPPC* variables should have a positive effect on trade, whereas *DIST* can be expected to have a negative sign. The impact of a common border and cultural affinities should be positive. *PTA* is expected to have a positive impact on trade flows. Meanwhile, the first key independent variable, *RoO-RI*, is expected to stifle aggregate trade between PTA partners. In contrast, *FACIL* should—through its components of de minimis diagonal and full cumulation, and drawback, which expand the pool of intermediate goods available to producers, and self-certification, which can be hypothesized to reduce exporters' administrative costs of complying with the RoO regime—have a positive impact on trade flows.

Table 5.1 reports the results for all country pairs in the sample and for the subset of PTA pairs. The results on the traditional gravity variables are as expected. The basic gravity model used in several studies to examine the effects of regional integration shows that PTAs have a positive effect on aggregate trade flows. However, and as expected, rules of origin, a key market access provision in virtually all PTAs, has a negative sign and is significant at the 1 percent level. This is the first main finding of this study: restrictive product-specific RoO undermine aggregate trade. Indeed, stringent RoO are key in countering the PTA-inspired boost to trade: the difference in the coefficient for the PTA variable in columns I and II (i.e., 2.417 – 0.550 = 1.867) approximates the negative coefficient of the RoO variable (–1.482). This finding provides empirical ground for the suspicion that what one hand gives in tariff liberalization in PTAs, the other hand takes in restrictive RoO.

---

[13] Indeed, Anderson and van Wincoop (2001) suggest that empirically, the inclusion of country fixed effects captures multilateral resistance and thus corrects misspecification.

Table 5.1 Effects of Restrictive RoO and Sectoral Selectivity of RoO on Trade, 1981–2001

	Dependent variable: $\ln(V_{ij})$					Dependent variable: $\ln(V_{ij})$					
	All Pairs, 1981–2001			PTA Pairs, 1981–2001		All Pairs, 1981–2001		PTA Pairs, 1981–2001		PTA Pairs, 1991–2001	
Independent variables	I	II	III	IV	V	VI	VII	VIII	IX	X	XI
$\ln(GDP_i)$	0.224	0.206	0.207	0.800	0.782	0.207	0.207	0.797	0.789	0.437	0.434
	(8.18)**	(7.55)**	(7.58)**	(9.86)**	(9.68)**	(7.58)**	(7.56)**	(9.80)**	(9.72)**	(4.86)**	(4.84)**
$\ln(GDP_j)$	0.464	0.403	0.406	0.530	0.480	0.405	0.403	0.532	0.512	−0.216	−0.197
	(10.58)**	(9.20)**	(9.27)**	(3.04)**	(2.76)**	(9.22)**	(9.17)**	(3.04)**	(2.93)**	(0.94)	(0.86)
$\ln(GDPPC_i)$	0.378	0.398	0.397	−0.533	−0.516	0.393	0.393	−0.532	−0.520	−0.568	−0.561
	(13.74)**	(14.51)**	(14.46)**	(8.82)**	(8.57)**	(14.31)**	(14.30)**	(8.79)**	(8.60)**	(9.00)**	(8.90)**
$\ln(GDPPC_j)$	0.601	0.659	0.657	−0.347	−0.304	0.649	0.650	−0.35	−0.327	0.106	0.102
	(14.40)**	(15.82)**	(15.76)**	(2.64)*	(2.32)*	(15.54)**	(15.56)**	(2.66)**	(2.49)*	(0.68)	(0.65)
$\ln(DIST_{ij})$	−1.234	−1.222	−1.218	−1.158	−1.151	−1.231	−1.228	−1.183	−1.182	−1.253	−1.253
	(185.94)**	(183.73)**	(182.75)**	(47.45)**	(47.29)**	(185.22)**	(184.45)**	(49.01)**	(49.09)**	(45.61)**	(45.70)**
$BORDER_{ij}$	0.27	0.238	0.244	0.504	0.481	0.241	0.245	0.507	0.489	0.539	0.519
	(10.32)**	(9.12)**	(9.37)**	(11.71)**	(11.19)**	(9.22)**	(9.37)**	(11.78)**	(11.34)**	(10.82)**	(10.40)**
$COMLANG_{ij}$	0.354	0.334	0.337	−0.031	−0.013	0.334	0.335	−0.013	−0.002	0.105	0.117
	(24.39)**	(23.07)**	(23.26)**	(0.54)	(0.23)	(22.99)**	(23.06)**	(0.23)	(0.04)	(1.68)	(1.87)
COL_{ij}	1.287	1.295	1.294	0.802	0.765	1.285	1.282	0.846	0.819	1.055	1.014
	(41.74)**	(42.07)**	(42.04)**	(7.99)**	(7.63)**	(41.68)**	(41.60)**	(8.43)**	(8.17)**	(8.19)**	(7.87)**

(continued on next page)

Table 5.1 Effects of Restrictive RoO and Sectoral Selectivity of RoO on Trade, 1981–2001 *(continued)*

	Dependent variable: $\ln(V_{ij})$					Dependent variable: $\ln(V_{ij})$					
	All Pairs, 1981–2001			PTA Pairs, 1981–2001		All Pairs, 1981–2001		PTA Pairs, 1981–2001		PTA Pairs, 1991–2001	
Independent variables	I	II	III	IV	V	VI	VII	VIII	IX	X	XI
$COMCOL_{ij}$	0.643	0.618	0.627	0.715	0.720	0.625	0.632	0.685	0.676	0.621	0.613
	(39.11)**	(37.67)**	(38.11)**	(14.79)**	(14.93)**	(38.01)**	(38.38)**	(14.13)**	(13.97)**	(10.55)**	(10.44)**
PTA_{ij}	0.550	2.417	2.341			0.879	0.643				
	(28.56)**	(38.53)**	(36.90)**			(36.51)**	(15.66)**				
$\ln(RoO\text{-}RI_{ij})$		−1.482	−1.676	−0.637	−0.715						
		(31.26)**	(31.49)**	(6.91)**	(7.74)**						
$\ln(RoO\text{-}SD_{ij})$						−0.942	−1.144	0.095	−0.048	−0.14	−0.252
						(22.71)**	(22.74)**	(1.13)	(0.55)	(1.49)	(2.63)**
$FACIL_{ij}$			0.189		0.474		0.181		0.376		0.319
			(8.02)**		(8.47)**		(7.10)**		(6.85)**		(5.53)**
Constant	2.597	−1.281	−1.363	−3.806	−3.336	−1.137	−1.067	−4.704	−4.779	19.176	18.351
	(2.59)**	(1.28)	(1.36)	(1.00)	(0.88)	(1.13)	(1.06)	(1.23)	(1.25)	(3.83)*	(3.67)**
Observations	185,497	185,491	185,491	11,920	11,920	185,497	185,497	11,926	11,926	8,857	8,857
Adjusted R-squared	0.73	0.73	0.73	0.88	0.88	0.73	0.73	0.88	0.88	0.88	0.88
Year fixed effects	Yes	Yes	Yes	Yes	Yes	Yes	Yes	Yes	Yes	Yes	Yes
Importer and exporter fixed effects	Yes	Yes	Yes	Yes	Yes	Yes	Yes	Yes	Yes	Yes	Yes

Note: Absolute value of t-statistics in parentheses.

* significant at 5 percent level; ** significant at 1 percent level.

Column III incorporates the *FACIL* variable. As expected, *FACIL* has a positive and significant effect on trade. This is the second main finding of this chapter: the combined effect of regime-wide variables that instill flexibility into the application of product-specific RoO boosts trade.

Columns IV and V show that the results on RoO and *FACIL* hold also for the subsample of PTA pairs. RoO undermine aggregate trade flows among PTA pairs; however, and importantly, the opposite effect of permissive facilitation terms compensates for this negative impact of product-specific RoO.[14] Indeed, this is an important result, because a regression incorporating all pairs may have an endogeneity problem: countries do not select randomly into PTAs, but may choose to enter PTAs with the partners with which they trade the most—which, in turn, might cause the effect of RoO on trade to appear excessively accentuated. The policy implication is clear: PTA members adopting stringent product-specific RoO are well-advised to adopt lenient regime-wide RoO. (The individual effect of each *FACIL* component is explored below.)

Another important question is whether RoO regimes with marked intraregime variation across products in levels of RoO restrictiveness—regimes with high levels of sectoral selectivity or "peak RoO"—have greater negative effects on trade than regimes with an across-the-board rule of origin. Work on the structure of tariff regimes shows that regimes populated by tariff peaks can have stronger negative effects on trade and even be more susceptible to corruption than regimes with homogeneous tariffs, ceteris paribus.[15] We explore the relevance of RoO peaks by estimating (5.1) but replacing *RoO-RI* with *RoO-SD*:

$$\begin{aligned}\ln(V_{ij}) = \beta_0 &+ \beta_1 \ln(GDP_i) + \beta_2 \ln(GDP_j) + \beta_3 \ln(GDPPC_i), \\ &+ \beta_4 \ln(GDPPC_i) + \beta_5 \ln(DIST_{ij}) + \beta_6 (BORDER_{ij}) \\ &+ \beta_7 (COMLANG_{ij}) + \beta_8 (COL_{ij}) + \beta_9 (COMCOL_{ij}) \\ &+ \beta_{10} (PTA_{ij}) + \beta_{11} \ln(RoO\text{-}SD_{ij}) + \beta_{12} (FACIL_{ij}) + \varepsilon\end{aligned} \tag{5.2}$$

[14] To be sure, the facilitation term may pick up and thus proxy for some other trade-enhancing variables of PTAs, such as sturdy regulations on the use of emergency safeguards.
[15] See, for instance, Gatti (1999).

where $RoO\text{-}SD_{ij}$ is the standard deviation of *RoO-RI* values within a regime.

Note that there are two complementary reasons why *RoO-SD* would have a negative effect on trade. First, *RoO-SD* necessarily captures some of the effects of the *RoO-RI* variable because of the correlation between the two variables: the most restrictive RoO regimes—those based on the NAFTA and Pan-Euro models—also have the highest *RoO-SD* values. Conversely, regimes with an across-the-board rule and hence zero *RoO-SD* are empirically also the less restrictive ones. However, and second, regimes with high *RoO-SD* values—regimes with peak *RoO-RI*—are those where the high *RoO-SD* is produced by the existence of some *RoO-RI* values taking very high levels; it is thus the existence of RoO peaks—rather than overall level of *RoO-RI*—that is in model (5.2) expected to reduce trade.[16]

Columns VI–XI of Table 5.1 present the results. As expected, *RoO-SD* has a negative effect on trade. The finding allows us to conclude that greater sectoral selectivity in RoO regimes undermines trade. *FACIL*, meanwhile, has a positive and significant effect on trade. This provides further evidence that flexible regime-wide RoO can help boost aggregate trade flows. This is the third major result of this chapter: high levels of sectoral selectivity in RoO undermine aggregate trade.

The results are less resounding when *RoO-SD* is examined in the subsample of PTA pairs. However, this is due to the construction of the data. Apart from the Canada-U.S. FTA of 1989, all RoO regimes in the sample that were formed prior to 1991 feature an across-the-board rule of origin, which implies that *RoO-SD* values are basically zero until the 1990s. Indeed, column XI shows that *RoO-SD* reacquires its negative and significant sign when the sample is limited to the years of the rise of complex RoO regimes (1991–2001).[17]

---

[16] In other words, a three-product PTA with *RoO-RI* values of 4, 4, and 4 (i.e., *RoO-RI* average of 4 and *RoO-SD* of 0) should be less detrimental to trade than a three-product PTA with *RoO-RI* values of 2, 3, and 7 (i.e., *RoO-RI* average of 4 but *RoO-SD* value of 2.64).

[17] Robustness checks later in the chapter show that the results for all pairs rather than PTA pairs only are also more marked when the effect of *RoO-SD* on trade in the 1990s only is estimated.

The marked positive effect of *FACIL* on trade begs the question of the individual contributions of the five component parts of *FACIL*. We estimate the effects of the *FACIL* components through the following regression:

$$\begin{aligned}\ln\left(V_{ij}\right) = {} & \beta_0 + \beta_1 \ln\left(GDP_i\right) + \beta_2 \ln\left(GDP_j\right) + \beta_3 \ln\left(GDPPC_i\right), \\ & + \beta_4 \ln\left(GDPPC_j\right) + \beta_5 \ln\left(DIST_{ij}\right) + \beta_6\left(BORDER_{ij}\right) \\ & + \beta_7\left(COMLANG_{ij}\right) + \beta_8\left(COL_{ij}\right) + \beta_9\left(COMCOL_{ij}\right) \\ & + \beta_{10}\left(PTA_{ij}\right) + \beta_{11} \ln\left(RoO\text{-}RI_{ij}\right) + \beta_{12}\left(DE\ MINIMIS_{ij}\right) \\ & + \beta_{13}\left(CUMUDIAG_{ij}\right) + \beta_{14}\left(CUMUFULL_{ij}\right) \\ & + \beta_{15}\left(DRAWBACK_{ij}\right) + \beta_{16}\left(SELFCERT_{ij}\right) + \varepsilon\end{aligned} \tag{5.3}$$

where

$DE\ MINIMIS_{ij}$ takes the percentage value of de minimis provided by the PTA (i.e., between 0 and 15 percent);

$CUMUDIAG_{ij}$ is a dummy variable that takes value 1 when the PTA binding the two countries allows diagonal cumulation and 0 otherwise;

$CUMUFULL_{ij}$ is a dummy variable that takes value 1 when the PTA binding the two countries allows full cumulation and 0 otherwise;

$DRAWBACK_{ij}$ is a dummy variable that takes value 1 when the PTA binding the two countries allows or does not explicitly prohibit the use of drawback and 0 otherwise; and

$SELFCERT_{ij}$ is a dummy variable that takes value 1 when the PTA binding the two countries allows self-certification and 0 otherwise.

The other variables are as in (5.1).

Table 5.2 presents the results for all pairs and PTA pairs. De minimis, full cumulation, drawback, and self-certification all enter with a positive sign and are significant at the 1 percent level. Diagonal cumulation is

Table 5.2 Effects of RoO De Minimis, Cumulation, Drawback, and Self-Certification on Aggregate Trade, 1981–2001

	Dependent variable: $\ln(V_{ij})$	
	All Pairs, 1981–2001	PTA Pairs, 1981–2001
Independent variables	**I**	**II**
$\ln(GDP_j)$	0.199	0.772
	(7.27)**	(9.56)**
$\ln(GDP_i)$	0.381	0.443
	(8.67)**	(2.55)*
$\ln(GDPPC_j)$	0.401	−0.506
	(14.62)**	(8.41)**
$\ln(GDPPC_i)$	0.672	−0.275
	(16.12)**	(2.10)*
$\ln(DIST_{ij})$	−1.217	−1.151
	(182.63)**	(46.87)**
$BORDER_{ij}$	0.238	0.471
	(9.11)**	(10.97)**
$COMLANG_{ij}$	0.329	−0.007
	(22.66)**	(0.13)
COL_{ij}	1.299	0.722
	(41.77)**	(7.20)**
$COMCOL_{ij}$	0.631	0.734
	(38.35)**	(14.93)**
PTA_{ij}	1.394	
	(11.61)**	
$\ln(RoO\text{-}RI_{ij})$	−1.309	−0.744
	(20.22)**	(7.91)**
$DE\ MINIMIS_{ij}$	0.037	0.067
	(5.52)**	(4.64)**
$CUMUDIAG_{ij}$	0.127	−0.329
	(1.58)	(2.65)**
$CUMUFULL_{ij}$	0.215	0.735
	(4.11)**	(8.41)**
$DRAWBACK_{ij}$	0.838	0.031
	(10.03)**	(0.29)
$SELFCERT_{ij}$	0.868	0.858
	(10.04)**	(5.59)**
Constant	−0.617	−1.729
	(0.61)	(0.45)
Observations	185,491	11,920
Adjusted R-squared	0.73	0.88
Year fixed effects	Yes	Yes
Importer and exporter fixed effects	Yes	Yes

Note: Absolute value of t-statistics in parentheses.

* significant at 5 percent level; ** significant at 1 percent level.

positive and significant at the 10 percent level; however, this may also be because of the high correlation between de minimis and diagonal cumulation. Notable are the highly positive effects of full cumulation (which markedly expands the geographical scope of intermediate goods) and self-certification (which cuts the steps required for an exporter to certify the origin of a shipment) on aggregate trade flows. The results for the sample of PTA pairs are similar, although correlation among three variables—de minimis, diagonal cumulation, and drawback—likely affects the results to an extent.

Do RoO Divert Trade in Intermediates?

Rules of origin are first and foremost geared toward affecting the input composition of goods. As such, they can be expected to have particularly important effects on trade in intermediate goods. This subsection assesses such effects by estimating the impact of the restrictiveness of product-specific RoO in final goods on trade in intermediate goods in five major manufacturing sectors—chemicals, machinery, textiles, television and radio transmitters, and vehicles. Sectors are here defined as divisions of the ISIC Revision 3 classification system (Divisions 24 for chemicals, 29 for machinery, 17 for textiles, 32 for television and radio transmitters, and 34 for vehicles). The dependent variable in each sector is the total imports of a bundle of Harmonized System 6-digit-level intermediate products used intensively in the production of the HS 6-digit-level final goods falling in the ISIC Division (here, "sector") in question. The correspondence between ISIC and HS is obtained from the United Nations. We use divisions rather than higher levels of disaggregation, such as groups, of the ISIC system, since a given country may not have any comparative advantages when product categories are highly disaggregated and sectors narrowly defined.[18] The details on the construction of the data set are discussed in Appendix 5.2.

[18] Dihel and Walkenhorst (2002) note that the problem dissipates once sectors are defined broadly enough, as potential for intra-industry trade expands.

Empirical Specification

We explore the impact of RoO in final goods on imports in intermediates by estimating the following equation using OLS:

$$\begin{aligned}\ln\left(INPUT_{ijs}\right) = {} & \beta_0 + \beta_1 \ln\left(GDP_i\right) + \beta_2 \ln\left(GDP_j\right), \\ & + \beta_3 \ln\left(GDPPC_i\right) + \beta_4 \ln\left(GDPPC_j\right) + \beta_5 \ln\left(DIST_{ij}\right) \\ & + \beta_6\left(BORDER_{ij}\right) + \beta_7\left(COMLANG_{ij}\right) \\ & + \beta_8\left(COL_{ij}\right) + \beta_9\left(COMCOL_{ij}\right) \\ & + \beta_{10} \ln\left(RoO\text{-}RI\text{-}FINAL_{ijs}\right) + \beta_{11}\left(FACIL_{ij}\right) + \varepsilon\end{aligned} \qquad (5.4)$$

where

$INPUT_{ijs}$ is the value of intermediate imports into country *i* from country *j* in sector *s*; and

$RoO\text{-}RI\text{-}FINAL_{ijs}$ is the average of the restrictiveness of RoO values (as measured at the 6-digit level of disaggregation) in final goods in sector *s*.

The other variables are defined as in (5.1).

The expectation is now that the key independent variable, $RoO\text{-}RI\text{-}FINAL_{ijs}$, will be *positively* related to trade flows: stringent RoO in final goods should encourage trade in intermediates in the PTA area at the expense of sourcing by the PTA partners from ROW. *FACIL* should, as above, be positively related to trade flows between the partners.

Importantly here, the model does not include the *PTA* variable. This is because although a PTA should and does reduce barriers to trade between partners *on average* in the tariff universe as a whole and does so immediately in the first year of the PTA, its liberalizing impact on trade in the five narrowly defined bundles of intermediate goods examined here is questionable for two reasons.

First, the *PTA* dummy per se is a very crude measure of regional integration agreements, each of which incorporates a great many disciplines and enormous variation across product categories in the discipline of market access.

Second, the *PTA* dummy may be completely inapplicable to any given narrow subset of the tariff lines included in the PTA, such as the small bundles of intermediate goods analyzed here—which make up only between 0.2 percent (textiles) and 3.6 percent (vehicles) of the total of about 5,000 6-digit tariff lines in the negotiated tariff universe. It is hardly self-evident that tariffs in that particular bundle are being dropped either immediately or completely in any given PTA much less across all PTAs included in this study—or cut down even after repeated rounds of tariff phaseouts.

In other words, PTA-inspired trade liberalization may be subject to significant time lags in certain intermediate goods and/or sensitive sectors; the onset of a PTA per se, ceteris paribus, may thus entail a markedly lower or no boost to trade between the partners in the narrow bundles of intermediates than it does at the aggregate level. Indeed, the regressions we conducted with models that contained (1) both *RoO-RI-FINAL* and *PTA*, and (2) *RoO-RI-FINAL*, *PTA*, and *FACIL*, the coefficient for *PTA* behaves inconsistently across regressions and most often acquires a negative sign. The variable may simply capture the effects of the existing barriers remaining to trade in the small bundles of intermediate goods considered here.

In contrast to the *PTA* variable, *RoO-RI-FINAL* and *FACIL* can be expected to have important explanatory power for trade flows of intermediates for two reasons. First, each intermediate good in each of the five bundles is used very intensively in the production of the final goods in the examined division. As such, unlike the *PTA* variable, which is insensitive to intrasectoral variations in market access, *RoO-RI-FINAL* is a highly targeted variable arbitrating the flow of trade in the selected bundle of intermediate goods, in particular, and takes effect immediately at the onset of the PTA. Second, *FACIL*, unlike *PTA*, applies by and large similarly across products in the entire tariff universe and is, like *RoO-RI-FINAL*, applied immediately upon the launch of the PTA. Note that since the *PTA* indicator has poor predictive value in the kind of enterprise we are carrying out—estimation of the determinants of trade in a narrow bundle of intermediate goods—circumscribing the sample by the *PTA* variable to examine flows among PTA pairs only is also theoretically unsound.

Table 5.3 summarizes the regression results according to the variables of interest.[19] The key independent variables, *RoO-RI-FINAL* and *FACIL*, are, as expected, positively related to trade in intermediate goods. This is the fourth major result of this chapter: the restrictiveness of RoO in final goods encourages trade in intermediate products. This finding serves as evidence for the long-suspected impact of RoO on input trade—an impact that could divert trade in intermediates from ROW to the PTA area. In political economy terms, the finding provides grounds for believing that the growing propensity toward fragmentation of global production presents a threat to high-cost domestic input providers—which see an opportunity in RoO to reduce the incentives for final goods producers to shift to sourcing from lower-cost suppliers abroad, and as such, to stay afloat in the face of globalization. Thus, it would not be a coincidence that the selectivity and restrictiveness of RoO around the world have increased over time.

Note that inclusion of the *FACIL* variable reduces the coefficient of the *RoO-RI-FINAL* variable by roughly the amount of the coefficient of *FACIL*; as such, it appears to be the combined effect of *RoO-RI-FINAL* and *FACIL* that serves to boost trade in intermediates.[20] This result stands in clear contrast to the regressions at the aggregate level, where *RoO-RI* and *FACIL* pulled in different directions. Indeed, even in regressions conducted at the aggregate level that did not include the *PTA* variable,

---

[19] The dependent variable is here expanded to the log of trade + 1. This is because the use of only positive flows restricts each sample to somewhere between 19,000 observations (textiles) and 65,000 observations (vehicles); because of the limited samples, a large set of the *RoO-RI-FINAL* values used to estimate the impact of RoO in final goods on the behavior of the flows in intermediate goods falls outside the pairs with positive trade flows (from 46 percent of all *RoO-RI-FINAL* values in vehicles to 77 percent in textiles). In other words, the explanatory value of the *RoO-RI* variable is greatly curbed by limiting the estimation to the pairs with positive values only; the "true" impact of RoO on trade can be discerned only by including in the sample also pairs with zero trade flows. In sharp contrast, the loss of *RoO-RI* values at the aggregate level when the regressions are estimated with the log of trade is below 10 percent.

[20] Thus, omitting either would lead to attributing too much weight to each individual variable.

Table 5.3 Effects of Sectoral Restrictiveness of RoO in Final Goods and Facilitation Terms on Trade in Intermediates, 1988–2001

Chemicals		
RoO-RI-FINAL	0.984 (64.96)**	0.339 (9.45)**
FACIL		0.474 (19.81)**
Observations	237,708	237,708
Adjusted R-squared	0.43	0.43
Machinery		
RoO-RI-FINAL	0.928 (67.56)**	0.496 (14.73)**
FACIL		0.333 (14.06)**
Observations	237,715	237,715
Adjusted R-squared	0.45	0.45
Television and Radio Transmitters		
RoO-RI-FINAL	1.002 (63.85)**	0.583 (15.25)**
FACIL		0.326 (12.01)**
Observations	237,708	237,708
Adjusted R-squared	0.47	0.47
Textiles		
RoO-RI-FINAL	0.407 (54.47)**	0.347 (18.31)**
FACIL		0.050 (3.42)**
Observations	237,708	237,708
Adjusted R-squared	0.30	0.30
Vehicles		
RoO-RI-FINAL	1.000 (59.63)**	0.603 (14.66)**
FACIL		0.311 (10.55)**
Observations	237,708	237,708
Adjusted R-squared	0.50	0.50

Note: Absolute value of *t*-statistics in parentheses. All regressions with year and exporter and importer fixed effects.
* significant at 5 percent level; ** significant at 1 percent level.

RoO-RI entered with a negative and significant sign and *FACIL* with a positive and significant sign. This further warrants concluding that the restrictiveness of RoO plays an inherently different role at the sectoral than at the aggregate level in arbitrating trade flows. The effect of *FACIL* appears less important in textiles. This may be a result of the fact that many RoO regimes define de minimis, one of the key components of *FACIL*, for textiles in terms of weight rather than in terms of value: basing de minimis on the weight principle may reduce the usefulness of de minimis.

The next set of estimations explores the impact of the complexity or sectoral selectivity of RoO in final goods on imports in intermediates by replacing *RoO-RI-FINAL* by *RoO-SD-FINAL* through the following equation:

$$\begin{aligned}\ln\left(INPUT_{ijs}\right) = \beta_0 + \beta_1 \ln\left(GDP_i\right) + \beta_2 \ln\left(GDP_j\right), \\ + \beta_3 \ln\left(GDPPC_i\right) + \beta_4 \ln\left(GDPPC_j\right) + \beta_5 \ln\left(DIST_{ij}\right) \\ + \beta_6\left(BORDER_{ij}\right) + \beta_7\left(COMLANG_{ij}\right) \\ + \beta_8\left(COL_{ij}\right) + \beta_9\left(COMCOL_{ij}\right) \\ + \beta_{10} \ln\left(RoO\text{-}SD\text{-}FINAL_{ijs}\right) + \beta_{11}\left(FACIL_{ij}\right) + \varepsilon\end{aligned} \quad (5.5)$$

where $RoO\text{-}SD\text{-}FINAL_{ijs}$ is the standard deviation of the restrictiveness of RoO values (as measured at the 6-digit level of disaggregation) in final goods in sector *s*. The expectation is as above: regimes with high levels of sectoral selectivity in the restrictiveness of their RoO in final goods should have a positive impact on trade in intermediates. However, whereas *RoO-SD* at the aggregate level may have captured some of the effects of *RoO-RI*, given the high level of correlation between the two variables, this is not the case in intermediate goods. For example, whereas *RoO-RI-FINAL* is very high (at 5–7 on the RoO index scale) in textiles at the HS 6-digit level in most PTAs, *RoO-SD-FINAL*—the variation in the *RoO-RI* levels across final goods *within a division* rather than across all goods within a PTA—is very low, as the *RoO-RI* values vary little across products in the five examined divisions in most RoO regimes analyzed here. Thus, the sectoral regressions should reflect particularly well the genuine effects of RoO peaks.

The results are reported in Table 5.4. They are consistent across the models: the sectoral selectivity of RoO in final goods is positively and significantly related to trade in intermediate goods. *FACIL*, meanwhile, continues to boost trade. The only exception is again its inefficacy in textiles. As above, it is the combined effect of *FACIL* and *RoO-SD-FINAL* that encourages trade between the PTA partners. This is the fifth key result of this chapter: RoO peaks in final goods encourage trade in intermediate products.

Learning to Play by the Rules: Effects of RoO Over Time

How do the trade effects of RoO vary over time? There are two plausible answers. First, given that the restrictiveness and selectivity of RoO around the world has increased over time, RoO could be expected to obstruct trade flows increasingly each year. However, and second, the effects of RoO may also decrease over time, given that exporters learn to comply with product-specific RoO and to take advantage of the facilitation terms and/or alter their production strategies to meet the RoO requirements. This "RoO learning" implies that the growing stringency of RoO around the world does not necessarily translate into growing "RoO interference" over time.

We examine these possibilities by running (5.1) as a panel for 1981–2001 but interacting *RoO-RI* and *FACIL*, respectively, with a year dummy. This allows an examination of whether the response of trade to rules of origin is significantly different in any given year from the reference year of 1981, when few PTAs, much less PTAs with demanding or complex RoO, were in place. The procedure also allows the year-by-year effects to be contrasted with one another. The model is as follows:

$$
\begin{aligned}
\ln\left(V_{ij}\right) = \beta_0 &+ \beta_1 \ln\left(GDP_i\right) + \beta_2 \ln\left(GDP_j\right) + \beta_3 \ln\left(GDPPC_i\right), \qquad (5.6)\\
&+ \beta_4 \ln\left(GDPPC_j\right) + \beta_5 \ln\left(DIST_{ij}\right) + \beta_6\left(BORDER_{ij}\right)\\
&+ \beta_7\left(COMLANG_{ij}\right) + \beta_8\left(COL_{ij}\right)\\
&+ \beta_9\left(COMCOL_{ij}\right) + \beta_{10}(PTA_{ij})\\
&+ \beta_{11} \ln\left(RoO\text{-}RI_{ij}\right) + \beta_{12}\left(FACIL_{ij}\right)\\
&+ \beta_{13} \ln\left(RoO\text{-}RI{*}YEAR_{ij}\right) + \varepsilon
\end{aligned}
$$

Table 5.4 Effects of Sectoral Selectivity of RoO in Final Goods and Facilitation Terms on Trade in Intermediates, 1988–2001

Chemicals		
RoO-SD-FINAL	4.321 (81.61)**	3.695 (47.06)**
FACIL		0.162 (10.85)**
Observations	237,721	237,721
Adjusted *R*-squared	0.43	0.43
Machinery		
RoO-SD-FINAL	5.519 (82.05)**	4.605 (48.35)**
FACIL		0.185 (13.53)**
Observations	237,721	237,721
Adjusted *R*-squared	0.45	0.45
Television and Radio Transmitters		
RoO-SD-FINAL	7.137 (71.27)**	5.225 (40.05)**
FACIL		0.330 (22.82)**
Observations	237,721	237,721
Adjusted *R*-squared	0.47	0.47
Textiles		
RoO-SD-FINAL	1.279 (67.66)**	1.264 (43.90)**
FACIL		0.006 (0.66)
Observations	237,721	237,721
Adjusted *R*-squared	0.30	0.30
Vehicles		
RoO-SD-FINAL	4.985 (20.71)**	2.847 (11.76)**
FACIL		0.682 (56.12)**
Observations	237,721	237,721
Adjusted *R*-squared	0.50	0.50

Note: Absolute value of *t*-statistics in parentheses. All regressions with year and exporter and importer fixed effects.
* significant at 5 percent level; ** significant at 1 percent level.

where $RoO\text{-}RI^{*}YEAR_{ij}$ is an interaction term for *RoO-RI* and a given year in the set (1982–2001). Table 5.5 presents the results for all pairs and the subsample of PTA pairs.

The *RoO-RI**YEAR variable is, ceteris paribus, significantly different from the reference category of 1981 for most years in the regression containing the entire sample. The negative trend from the 1981 level accentuates in the early 1980s around the formation of such integration schemes as LAIA, ANZCERTA, and SPARTECA, and then again upon the wave of regionalism in the Americas, Europe, and Southeast Asia. However, the evolution of the coefficients over time reveals a downward trend in the negative pressure of RoO on trade, which, in turn, suggests that "RoO learning" gradually reduces "RoO interference"—that is, that exporters learned to comply with RoO and potentially also altered their production strategies to better meet the RoO requirements, so that the interference level gradually converged back to that of 1981.[21] To be sure, whether such retailoring of production strategies follows an economic logic or, rather, leads to allocational inefficiencies is clearly debatable.

Interestingly, however, the response of trade to RoO among PTA pairs is significantly different from that in 1981 only in eight years. This may again suggest some endogeneity issues, but could also simply indicate that exporters and producers in the PTA partners were equally or even better equipped to deal with RoO (or evade RoO at lower costs) in 2001 than in 1981; ex ante altered their sourcing strategies to comply with RoO requirements; and, indeed, in a strategy that is not as readily available to extra-PTA producers, themselves lobbied for RoO tailored to accommodate their existing production and sourcing patterns—and even to obstruct extra-PTA producers from entering the PTA market.[22]

Importantly, however, there are three further factors potentially contributing to the decline in RoO interference in the sample with all

---

[21] A similar trend occurs in the cross-sectional regressions.

[22] For empirical work on the endogeneity of RoO to political pressures, see Estevadeordal (2000) and Suominen (2004).

Table 5.5 Interactive Effect of Time and RoO on Trade, 1981–2001

	All countries		PTA members	
	$\ln(V_{ij})$		$\ln(V_{ij})$	
Independent variables	Coefficient	*t*-statistic	Coefficient	*t*-statistic
$\ln(GDP_j)$	0.208	(7.61)**	0.778	(9.59)**
$\ln(GDP_i)$	0.422	(9.60)**	0.704	(3.96)**
$\ln(GDPPC_j)$	0.396	(14.42)**	−0.530	(8.75)**
$\ln(GDPPC_i)$	0.646	(15.49)**	−0.455	(3.42)**
$\ln(DIST_{ij})$	−1.223	(180.44)**	−1.151	(47.36)**
$BORDER_{ij}$	0.251	(9.59)**	0.477	(11.11)**
$COMLANG_{ij}$	0.341	(23.51)**	−0.014	(0.26)
COL_{ij}	1.288	(41.82)**	0.754	(7.55)**
$COMCOL_{ij}$	0.629	(38.27)**	0.729	(15.15)**
PTA_{ij}	2.338	(36.56)**		
$\ln(RoO\text{-}RI_{ij})$	−1.482	(17.46)**	−1.115	(5.53)**
$FACIL_{ij}$	0.199	(8.43)**	0.456	(8.15)**
$RoO\text{-}RI{*}1982_{ij}$	−0.150	(4.24)**	−0.023	(0.26)
$RoO\text{-}RI{*}1983_{ij}$	−0.182	(5.23)**	−0.028	(0.32)
$RoO\text{-}RI{*}1984_{ij}$	−0.181	(5.21)**	0.081	(0.91)
$RoO\text{-}RI{*}1985_{ij}$	−0.162	(4.69)**	0.141	(1.61)
$RoO\text{-}RI{*}1986_{ij}$	−0.144	(4.28)**	0.233	(2.73)**
$RoO\text{-}RI{*}1987_{ij}$	−0.120	(3.60)**	0.218	(2.62)**
$RoO\text{-}RI{*}1988_{ij}$	−0.103	(3.10)**	0.203	(2.45)*
$RoO\text{-}RI{*}1989_{ij}$	−0.078	(2.33)*	0.161	(1.96)*
$RoO\text{-}RI{*}1990_{ij}$	−0.060	(1.82)	0.121	(1.55)
$RoO\text{-}RI{*}1991_{ij}$	−0.069	(2.10)*	0.174	(2.23)*
$RoO\text{-}RI{*}1992_{ij}$	−0.039	(1.19)	0.098	(1.27)
$RoO\text{-}RI{*}1993_{ij}$	−0.063	(2.09)*	−0.013	(0.18)
$RoO\text{-}RI{*}1994_{ij}$	−0.094	(3.48)**	0.031	(0.44)
$RoO\text{-}RI{*}1995_{ij}$	−0.083	(3.14)**	0.086	(1.24)
$RoO\text{-}RI{*}1996_{ij}$	−0.084	(3.17)**	0.130	(1.87)
$RoO\text{-}RI{*}1997_{ij}$	−0.082	(3.15)**	0.115	(1.67)
$RoO\text{-}RI{*}1998_{ij}$	−0.065	(2.51)*	0.185	(2.69)**
$RoO\text{-}RI{*}1999_{ij}$	−0.053	(2.07)*	0.230	(3.34)**
$RoO\text{-}RI{*}2000_{ij}$	−0.033	(1.27)	0.232	(3.32)**
$RoO\text{-}RI{*}2001_{ij}$	−0.009	(0.36)	0.240	(3.55)**
Constant	−1.034	(1.05)	−7.129	(1.88)
Observations	185,491		11,920	
Adjusted R-squared	0.73		0.88	
Year fixed effects	Yes		Yes	
Importer and exporter fixed effects	Yes		Yes	

Note: Absolute value of *t*-statistics in parentheses.

* significant at 5 percent level; ** significant at 1 percent level.

pairs. First, the *RoO-RI* variable may simply capture some of the effects of the onset of the tariff phaseouts in the newer PTAs—which is not necessarily fully captured by the *PTA* dummy, which remains constant after the first year of any PTA.

Second, and more interestingly, the lowering of preferential tariffs also increased exporters' incentives to qualify for preferences and hence learn to comply with RoO. Indeed, that RoO interference declines (1) in the early 1990s, when the truly liberalizing PTAs emerge to replace the older schemes, many of which, such as LAIA, had patchy records at tariff lowering, and (2) in the mid-1990s upon the kick-in of the preferences of the major PTAs, such as NAFTA and the EEA agreement, suggests that the attraction of preferences gradually overwhelms the burdens of RoO.

Third, and contrary to the second point, the multilateral lowering of tariffs and nontariff barriers resulting particularly from the conclusion of the Uruguay Round in 1994 may have reduced the relevance of RoO: exporters may simply have started circumventing RoO altogether by paying the (declining) MFN tariff to enter a PTA member's market. This would happen particularly in product categories—admittedly rare—where the preferential tariffs are high and preferential liberalization is very slow, yet multilateral liberalization is speedy and substantial.

We explored this "circumvention hypothesis" by including in model (5.4) a dummy for WTO members, which takes the value of 1 starting in year 1995 for all pairs where both the importer and the exporter signed the 1994 Marrakech Agreement. As expected, the dummy, despite its crudeness given the vast variation in the WTO signatories' tariff-lowering commitments, enters with a positive and highly significant sign. However, this does not necessarily still mean that exporters circumvented RoO, merely that the lowered barriers to trade propelled trade flows along. The overall year-by-year behavior of *RoO-RI* remains unaltered and significant even when the *WTO* dummy is included.

If exporters learn to comply with product-specific RoO over time, might they also draw greater advantage from the facilitation terms in RoO regimes? The following equation modifies (5.4) to explore this question:

$$\ln(V_{ij}) = \beta_0 + \beta_1 \ln(GDP_i) + \beta_2 \ln(GDP_j) + \beta_3 \ln(GDPPC_i), + \beta_4 \ln(GDPPC_j) + \beta_5 \ln(DIST_{ij}) + \beta_6 (BORDER_{ij}) + \beta_7 (COMLANG_{ij}) + \beta_8 (COL_{ij}) + \beta_9 (COMCOL_{ij}) + \beta_{10} (PTA_{ij}) + \beta_{11} \ln(RoO\text{-}RI_{ij}) + \beta_{12} (FACIL_{ij}) + \beta_{13} (FACIL*YEAR_{ij}) + \varepsilon \quad (5.7)$$

where $FACIL*YEAR_{ij}$ is an interaction term for *FACIL* and a given year in the set (1982–2001).

The results in Table 5.6 show that the response of trade to *FACIL* becomes significantly different in the 1990s from the response in 1981.[23] This is not surprising given that the regimes of the 1990s—those with the most restrictive product-specific RoO—also include the relatively most flexible facilitation terms.

Again, however, the response is not significantly different from that in 1981 among PTA pairs. This may mean that intra-PTA exporters were throughout the sample period able to use facilitation terms to their advantage and/or, again, tailored these terms ex ante to meet their preferences. However, it may also indicate that facilitation terms per se over time were less relevant to intra- than extra-PTA exporters, which may have resulted from the likely endogeneity of product-specific RoO to intra-PTA exporters' preferences. If product-specific RoO over time posed few hurdles to compliance to begin with in comparison to the reference year of 1981, the facilitation terms will not be of much greater use at any time since 1981 than they were in 1981, either. Nonetheless, facilitation terms do play a statistically significant role in intra-PTA trade flows in 1987–88 and in 1995–96; the impact during these years is just not too different from that in 1981.

Figure 5.1 summarizes the effects of *RoO-RI* and *FACIL* on trade over time for the entire sample.[24] Notable in both the figure and Table 5.6

[23] That *FACIL* per se becomes insignificant may be due to some colinearity between *FACIL* and the *FACIL*YEAR* variables.

[24] These are calculated as exp(coef. *RoO-RI*YEAR*) – 1 and exp(coef. FACIL**YEAR*) – 1, respectively.

Table 5.6 | Interactive Effect of Time and Facilitation Terms on Trade 1981–2001

	All countries		PTA members	
	$\ln(V_{ij})$		$\ln(V_{ij})$	
Independent variables	Coefficient	*t*-statistic	Coefficient	*t*-statistic
$\ln(GDP_j)$	0.210	(7.68)**	0.757	(9.26)**
$\ln(GDP_i)$	0.425	(9.68)**	0.385	(2.16)*
$\ln(GDPPC_j)$	0.396	(14.43)**	−0.521	(8.63)**
$\ln(GDPPC_i)$	0.646	(15.48)**	−0.261	(1.96)*
$\ln(DIST_{ij})$	−1.219	(182.83)**	−1.149	(47.15)**
$BORDER_{ij}$	0.246	(9.41)**	0.484	(11.25)**
$COMLANG_{ij}$	0.339	(23.41)**	−0.014	(0.01)
COL_{ij}	1.292	(41.99)**	0.770	(7.68)**
$COMCOL_{ij}$	0.628	(38.19)**	0.716	(14.86)**
PTA_{ij}	2.367	(37.12)**		
$\ln(RoO\text{-}RI_{ij})$	−1.729	(31.92)**	−0.686	(7.40)**
$FACIL_{ij}$	0.058	(0.06)	0.397	(4.19)**
$FACIL*1982_{ij}$	0.029	(0.03)	0.017	(0.02)
$FACIL*1983_{ij}$	0.018	(0.02)	0.208	(1.99)*
$FACIL*1984_{ij}$	0.014	(0.01)	0.256	(2.45)*
$FACIL*1985_{ij}$	0.036	(0.04)	0.239	(2.31)*
$FACIL*1986_{ij}$	0.045	(0.05)	0.227	(2.21)*
$FACIL*1987_{ij}$	0.085	(0.08)	0.221	(2.19)*
$FACIL*1988_{ij}$	0.099	(0.10)	0.152	(0.15)
$FACIL*1989_{ij}$	0.150	(2.08)*	0.159	(0.16)
$FACIL*1990_{ij}$	0.155	(2.17)*	0.061	(0.06)
$FACIL*1991_{ij}$	0.140	(1.96)*	0.094	(0.09)
$FACIL*1992_{ij}$	0.199	(2.81)**	0.059	(0.06)
$FACIL*1993_{ij}$	0.176	(2.56)*	0.000	(0.00)
$FACIL*1994_{ij}$	0.122	(1.92)*	0.010	(0.01)
$FACIL*1995_{ij}$	0.138	(2.17)*	0.025	(0.02)
$FACIL*1996_{ij}$	0.139	(2.20)*	0.051	(0.05)
$FACIL*1997_{ij}$	0.137	(2.20)*	0.007	(0.01)
$FACIL*1998_{ij}$	0.173	(2.77)**	0.091	(0.09)
$FACIL*1999_{ij}$	0.192	(3.10)**	0.134	(0.13)
$FACIL*2000_{ij}$	0.235	(3.81)**	0.067	(0.07)
$FACIL*2001_{ij}$	0.289	(4.80)**	0.040	(0.04)
Constant	−1.165	(1.19)	−0.939	(0.25)
Observations	185,491		11,920	
Adjusted R-squared	0.73		0.88	
Year fixed effects	Yes		Yes	
Importer and exporter fixed effects	Yes		Yes	

Note: Absolute value of *t*-statistics in parentheses.

* significant at 5 percent level; ** significant at 1 percent level.

Figure 5.1 | Effect of *RoO-RI* and *FACIL* on Aggregate Trade, 1981–2001

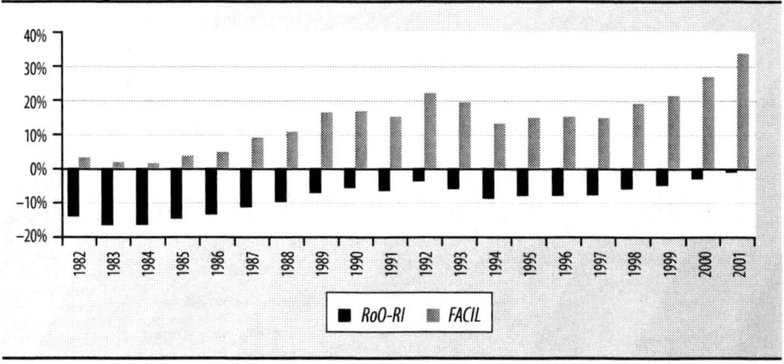

Source: Authors' calculations.

is a jump in the effect of RoO in the 1993–95 period, which captures the entry into force of many important PTAs in 1992–95. However, the jump in "RoO interference" is compensated for by the simultaneous entry into effect of the relatively permissive facilitation terms of agreements based on the Pan-Euro and NAFTA models; the overall effects thus remain largely unaltered. Interestingly, however, the positive trend in *FACIL* appears to lag behind the negative effect of *RoO-RI* by some three years: whereas the negative *RoO-RI* peak takes place around 1993–94, the positive effect of *FACIL* actually drops before gaining steam in 1998.

These results further suggest that exporters learn to circumvent restrictive RoO by altering production strategies and taking advantage of *FACIL* only a few years into the demanding RoO regimes. In other words, the decline in the negative effect of *RoO-RI* and growth in the positive effect of *FACIL* coincide some three years into a PTA. Education, particularly among extra-PTA export groups, about the requirements of RoO as well as the opportunities provided by the facilitation terms well before the onset of a negotiated PTA would likely reduce such a time lag. Such a task is complicated, however, by the fact that RoO tend to be among the last items that are agreed upon in PTA negotiations. To be sure, a fast and deep preferential tariff phaseout schedule built into a PTA would likely also reduce the lag by providing exporters with an incentive to qualify for PTA-provided preferences. Meanwhile, prompt MFN tariff liberalization by the PTA partners would eliminate the relevance of RoO to both intra- and extra-PTA exporters alike.[25]

Results in Sum

In sum, the exercises have yielded four main results: (1) both the restrictiveness and selectivity of rules of origin have an adverse effect on aggregate trade flows; (2) regime-wide RoO—and particularly the combined effects of such RoO—that are designed to add leniency to the application of product-specific RoO boost trade; (3) restrictive and selective rules of origin in final goods markedly increase trade in intermediates; and (4) exporters learn to apply RoO over time, which is reflected in (a) the decreasing relevance of RoO, as evident in the analysis of aggregate trade flows, for creating disincentives for exporters to qualify for PTA-provided preferential treatment; and (b) the growing importance of RoO in diverting trade in intermediates to flow between the parties applying RoO.

Robustness Checks

Table 5.7 reports robustness checks of the estimations, including for trade weighted by total trade; limiting the sample to pairs with dependent

---

[25] We further explored the immediate net effect of the 1993–95 wave of PTAs (and restrictive RoO) by focusing on the years 1990–92, on the one hand, and the 1993–95 period, on the other. More specifically, we compared the average of coefficients of the *RoO-RI*YEAR* variable in 1990–92 to the average of coefficients of the variable in 1993–95 for the whole sample. The comparisons are calculated as exp(avg. coef. 90–92 – avg. coef. 93–95) – 1. We subsequently performed the same exercise comparing the 1990–92 period to the post-PTA wave period of 1998–2001. We also calculated the interannual differences for *FACIL*, but with the three-year period when the positive effects of *FACIL* appear to lag behind the negative effects of RoO. As such, the contrast was between the period 1993–95, when the new facilitation terms went into effect yet had scant beneficial effects, and 1998–2000, the period when exporters plausibly had learned to use the facilitation terms to their benefit. We subsequently performed the same exercise comparing the 1993–95 period to 2001. The results indicate that the hike in the negative impact of the restrictiveness of RoO on trade between the 1990–92 and the 1993–95 periods was some 2.4 percent; the effects dissipated fully by the 1998–2000 period. Meanwhile, in contrast to a low in 1993–95, *FACIL* increased its positive effects in 1998–2001 by 5.3 percent and in 2001 by 14.2 percent.

Table 5.7 Robustness Checks, Aggregate Trade, 1981–2001

	WIS (weight: ln (total imports))		Trade > $500,000		ln(Trade) 3sd from mean		ln(Trade) 2sd from mean		Excluding Pan-Euro pairs		Country-pair fixed effects				Country-pair random effects			
	$\ln(V_{ij})$		$\ln(V_{ij})$		$\ln(V_{ij})$		$\ln(V_{ij})$		$\ln(V_{ij})$		$\ln(V_{ij})$		$\ln(V_{ij})$ 1991–2001		$\ln(V_{ij})$		$\ln(V_{ij})$ 1991–2001	
Ind. var.	I	II	I	II	I	II	I	II	I	II	I	II	I	II	I	II	I	II
PTA	2.514	2.440	1.916	1.807	1.367	1.18	0.85	0.734	2.396	2.299	−0.101	−0.100	0.713	0.726	0.167	0.153	1.100	1.100
	(38.68)**	(37.19)**	(33.27)**	(30.90)**	(22.75)**	(18.89)**	(14.70)**	(12.23)**	(37.03)**	(34.97)**	(1.03)	(1.03)	(4.43)**	(4.50)**	(1.75)	(1.64)	(7.96)**	(7.97)**
ln ($RoO\text{-}RI_{ij}$)	−1.532	−1.716	−1.12	−1.332	−0.795	−0.989	−0.494	−0.626	−1.445	−1.641	0.264	0.148	−0.274	−0.383	0.155	−0.04	−0.462	−0.643
	(31.75)**	(31.69)**	(26.22)**	(28.23)**	(16.87)**	(19.61)**	(10.66)**	(12.55)**	(28.31)**	(29.16)**	(3.69)**	(1.63)	(2.46)*	(2.87)**	(2.27)*	(0.50)	(4.77)**	(5.59)**
FACIL		0.177		0.218		0.263		0.177		0.202		0.091		0.079		0.16		0.142
		(7.48)**		(10.56)**		(10.75)**		(7.16)**		(8.20)**		(2.07)*		(1.48)		(3.85)**		(2.91)**
PTA	0.907	0.685	0.700	0.436	0.515	0.213	0.317	0.143	0.904	−0.645	0.042	0.11	0.30	0.327	0.197	0.177	0.547	0.469
	(36.28)**	(16.35)**	(31.56)**	(11.71)**	(21.77)**	(5.12)**	(14.12)**	(3.53)**	(36.83)**	(15.09)**	(1.12)	(1.71)	(5.30)**	(3.83)**	(5.39)**	(2.82)**	(10.65)**	(5.94)**
ln ($RoO\text{-}SD_{ij}$)	−0.958	−1.147	−0.597	−0.811	−0.358	−0.566	−0.185	−0.308	−0.967	−1.206	0.434	0.494	0.043	0.062	0.366	0.348	−0.157	−0.216
	(23.08)**	(22.73)**	(16.15)**	(18.33)**	(8.02)**	(11.21)**	(4.09)**	(6.03)**	(19.38)**	(20.31)**	(7.76)**	(6.83)**	(0.56)	(0.70)	(6.68)**	(4.98)**	(2.22)*	(2.58)**
FACIL		0.168		0.197		0.227		0.134		0.198		−0.058		−0.022		0.017		0.063
		(6.58)**		(8.80)**		(8.76)**		(5.18)**		(7.42)**		(1.30)		(0.42)		(0.39)		(1.31)

Note: Absolute value of *t*-statistics in parentheses. All regressions with year dummies. Except for regressions with country-pair fixed effects, all regressions with importer and exporter dummies.
* significant at 5 percent level; ** significant at 1 percent level.

variable three and two standard deviations from the mean; limiting the sample to pairs with above US$500,000 in trade; excluding Pan-Euro pairs in order to verify that the Pan-Euro system alone does not drive the results; and including country-pair fixed effects and country-pair random effects. All regressions include year fixed effects, and except for those containing country-pair fixed and random effects, importer and exporter fixed effects.

The results remain robust. The country-pair dummies do seem to sap the explanatory power of the *RoO-RI* variable; however, in the regression for the years of the heyday of PTAs and the greatest number of positive *RoO-RI* and *RoO-SD* values in the data set, 1990–2001, *RoO-RI* again enters with a negative and significant sign, and *FACIL* acquires a positive and significant sign. It should also be kept in mind that it is not necessarily clear that country-pair fixed effects accomplish the task of capturing all the variables that are constant for a given country pair. Table 5.8 extends the robustness checks to the PTA pairs; again, the results remain robust.[26]

Given the possible instability in the regressions with country fixed effects, we run another specification that is less affected by measurement errors yet allows country-pair fixed effects to be controlled for. This is done by calculating the difference in all time-variant variables between 2001 and 1981, and 2001 and 1991, respectively, and running (5.1) with these calculated differentials.[27] Table 5.9 presents the results for the key variables of interest. They show that the increase in *RoO-RI* values over time stifles commerce, whereas the rise in the PTA value (from 0 to 1) helps boost trade. Changes in *FACIL* over time, meanwhile, have a less appreciable effect on trade—which may simply evince some of the

---

[26] Note that running country-pair fixed effects and country-pair random effects without year dummies enhances the robustness of all variables; indeed, *RoO-RI* in such specifications acquires significant values.

[27] Note that *RoO-RI* values can also decline during this time. For instance, the MERCOSUR-Chile RoO regime, formed in 1997, has a *RoO-RI* average of slightly above 3, whereas the regime for LAIA, the prior forum for preferential trade between Chile and MERCOSUR, has a *RoO-RI* of 4. Similarly, the accession of Austria, Finland, and Sweden to the EU in 1995 effectively dropped their bilateral *RoO-RI* values with all EU partners from nearly 5 to 1.

Table 5.8 Robustness Checks for PTA Pairs, Aggregate Trade, 1981–2001

	WLS (Weight: ln (total imports))		Trade > US$500,000		ln(Trade) 3sd from mean		ln 2sd from Mean		Excluding Pan-Euro pairs		Country-pair fixed effects		Country-pair random effects	
	$\ln(V_{ij})$		$\ln(V_{ij})$		$\ln(V_{ij})$		$\ln(V_{ij})$		$\ln(V_{ij})$		$\ln(V_{ij})$		$\ln(V_{ij})$	
Independent var.	I	II	I	II	I	II	I	II	I	II	I	II	I	II
$\ln(RoO\text{-}RI_{ij})$	−0.626	−0.705	−0.361	−0.441	−1.057	−1.196	−0.824	−0.887	−0.686	−0.738	−0.128	−0.242	−0.353	−0.615
	(7.32)**	(8.24)**	(5.78)**	(7.10)**	(8.89)**	(10.01)**	(6.43)**	(6.86)**	(7.20)**	(7.72)**	(0.73)	(1.37)	(2.49)*	(4.24)**
$FACIL_{ij}$				0.387		0.731		0.31		0.375		0.449		0.490
				(10.95)**		(9.13)**		(3.52)**		(5.47)**		(4.99)**		(7.68)**
$\ln(RoO\text{-}SD_{ij})$	0.053	−0.092	0.053	−0.238	0.130	−0.091	0.121	0.038	0.144	0.054	0.412	0.242	0.283	0.069
		(1.15)		(4.39)**	(1.20)	(0.81)	(0.99)	(0.30)	(1.57)	(0.57)	(3.71)**	(2.02)*	(2.98)**	(0.66)
$FACIL_{ij}$		0.377		0.317		0.626		0.219		0.246		0.324		0.325
		(7.51)**		(9.61)**		(7.63)**		(2.40)*		(3.73)**		(3.74)**		(4.79)**

Note: Absolute value of *t*-statistics in parentheses. All regressions with year dummies. Except for regressions with country-pair fixed effects, all regressions with importer and exporter are dummies.
* significant at 5 percent level; ** significant at 1 percent level.

Table 5.9 Effects of Changes in *PTA*, *RoO-RI*, and *FACIL* on Changes in Trade over One and Two Decades

Dependent variable: ln[(*V2001*) – (*V1991*) + 1]		
	I	II
PTA01–PTA91	1.523 (3.24)**	1.098 (2.09)*
RoO-RIØ1–RoO-RI91	–0.873 (3.12)**	–0.995 (3.46)**
FACIL01–FACIL91		0.393 (1.81)
Dependent variable: ln[(*V2001* – *V1981*) + 1]		
	I	II
PTA01–PTA81	2.015 (4.79)**	1.591 (3.34)**
RoO-RIØ1–RoO-RI81	–0.629 (2.39)*	–0.752 (2.78)**
FACILØ1–FACIL81		0.412 (1.90)

Note: Absolute value of *t*-statistics in parentheses. All regressions with exporter and importer dummies.
* significant at 5 percent level; ** significant at 1 percent level.

same results as in Table 5.6. The results provide further indication of the robustness of the key variables.

Table 5.10 extends the robustness checks to the sectoral regressions. There is less leeway for conducting robustness checks at the sectoral level, given that diminishing the number of observations for the dependent variable causes too many *RoO-RI* values to drop out of the regression. However, robustness checks with trade weighted by total trade and country-pair fixed and random effects show that the sectoral effects remain significant and with the correct signs. The chemicals sector is the only exception; including *FACIL* in regressions with country-pair fixed and random effects saps explanatory power from the *RoO-RI* variable—which nonetheless is positive and significant when *FACIL* is not considered.

Table 5.10 Robustness Checks, Sectoral Trade, 1988–2001

	Dependent variable: $\ln(V_{ij}+1)$									
WLS (weight: ln (total imports))	**Chemicals**		**Machinery**		**Textiles**		**TV and radio transmitters**		**Vehicles**	
	I	II	I	II	I	II	I	II	I	II
ln(*RoO-RI*)	0.999	0.376	0.941	0.531	0.412	0.364	1.015	0.62	1.011	0.633
	(65.11)**	(10.33)**	(67.77)**	(15.59)**	(54.51)**	(18.95)**	(64.03)**	(16.03)**	(59.71)**	(15.23)**
FACIL		0.455		0.315		0.041		0.307		0.295
		(18.84)**		(13.17)**		(2.75)**		(11.21)**		(9.94)**
ln(*RoO-SD*)	4.296	3.642	5.528	4.602	2.197	1.381	7.117	5.173	5.143	3.014
	(80.74)**	(46.03)**	(81.57)**	(47.77)**	(50.97)**	(25.98)**	(70.70)**	(39.38)**	(21.06)**	(12.27)**
FACIL		0.168		0.187		0.188		0.336		0.684
		(11.16)**		(13.53)**		(26.11)**		(22.99)**		(55.92)**
Country-pair fixed effects										
ln(*RoO-RI*)	1.113	−0.162	1.019	0.199	0.440	0.417	1.219	0.320	1.114	0.237
	(51.87)**	(2.49)*	(53.43)**	(3.32)**	(43.42)**	(12.39)**	(56.09)**	(4.76)**	(46.94)**	(3.21)**
FACIL		0.957		0.656		0.02		0.729		0.719
		(20.81)**		(14.42)**		(0.71)		(14.15)**		(12.55)**
ln(*RoO-SD*)	4.352	3.844	1.114	4.055	1.742	0.833	6.784	4.027	4.087	1.487
	(65.17)**	(33.84)**	(46.94)**	(31.72)**	(35.77)**	(13.61)**	(57.45)**	(25.50)**	(14.73)**	(5.28)**
FACIL		0.142		0.254		0.265		0.584		0.872
		(5.53)**		(11.32)**		(24.46)**		(26.26)**		(46.47)**

(continued on next page)

Table 5.10 Robustness Checks, Sectoral Trade, 1988–2001 (*Continued*)

WLS (weight: ln (total imports))	Chemicals I	Chemicals II	Machinery I	Machinery II	Textiles I	Textiles II	TV and radio transmitters I	TV and radio transmitters II	Vehicles I	Vehicles II
	Dependent variable: $\ln(V_{ij}+1)$									
Country-pair random effects										
ln(*RoO-RI*)	1.136	−0.051	1.045	0.243	0.443	0.388	1.222	0.356	1.149	0.311
	(56.50)**	(0.89)	(58.02)**	(4.51)**	(46.39)**	(12.95)**	(59.34)**	(5.84)**	(51.50)**	(4.72)**
FACIL		0.891		0.639		0.049		0.699		0.683
		(22.03)**		(15.83)**		(1.95)		(15.14)**		(13.50)**
ln(*RoO-SD*)	4.480	3.780	5.401	4.178	1.845	0.920	7.011	4.207	4.274	1.602
	(70.08)**	(35.81)**	(67.95)**	(34.41)**	(38.98)**	(15.53)**	(61.00)**	(27.49)**	(15.70)**	(5.81)**
FACIL		0.194		0.274		0.26		0.576		0.888
		(8.33)**		(13.33)**		(25.90)**		(27.67)**		(50.95)**

Note: Absolute value of *t*-statistics in parentheses. WLS regressions with importer and exporter dummies. All regressions with year dummies.
* significant at 5 percent level; ** significant at 1 percent level.

Methodological Issues

The coding methodology for the variables and different RoO regimes is detailed in Appendix 5.1. There are three further methodological issues that warrant mentioning—and that if resolved, would add greater nuance to the estimations.

First, all the models assume homogeneous trade policy institutions beyond RoO regimes. One, for PTA members, the speed and extent of preferential tariff liberalization is assumed not to vary across agreements. Two, the model also assumes that all countries' MFN tariffs are alike. These assumptions are made because identifying the annual applied preferential and MFN tariffs for each country (much less for each country in each sector) is difficult. The latter assumption is justified in part by the fact that WTO member countries' MFN tariffs are increasingly harmonized as well as lowered by the multilateral trade rounds.

Second, RoO are used also in the Generalized System of Preferences schemes of the European Union and the United States, affecting bilateral preferential commerce between these entities, on the one hand, and dozens of developing countries, on the other. This chapter, however, has operationalized only RoO that apply in reciprocal liberalization schemes. This is to a good extent because the sectoral coverage of the GSP-provided preferences often varies by partner country, so that a given set of RoO applicable to one GSP beneficiary may not be applicable to another. Moreover, the product coverage and preferences provided by the GSP schemes often vary over time for any given beneficiary. These issues make coding the GSP RoO very time-consuming. However, in recent studies, Brenton (2004) and Inama (2004) show that GSP RoO do play an important role in arbitrating the odds for developing countries to qualify for GSP treatment.

Third, diagonal cumulation can have widely different implications for bilateral trade depending on the space where cumulation is allowed. For instance, cumulation like that with the United States that is permitted in the Canada-Israel FTA might have widely divergent effects should it be permitted with a smaller country, such as Jordan. Meanwhile, cumulation in the Pan-Euro zone, which incorporates more than a dozen parties, will likely have different implications for any given member than it would if the zone incorporated only three parties. The effects of the size of the cumulation area are, however, beyond this chapter and could be explored in future work.

Conclusion

This study has paved the way to capturing the trade effects of rules of origin. The empirical exercises carried out here provide preliminary evidence that restrictive rules of origin stifle trade and hence constrain the liberalizing potential of PTAs. However, we have also found that various regime-wide provisions, such as drawback and cumulation, can encourage trade and thus reduce the negative effects of stringent product-specific RoO. At the sectoral level, the findings indicate that restrictive RoO in final goods encourage trade in intra-PTA inputs. As such, restrictive RoO in final goods may result in trade diversion in intermediate goods.

Importantly, we also encounter a reduction in the negative effects of RoO over time; this can be attributed to exporters' learning to comply with product-specific RoO and to take full advantage of permissive regime-wide RoO, and/or adjusting their production strategies to meet the RoO requirements. Whether such RoO-driven adjustments are welfare-enhancing in the long run is questionable, but beyond the scope of this chapter. Also beyond this chapter, yet a highly important and a particularly fruitful focus for future research, are the effects of RoO on investment.

The policy implications of our findings are clear. Although RoO are not necessarily bad for sound economic decisions, restrictive RoO can be. Furthermore, the existing differences in the product-specific and regime-wide RoO *across* the different RoO regimes can, even in a simplified bi- or tripolar RoO world, make a difference in economic decisions and limit exporters' opportunities for diversifying markets. To be sure, preferential RoO matter only as long as there are MFN tariffs. Thus, the ultimate key to counteracting preferential RoO's negative effects lies in the success of multilateral liberalization. Should multilateral trade rounds result in deep MFN tariff lowerings and the proliferation of PTAs engender a dynamic of competitive liberalization worldwide, the importance of preferential RoO as gatekeepers of commerce would automatically dissolve.

Appendix 5.1 Coding Methodology for RoO in Gravity Data Set

This appendix details the coding methodology for various country pairs in the gravity data set.

PTA Indicators

The *PTA* dummy is set at 1 when a country pair belongs to the same FTA or CU. In the panel, *PTA* dummies and PTA-related provisions for a given year acquire positive values if the country pair is in or enters into a PTA no later than the first day of the year in question. Thus, a PTA that was launched on 1 January 2001 qualifies as a PTA for 2001, whereas a PTA that is launched, say, in February (or on 2 January, for that matter) of 2001 would not qualify as a PTA until the year 2002. The same rule applies to dates of countries' accessions to existing PTAs (such as Spain and Portugal to the European Community or Haiti to CARICOM).

Product-Specific RoO

The product-specific RoO include the restrictiveness of RoO in a given regime and the standard deviation of the restrictiveness of RoO values in the regime.

The average *RoO-RI* variable is the average of the 6-digit restrictiveness values in the different RoO regimes. The *RoO-RI* coding is based on the first rule of origin defined in the RoO protocol if two or more RoO alternatives are allowed for a given product. Although the RoO of the bulk of the PTAs have been coded, agreements for which restrictiveness values have yet to be calculated (such as Georgia-Kazakhstan) are coded as having a *RoO-RI* average of 4. For the years preceding Turkey's entry into a CU with the EU in 1996 (i.e., 1981–1995), its *RoO-RI* with the EU is also set at 4. Canada-U.S. FTA RoO that apply in 1989–93 are coded as 5, slightly below the NAFTA *RoO-RI* of 5.15.

The *RoO-RI* variable is set at 2 when the country pair is party to the same customs union, but the customs union is an aspiring one and hence "imperfect," that is, where RoO continue governing trade between members in the portion of the tariff universe for which agreement on a CET has not been reached. This "imperfect CU" rule applies to MERCOSUR, the Andean Community, CACM, CARICOM, and MERCOSUR. Except for MERCOSUR, which was launched in November 1991, each of the four imperfect CUs are treated similarly across years in the panel data. As such, the coding does not take into account the "relaunch" of these agreements in the early 1990s or the attendant alterations in RoO that the relaunch may have entailed.

For the sectoral regressions, *RoO-RI-FINAL* is the average restrictiveness value of the 6-digit level of final goods falling in the ISIC Revision 3 division under analysis.

The *RoO-SD* (*RoO-SD-FINAL*) variable is the regime-wide (sector-wide) standard deviation in the 6-digit *RoO-RI* (*RoO-RI-FINAL*) values.

Regime-Wide Variables

Regime-wide variables include de minimis, diagonal and full cumulation, drawback rule, self-certification, and the facilitation index.

As with the product-specific RoO, except for MERCOSUR, which was launched in November 1991, each of the four imperfect CUs are treated similarly across years in the panel data.

De Minimis

De minimis is coded as the percentage of de minimis permitted by the PTA. Between parties not belonging to a PTA or belonging to a perfect customs union, de minimis is set at 0.

Diagonal and Full Cumulation

Diagonal and full cumulation are set at 1 between states party to a PTA that allows for either or both of these systems of cumulation and at 0 otherwise (for pairs with a common PTA but without these cumulation provisions, for pairs without a common PTA, and for pairs with a common perfect customs union).

In the panel, for EFTA members that had bilateral FTAs with the European Community prior to the 1994 EEA agreement between the EU and the signatories to EFTA (Iceland, Norway, and Switzerland), diagonal cumulation is set at 1 in the bilateral FTAs and full cumulation at 0. When the EEA is launched, all EFTA members at the time (Austria, Finland, Iceland, Norway, Sweden, and Switzerland) are coded to have diagonal and full cumulation in their trade with EU members. When Austria, Finland, and Sweden accede to the EU in 1995, their external trade relations are adjusted to equal those of the EU member states.

Drawback

Drawback is coded as 1 between states party to a PTA that allows drawback or does not explicitly prohibit it and as 0 for pairs party to a PTA that explicitly bars drawback. It is also set at 0 between states not party to a common PTA and between states party to a common perfect customs union.

Self-Certification

Self-certification is set at 1 between states party to a PTA that requires self-certification rather than public certification or two-step private/public certification. It is set at 0 between states not party to a common PTA and between states party to a common perfect customs union.

Facilitation Index

The facilitation index is constructed on the basis of five regime-wide RoO (de minimis, diagonal and full cumulation, drawback, and self-certification). The latter four are set at 1 if the PTA allows for any of them (or does not explicitly bar drawback). De minimis is set at 0 if it is below 5 percent and at 1 if it is 5 percent or above. The index is subsequently constructed by summing the values for the five different components. The index is set at 0 between states not party to a common PTA and between states party to a common perfect customs union.

Regime-Wide Indicators for PTAs That Are Not Coded

The few country pairs for which a RoO value has not been computed here despite the existence of a common PTA (such as Georgia-Kazakhstan or Georgia-Russian Federation) are assumed *not* to have de minimis provisions, diagonal and full cumulation, or self-certification (i.e., these variables are set at 0), but are assumed to allow drawback.

Appendix 5.2 Construction of the Data Set for Intermediate Goods

This appendix details the construction of the data set for analyzing the effects of RoO in final goods on trade in intermediates in the five sectors examined in this chapter—chemicals, machinery, textiles, television and radio transmitters, and vehicles. Sectors are here defined as divisions of the ISIC Revision 3 classification system (Divisions 24 for chemicals, 29 for machinery, 17 for textiles, 32 for television and radio transmitters, and 34 for vehicles).

The data set is constructed as follows. The differentiation of the HS 6-digit-level products into intermediates and final goods is obtained from Suwa-Eisenmann's calculations based on the U.S. input-output table. The calculation of the dependent variable—total trade flows in intermediates—for each sectoral model includes here only the trade of a bundle of intermediate goods that are being used particularly intensively in the production of final goods in the examined division. The intensity of usage of an intermediate good in a given final good is also extracted from Suwa-Eisenmann's data. We exclude from the calculation the flows of intermediate goods used intensively in other divisions or not used intensively in any division in particular, but rather, moderately in many. This is because flows of intermediates would in either of these two cases be crucially influenced by RoO in final goods in the other divisions, rather than primarily by the RoO in the final goods in the division under analysis. Examples of 6-digit-level intermediate goods that are intensively used in the final goods of one particular division (rather than in many divisions) are man-made filaments in the textiles division and conveyor belts in the vehicles division.

The key independent variables, *RoO-RI-FINAL* and *RoO-SD-FINAL*, are the average sectoral restrictiveness and sectoral standard deviation (per the RoO restrictiveness index), respectively, of all 6-digit-level final goods (as defined as such per Suwa-Eisenmann's data) that fall within the ISIC division under analysis (per UN correspondences tables for ISIC and HS).

The construction of the data set for each of the five divisions is carried out in four steps:

Step 1. Choosing a major ISIC division and using a correspondence table to determine the HS 6-digit-level final goods falling in that division.

Step 2. Taking the average of the *RoO-RI-FINAL* and *RoO-SD-FINAL* values of the selected HS 6-digit-level final goods by division (as defined in step 1).

Step 3. Defining the bundle of the HS 6-digit intermediate goods that are used most intensively in the production of the HS 6-digit-level final goods in the examined division.

Step 4. Obtaining pairwise trade data by year in 1988–2001 at the 6-digit level for the selected intermediate goods from the United Nations Commodity Trade Statistics Database (UN COMTRADE) and aggregating the data into one "bundle-specific" measure for each pair for each year.

In sum, the ISIC division that is chosen dictates the choice of the HS 6-digit-level final goods for calculating the *RoO-RI* and *RoO-SD* values; the set of final goods, in turn, dictates the choice of the intermediate goods. Note that whereas all the final goods in a given set necessarily fall in the ISIC division under analysis, the intermediate goods used intensively to produce these final goods do not need to do so, but can hail from any divisions of the tariff universe. The relationship of the three sets of data can be depicted as follows:

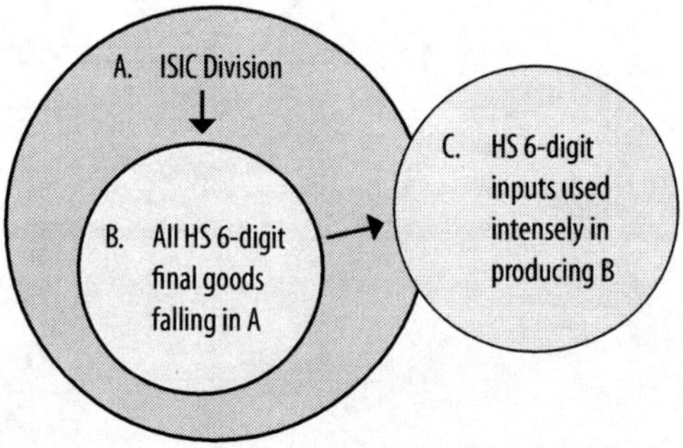

Appendix 5.3 Descriptive Statistics

Variable	Observations	Mean	Standard Deviation	Minimum	Maximum
$\ln(V_{ij})$	212,554	10.420	3.222	4.032	20.995
$\ln(GDP_j)$	379,513	23.354	2.441	17.379	29.829
$\ln(GDP_i)$	366,140	23.388	2.405	17.379	29.829
$\ln(GDPPC_j)$	377,696	7.633	1.602	4.439	13.396
$\ln(GDPPC_i)$	363,041	7.675	1.591	4.439	16.642
$\ln(DIST_{ij})$	490,823	8.757	0.781	4.394	9.899
$BORDER_{ij}$	500,606	0.017	0.130	0	1
$COMLANG_{ij}$	500,879	0.122	0.327	0	1
COL_{ij}	500,858	0.010	0.099	0	1
$COMCOL_{ij}$	500,842	0.118	0.323	0	1
PTA_{ij}	500,879	0.033	0.180	0	1
$\ln(RoO\text{-}RI_{ij})$	500,879	0.127	0.671	0	5.154
$\ln(RoO\text{-}RI_{ij} + 1)$	500,858	0.040	0.225	0	1.640
$\ln(RoO\text{-}SD_{ij})$	500,879	0.015	0.142	0	1.845
$\ln(RoO\text{-}SD_{ij} + 1)$	500,879	0.009	0.089	0	1.046
$FACIL_{ij}$	500,879	0.052	0.312	0	4.000
$DE\ MINIMIS_{ij}$	500,879	0.121	1.087	0	15.000
$CUMUDIAG_{ij}$	500,879	0.009	0.097	0	1
$CUMUFULL_{ij}$	500,879	0.005	0.068	0	1
$DRAWBACK_{ij}$	500,879	0.023	0.150	0	1
$SELFCERT_{ij}$	500,879	0.001	0.037	0	1

Appendix 5.4 Countries Included in the Sample

Algeria	Denmark	Italy
Angola	Dominica	Jamaica
Antigua and Barbuda	Dominican Republic	Japan
Argentina	Ecuador	Jordan
Armenia	Egypt	Kazakhstan
Australia	El Salvador	Kenya
Austria	Equatorial Guinea	Kiribati
Bangladesh	Estonia	Korea
Barbados	Ethiopia	Kuwait
Belarus	Fiji	Kirgiz Republic
Belgium	Finland	Lao People's Dem. Rep.
Belize	France	Latvia
Benin	Gabon	Lithuania
Bolivia	Gambia	Luxembourg
Brazil	Georgia	Madagascar
Bulgaria	Germany	Malawi
Burkina Faso	Ghana	Malaysia
Burundi	Greece	Maldives
Cameroon	Grenada	Mali
Canada	Guatemala	Malta
Cape Verde	Guinea	Mauritania
Central African Republic	Guinea-Bissau	Mauritius
Chad	Guyana	Mexico
Chile	Haiti	Moldova
China	Honduras	Mongolia
Colombia	Hong Kong	Morocco
Comoros	Hungary	Mozambique
Congo, Republic of	Iceland	Myanmar
Costa Rica	India	Nepal
Cote d'Ivoire	Indonesia	Netherlands
Croatia	Iran	New Zealand
Cuba	Iraq	Nicaragua
Cyprus	Ireland	Niger
Czech Republic	Israel	Nigeria

(continued on next page)

Appendix 5.4 Countries Included in the Sample *(Continued)*

Norway	Sierra Leone	Togo
Oman	Singapore	Tonga
Pakistan	Slovak Republic	Trinidad and Tobago
Panama	Slovenia	Tunisia
Papua New Guinea	Solomon Islands	Turkey
Paraguay	South Africa	Uganda
Peru	Spain	Ukraine
Philippines	Sri Lanka	United Arab Emirates
Poland	St. Kitts and Nevis	United Kingdom
Portugal	St. Lucia	United States
Qatar	St. Vincent and the Grenadines	Uruguay
Romania	Sudan	Vanuatu
Russia	Suriname	Venezuela
Rwanda	Sweden	Vietnam
Samoa	Switzerland	Yemen
Saudi Arabia	Syrian Arab Republic	Zambia
Senegal	Tanzania	Zimbabwe
Seychelles	Thailand	

Appendix 5.5 PTAs Included in the Tables and Graphs and the Empirical Specifications, with Years of Entry into Force and Full Names

PTA	Year of Entry	Full Name/Type
EC/EU	1958	European Community/European Union
EFTA	1960	European Free Trade Area
CACM	1961	Central American Common Market
EU - Malta	1971	
EU - Cyprus	1973	
CARICOM	1973	Caribbean Community
EU - Iceland	1973	
EU - Norway	1973	
EU - Switzerland	1973	
Bangkok Agreement	1976	
LAIA	1981	Latin American Integration Association
SPARTECA	1981	South Pacific Regional Trade and Economic Cooperation Agreement
ANZCERTA	1983	Australia - New Zealand Closer Economic Relations Trade Agreement
GCC	1983	Gulf Cooperation Council
SAARC	1985	South Asian Association for Regional Cooperation
U.S. - Israel	1985	
ECOWAS Trade Liberalisation Scheme	1990	Economic Community of West African States
MERCOSUR	1991	
Namibia - Zimbabwe	1992	
EFTA - Czech Republic	1992	Pan-Euro
EU - Czech Republic	1992	Pan-Euro
EU - Hungary	1992	Pan-Euro
EU - Slovak Republic	1992	Pan-Euro
EFTA - Slovak Republic	1992	Pan-Euro
EFTA - Turkey	1992	Pan-Euro
EU - Poland	1992	Pan-Euro
EU - Bulgaria	1993	Pan-Euro

(continued on next page)

Appendix 5.5 PTAs Included in the Tables and Graphs and the Empirical Specifications, with Years of Entry into Force and Full Names *(Continued)*

PTA	Year of Entry	Full Name/Type
AFTA	1993	ASEAN Free Trade Area
CEFTA	1993	Central European Free Trade Area/Pan-Euro
EFTA - Bulgaria	1993	Pan-Euro
EFTA - Israel	1993	PE
EFTA - Hungary	1993	Pan-Euro
EFTA - Poland	1993	Pan-Euro
EFTA - Romania	1993	Pan-Euro
EU - Romania	1993	Pan-Euro
BAFTA	1994	Baltic Free Trade Agreement/Pan-Euro
COMESA	1994	Common Market for Eastern and Southern Africa
EEA	1994	European Economic Area/Pan-Euro
NAFTA	1994	North American Free Trade Agreement
Georgia - Russia	1994	
G3	1995	Group of Three
EFTA - Slovenia	1995	Pan-Euro
EU - Latvia	1995	Pan-Euro
EU - Lithuania	1995	Pan-Euro
EU - Estonia	1995	Pan-Euro
Mexico - Bolivia	1995	
Mexico - Costa Rica	1995	
Romania - Moldova	1995	
Kirgiz Republic - Kazakhstan	1995	
EU - Turkey	1996	
EFTA - Estonia	1996	Pan-Euro
EFTA - Latvia	1996	Pan-Euro
EFTA - Lithuania	1996	Pan-Euro
Slovenia - Latvia	1996	Pan-Euro
MERCOSUR - Chile	1996	
Georgia - Ukraine	1996	

(continued on next page)

Appendix 5.5 PTAs Included in the Tables and Graphs and the Empirical Specifications, with Years of Entry into Force and Full Names *(Continued)*

PTA	Year of Entry	Full Name/Type
Georgia - Azerbaijan	1996	
Czech Republic - Lithuania	1997	Pan-Euro
Poland - Lithuania	1997	Pan-Euro
Slovak Republic - Israel	1997	Pan-Euro
Slovenia - Estonia	1997	Pan-Euro
Czech Republic - Israel	1997	PE
Czech Republic - Latvia	1997	Pan-Euro
Slovak Republic - Latvia	1997	Pan-Euro
Slovak Republic - Lithuania	1997	Pan-Euro
Slovenia - Lithuania	1997	Pan-Euro
Turkey - Israel	1997	PE
Canada - Chile	1997	
Canada - Israel	1997	
MERCOSUR - Bolivia	1997	
Czech Republic - Estonia	1998	Pan-Euro
Hungary - Turkey	1998	Pan-Euro
Romania - Turkey	1998	Pan-Euro
Slovak Republic - Estonia	1998	Pan-Euro
Slovak Republic - Turkey	1998	Pan-Euro
Turkey - Lithuania	1998	Pan-Euro
Czech Republic - Turkey	1998	Pan-Euro
Hungary - Israel	1998	PE
Poland - Israel	1998	PE
Slovenia - Croatia	1998	PE
Slovenia - Israel	1998	PE
EU - Tunisia	1998	
Mexico - Nicaragua	1998	
EU - Tunisia	1998	
Georgia - Armenia	1998	
EU - Slovenia	1999	Pan-Euro

(continued on next page)

Appendix 5.5 PTAs Included in the Tables and Graphs and the Empirical Specifications, with Years of Entry into Force and Full Names *(Continued)*

PTA	Year of Entry	Full Name/Type
Poland - Latvia	1999	Pan-Euro
Chile - Mexico	1999	
Turkey - Bulgaria	1999	
EFTA - Morocco	1999	
Georgia - Kazahkstan	1999	
FSRs	1999	Former Soviet Republics
Hungary - Lithuania	2000	Pan-Euro
Poland - Turkey	2000	Pan-Euro
Turkey - Latvia	2000	Pan-Euro
Turkey - Slovenia	2000	Pan-Euro
Hungary - Latvia	2000	Pan-Euro
Turkey - Slovenia	2000	Pan-Euro
EU - Israel	2000	PE
SADC	2000	Southern African Development Community
EU - Mexico	2000	
EU - South Africa	2000	
Mexico - Israel	2000	
EU - Morocco	2000	
New Zealand - Singapore	2001	
U.S. - Jordan	2001	
EFTA - Mexico	2001	
Hungary - Estonia	2001	Pan-Euro
EFTA - Croatia	2002	PE
EU - Croatia	2002	PE
CACM - Chile	2002	
JSEPA	2002	Japan - Singapore Economic Partnership Agreement
Chile - Costa Rica	2002	
Canada - Costa Rica	2002	
SAFTA	2003	Singapore - Australia Free Trade Agreement
EU - Chile	2003	

(continued on next page)

Appendix 5.5 PTAs Included in the Tables and Graphs and the Empirical Specifications, with Years of Entry into Force and Full Names *(Continued)*

PTA	Year of Entry	Full Name/Type
EFTA - Singapore	2003	
Chile - South Korea	2003	
U.S. - Chile	2003	
EFTA - Chile	2003	
CAFTA	2004 (signed)	

Note: The Pan-Euro system was launched in 1997. RoO protocols of FTAs forged prior to that by the EU were revised to be compatible with the Pan-Euro model. PE indicates RoO protocols that are basically identical to the Pan-Euro model in product-specific RoO, but diverge from the Pan-Euro model in some regime-wide provisions, most notably by not being part of the Pan-Euro system of diagonal cumulation. Entry dates obtained from the World Trade Organization and the Organization of American States.

Appendix 5.6 Member States of Selected PTAs

PTA	Members
AFTA	Brunei Darussalam, Cambodia, Indonesia, Laos, Malaysia, Myanmar, Philippines, Singapore, Thailand, Vietnam
ANZCERTA	Australia, New Zealand
BAFTA	Estonia, Latvia, Lithuania
Bangkok Agreement	Bangladesh, China, India, Republic of Korea, Laos, Sri Lanka
CACM	Costa Rica, El Salvador, Guatemala, Honduras, Nicaragua
CARICOM	Antigua and Barbuda, The Bahamas, Barbados, Belize, Dominica, Grenada, Guyana, Haiti, Jamaica, Montserrat, St. Lucia, St. Kitts and Nevis, St. Vincent and the Grenadines, Suriname, Trinidad and Tobago
CEFTA	Bulgaria, Czech Republic, Hungary, Poland, Romania, Slovak Republic, Slovenia
COMESA	Angola, Burundi, Comoros, Democratic Republic of Congo, Djibouti, Egypt, Eritrea, Ethiopia, Kenya, Madagascar, Malawi, Mauritius, Namibia, Rwanda, Seychelles, Sudan, Swaziland, Uganda, Zambia, Zimbabwe
EEA	European Union, Iceland, Liechtenstein, Norway
EFTA	Iceland, Liechtenstein, Norway, Switzerland
ECOWAS	Benin, Burkina Faso, Cape Verde, Ivory Coast, Gambia, Ghana, Guinea, Guinea Bissau, Mali, Liberia, Niger, Nigeria, Senegal, Sierra Leone, Togo, Namibia, Zimbabwe
FSRs	Belarus, Kazakhstan, Kirgiz Republic, Russia
G3	Mexico, Colombia, Venezuela
GCC	Bahrain, Kuwait, Oman, Qatar, Saudi Arabia, United Arab Emirates
JSEPA	Japan, Singapore

LAIA	Argentina, Bolivia, Brazil, Chile, Colombia, Cuba, Ecuador, Mexico, Paraguay, Peru, Uruguay, Venezuela
MERCOSUR	Argentina, Brazil, Paraguay, Uruguay
NAFTA	Canada, Mexico, United States
SADC	Angola, Botswana, Lesotho, Malawi, Mauritius, Mozambique, Namibia, South Africa, Swaziland, Tanzania, Zambia, Zimbabwe
SPARTECA	Australia, New Zealand, Cook Islands, Fiji, Kiribati, Marshall Islands, Micronesia, Nauru, Niue, Papua New Guinea, Solomon Islands, Tonga, Tuvalu, Vanuatu, Western Samoa

References

Anderson, J. 1979. "A Theoretical Foundation for the Gravity Equation." *American Economic Review* 69(1):106–16.

Anderson, J., and E. van Wincoop. 2001. "Gravity with Gravitas: A Solution to the Border Puzzle." NBER Working Paper No. 8079. Cambridge, MA: National Bureau of Economic Research.

Appiah, A. J. 1999. "Applied General Equilibrium Model of North American Integration with Rules of Origin." Ph.D. diss., Simon Fraser University, Vancouver, British Columbia, Canada.

Bayoumi, Tamim, and Barry J. Eichengreen. 1995. "Is Regionalism Simply a Diversion? Evidence from the Evolution of the EC and EFTA." IMF Working Paper No. 95/109. Washington, DC: International Monetary Fund.

Bergstrand, J. H. 1985. "The Gravity Equation in International Trade: Some Microeconomic Foundations and Empirical Evidence." *Review of Economics and Statistics* 20:474–81.

———. 1989. "The Generalized Gravity Equation, Monopolistic Competition, and the Factor-Proportions Theory in International Trade." *Review of Economic and Statistics* 71(1):143–53.

———. 1990. "The Heckscher-Ohlin-Samuelson Model, the Linder Hypothesis and the Determinants of Bilateral Intra-industry Trade." *Economic Journal* 100:1216–29.

Bertolini, P., and M. Montanari. 2002. "The Different Effects of the Europe Agreements on EU-CEECs Trade: A Sector Analysis." Department of Business Administration and Economics, Justus-Liebig-Universität Giessen, Giessen, Germany. Unpublished.

Brenton, P. 2004. "Integrating the Least Developed Countries into the World Trading System: The Current Impact of EU Preferences under Everything but Arms." Unpublished.

Brenton, P., and F. Di Mauro. 1998. "Trade in Sensitive Industrial Products between the EU and the CEECs: A Potential Yet to be Fulfilled." CEPS Working Document No. 199. Brussels: Centre for European Policy Studies.

Cadot, O., J. de Melo, A. Estevadeordal, A. Suwa-Eisenmann, and B. Tumurchudur. 2002. "Assessing the Effect of NAFTA's Rules of Origin." Unpublished.

Deardorff, A. 1997. "Determinants of Bilateral Trade: Does Gravity Work in a Classical World?" In J. Frankel (ed.), *The Regionalization of the World Economy*. Chicago: University of Chicago Press.

Dihel, N., and P. Walkenhorst. 2002. "European Union Trade and Non-Tariff Measures." Paper presented at the Fifth Annual Conference on Global Economic Analysis, Taipei, Taiwan, June 5–7.

Duttagupta, Rupa, and Arvind Panagariya. 2003. "Free Trade Areas and Rules of Origin: Economics and Politics." IMF Working Paper No. 03/229. Washington, DC: International Monetary Fund.

Estevadeordal, A. 2000. "Negotiating Preferential Market Access: The Case of the North American Free Trade Agreement." *Journal of World Trade* 34(1):141–66.

Frankel, Jeffrey A., with Ernesto Stein and Shang-Jin Wei. 1997. *Regional Trading Blocs in the World Economic System*. Washington, DC: Institute for International Economics.

Fujita, M., P. Krugman, and A. J. Venables. 1999. *The Spatial Economy: Cities, Regions, and International Trade.* Cambridge, MA: MIT Press.

Gatti, R. 1999. "Corruption and Trade Tariffs, or a Case for Uniform Tariffs." Working Paper No. 2216. Washington, DC: World Bank.

Ghosh, S., and S. Yamarik. 2004. "Does Trade Creation Measure Up? A Re-examination of the Effects of Regional Trading Arrangements." *Economics Letters* 82:213–19.

Grossman, Gene M., and Elhanan Helpman. 1991. *Innovation and growth in the global economy*. Cambridge, MA: MIT Press.

Helpman, Elhanan, and Paul A. Krugman. 1985. *Market Structure and Foreign Trade: Increasing Returns, Imperfect Competition, and the International Economy.* Cambridge, MA: MIT Press.

Inama, S. 2004. "Rules of Origin in GSP and ACP." Working Paper. New York: United Nations Conference on Trade and Development.

Ju, J., and K. Krishna. 1998. "Firm Behavior and Market Access in a Free Trade Area with Rules of Origin." NBER Working Paper No. 6857. Cambridge, MA: National Bureau of Economic Research.

Krishna, K., and A. O. Krueger. 1995. "Implementing Free Trade Areas: Rules of Origin and Hidden Protection." In A. Deardorff, J. Levinsohn, and R. Stern (eds.), *New Directions in Trade Theory.* Ann Arbor: University of Michigan Press.

Krueger, A. O. 1993. "Free Trade Agreements as Protectionist Devices: Rules of Origin." NBER Working Paper No. 4352. Cambridge, MA: National Bureau of Economic Research.

Leejour, A. M., R. de Mooji, and R. Nahuis. 2001. "EU Enlargement: Economic Implications for Countries and Industries." CPB Document No. 11. The Hague: Netherlands Bureau for Economic Policy Analysis (CPB).

Linnemann, H. 1966. *An Econometric Study of International Trade Flows.* Amsterdam: North-Holland.

Maskus, K., J. S. Wilson, and T. Otsuki. 2000. "Quantifying the Impact of Technical Barriers to Trade: A Framework for Analysis." Working Paper No. 2512. Washington, DC: World Bank.

McLaren, John. 2000. "'Globalization' and Vertical Structure." *American Economic Review* 90(5):1239–54.

Moenius, J. 1999. "Information versus Product Adaptation: The Role of Standards in Trade." Working Paper. Redlands, CA: University of Redlands.

———. 2000. "Three Studies on Trade Barriers and Trade Volumes." Ph.D. diss., University of California, San Diego.

Pöyhönen, P. 1963. "A Tentative Model for the Volume of Trade between Countries." *Weltwirtschftliches Archiv* 90(1):93–99.

Schumacher, D., and P. Trubswetter. 2000. "Volume and Comparative Advantage in East-West Trade." DIW Discussion Paper No. 223. Berlin: German Institute for Economic Research (DIW).

Suominen, K. 2004. "Rules of Origin in Global Commerce." Ph.D. diss., University of California, San Diego.

Tinbergen, J. 1962. "An Analysis of World Trade Flows." In Jan Tinbergen (ed.), *Shaping the World Economy*. New York: Twentieth Century Fund.

Viner, J. 1950. *The Customs Union Issue.* New York: Carnegie Endowment for International Peace.

Vittas, H., and P. Mauro. 1997. Implications of the Opening Up of Eastern Europe for Germany, Switzerland and Portugal." In S. Black (ed.), *Europe's Economy Looks East*. Washington, DC: American Institute for Contemporary Studies.

Wilson, J. S., and T. Otsuki. 2001. "Global Trade and Food Safety: Winners and Losers in a Fragmented System." Working Paper No. 2689. Washington, DC: World Bank.

CHAPTER 6

How Do Rules of Origin Affect Investment Flows? Some Hypotheses and the Case of Mexico*

Antoni Estevadeordal, José Ernesto López-Córdova, and Kati Suominen

Rules of origin are a powerful trade policy instrument arbitrating firms' sourcing and investment decisions around the world. However, the effects of RoO on investment flows have received scant empirical attention. Indeed, the notion that RoO could independently affect foreign direct investment (FDI) is relatively new even in the theoretical realm (Rodriguez, 2001). The purpose of this chapter is to start mending this gap. We develop hypotheses on the potential effects of the restrictiveness of RoO on FDI and conduct a preliminary empirical exercise on the impact of NAFTA's product-specific RoO on FDI in 122 manufacturing industries in Mexico in 1994–2000.

The main notion emerging from this chapter is that both restrictive and flexible RoO can attract investment. Restrictive RoO—RoO that compel producers to obtain inputs or carry out production processes within the PTA area rather than from the globally most efficient source or in the globally most efficient location—can encourage investment particularly in upstream sectors and protectionist downstream sectors, whereas flexible RoO can attract FDI in globalized sectors—sectors

* This chapter is a modified version of Estevadeordal, López-Córdova, and Suominen (2006).

where producers rely or expect to rely on genuinely global sourcing strategies. Our empirical results indicate that NAFTA RoO have played a central role in foreign investors' assessment of the cost of locating production in Mexico and that FDI in post-NAFTA Mexico has flowed in sectors with flexible RoO. However, we also find that flexible RoO in downstream industries encourage investment upstream. Both findings suggest that NAFTA-era investment in Mexican final and intermediate goods industries has come from efficient, globally competitive firms thriving on flexible RoO.

This study focuses on the investment effects of RoO, a market access discipline included in virtually all preferential trading arrangements. There are no comparable empirical studies. Theoretical treatments are also very limited. Rodriguez (2001), focusing on content protection, the domestic analogue of preferential RoO, shows that restrictive RoO can lead to an inefficient relocation of production among PTA partners.

Besides pioneering in exploring the RoO-FDI nexus, this study strives to foster the incipient understanding of the relationship between FDI and trade disciplines embedded in PTAs. Indeed, one of the key motivations for developing countries in particular to form and join PTAs has been to attract FDI. Some ways in which PTAs can spur investment include greater competition, new opportunities for exploiting scale economies, and dynamic effects, such as permanent growth once the initial efficiency and output gains increase factor rewards.[1] However, the bulk of empirical work on PTAs and FDI has centered on assessing aggregate

---

[1] See, for example, Eden (2001), World Bank (2000), Blomström and Kokko (1997), and Baldwin (1989).

To be sure, FDI can also be seen as exogenous to economic growth in the PTA market and thus to subsequent FDI in the sense of generating spillover effects, such as technology diffusion, technical assistance, and training (Blomström and Kokko, 1997: 13). As such, a virtuous cycle of FDI and growth can result (Baldwin, 1989). The World Bank (2000: 38–39) notes that tariff-jumping FDI can reduce real incomes—even though most usually, the benefits of FDI outweigh the costs, and FDI can be expected to stimulate local production in related industries, technology transfer, productivity in neighboring firms, exports, and incomes.

pre- and post-PTA flows and analyzing the PTA area as whole.[2] Few analysts have (1) examined the cross-sectoral variation in FDI flows in PTA members once the PTA has been set in motion or (2) considered the effects of PTAs on FDI in individual PTA partner countries.[3] This study strives to accomplish both tasks by focusing on Mexico, a NAFTA member, employing industry-level data on FDI flows and operationalizing the actual contractual provisions of PTAs—RoO, preferential tariffs, and

---

[2] The existing theories have yielded few conclusive predictions about the relationship between PTAs and FDI, and the existing empirical works have offered mixed results. See, for example, Behrman (1972) on the Latin American Free Trade Agreement; Mytelka (1979) on the Andean Community; Bulmer-Thomas (1982) on the Central American Common Market; Chudnovsky (2001) on the Southern Common Market; and Winters (1996), Balasubramanyam and Greenway (1992), Dunning (1992), Molle and Morsnik (1991), Lipsey (1990), Pelkmans (1984), Mayes (1983), O'Farrell (1983), and Franko (1976) on the European Community.

[3] In the case of Mexico, Waldkirch (2001) finds that had NAFTA not been formed, intra-regional FDI flows would have been 42 percent lower between 1994 and the end of 1999. The World Bank (2000) speculates that extraregional investors may have redirected part of their FDI from the United States and Canada to Mexico following NAFTA's implementation. Blomström and Kokko (1997) argue, albeit without presenting empirical evidence, that the agreement has been instrumental in inducing extraregional investors to move to Mexico in order to enjoy preferential access to the North American market. Blomström, Kokko, and Globerman (1998) posit that it is not possible to conclude that there has been an intensification of either intra- or extraregional FDI in Mexico since NAFTA. Eden (2001) discerns the impact of NAFTA from qualitative changes in firm behavior: the agreement has made North America a single spatial unit, resulting in locational reshuffling and integration of the three countries' industries into regional production networks, particularly in the automotive sector.

NAFTA's predecessor, the 1989 Canada-U.S. Free Trade Agreement (CUSFTA), is seen as having had relatively little influence on FDI patterns in Canada, mainly because much of the trade between Canada and the United States had been liberalized long before CUSFTA was established (Blomström and Kokko, 1997). The impact of NAFTA on the United States and Canada in terms of FDI is also judged as being rather neutral, as most effects should have taken place since CUSFTA (Rugman and Gestrin, 1993). Little (1996) finds that U.S. and Canadian firms tend to rely on trade rather than on FDI to serve the binational market. However, Hanson (1996) finds that NAFTA has influenced the relocation of U.S. manufacturing production to the U.S.-Mexico border region, particularly in cases where transportation costs play a central role in considerations of industry location. Hanson (1998) finds a similar pattern of relocation in Mexico to the northern border. The ITC (1997) concludes that production sharing along the U.S.-Mexican border will continue to expand as a result of the complementarities of the U.S. and Mexican economies.

rules governing foreign entry.[4] By disaggregating a PTA into its component parts, we strive to help disentangle the investment effects of the various PTA provisions from one another, as well as from the manifold competing explanations beyond PTAs, such as comparative advantages of the FDI target country. As such, our findings are not limited to those on RoO alone; we also encounter evidence that both preferential tariffs and limits on investment permitted under NAFTA have the expected significant effect on the patterns of FDI—a result that can have immediate implications for the design of PTAs.

The first section of this chapter discusses the potential effects of RoO on FDI. The second section reviews the patterns of sectoral FDI flows in Mexico during the first seven years of NAFTA, explores the structure of our key independent variable, NAFTA RoO, and puts forth the empirical specifications. The third section concludes.

RoO and FDI: Is There a Connection?

Do rules of origin help arbitrate FDI flows? There are at least three reasons to believe they do.

First, there are two ways in which restrictive RoO in particular can work to boost investment. For one, stipulating that a high share of the cost of production must arise within the PTA area, stringent RoO can lock final goods producers into obtaining supplies and/or performing production processes within the PTA area even if supplies and production in the rest of the world are cheaper. As such, demanding RoO downstream

[4] PTAs can also foster the odds for FDI inflows by helping to enhance domestic policy credibility in the member countries. Indeed, whereas the proliferating bilateral investment treaties tend to contribute to negative integration—they preclude certain policies that would discriminate against investment, rather than requiring policies that encourage investment—PTAs hold the potential to motivate investment by seeking to create a more predictable policy environment for foreign investors and by adding credibility to government policies (Winters, 2000: 5–6). The case is seen as accentuated in North-South PTAs when the northern country is willing and able to enforce investment-encouraging club rules (Winters, 2000: 6). FDI inflows could also receive a boost should the PTA institutionalize or lock in the elimination of trade-related investment measures—requirements on foreign affiliates to satisfy certain export targets—or guarantee strong investor property rights that reduce the risk of expropriation (Blomström and Kokko, 1997: 9).

provides PTA-based intermediate goods producers a specter of higher rents, which, in turn, should attract foreign intermediate producers to locate to the PTA area.

Moreover, by requiring a certain cost share of the final good to arise within the PTA, RoO can alter the margins of comparative advantage between a PTA member and a nonmember, in essence expanding the *range* of intermediate goods produced (and/or production processes carried out) in the PTA area—and do so even if the PTA area is not the globally most efficient location of production (Rodriguez, 2001). Thus, FDI can also flow to "new" intermediate industries—industries in which the PTA partners do not have a comparative advantage in the non-PTA equilibrium. In short, RoO can induce both more and a wider ranger of intermediates to be produced (or production processes to be performed) within the PTA area, which, in turn, can be expected to attract investment in intermediate industries.[5]

However, and second, it could be expected that flexible, nonbinding RoO[6] will be conducive to investment in downstream industries that procure inputs from around the world (and strive to qualify for PTA-conferred preferences). Investors in these industries would likely favor flexible RoO even if intra-PTA suppliers were relatively efficient in order to hedge against future increases in the relative cost of intra-PTA supplies and/or unforeseen inadequacies in intra-PTA production technologies.[7] The attraction of flexible RoO is accentuated (1) in sectors where the linkages between different stages of production in the industry are tight, so that downstream producers with global sourcing and production links would be hard pressed to locate appropriate components, identify appropriate input producers, and/or forge new contracts in the PTA area

---

[5] This implies that RoO will cause intermediate industries to migrate from nonmember countries to the FTA area, shift the margin of comparative advantage between the FTA members and nonmembers, and thus have direct implications for nonmember countries (Rodriguez, 2001).

[6] We follow Krishna (2004) in defining as binding those RoO that render the choice of inputs different from the non-RoO unconstrained equilibrium. Binding RoO thus imply additional costs to the consumers of the inputs.

[7] See Suominen (2004a, 2004b) for the policy preferences of import- and export-competing up- and downstream producers over RoO.

even if they did locate there,[8] and (2) in sectors where the production chain cannot be conveniently sliced up so as to enable the allocation of production within and outside the PTA area in a cost-efficient manner—that is, moving to the PTA area only the part of operations that allows the RoO to be met.

Firms that have established or plan to establish extensive sourcing and production links in extra-PTA countries are likely deterred from investing in the PTA area in the presence of stringent RoO. However, stringent RoO can encourage "RoO-jumping" investment—investment that is diverted to the PTA area in order to circumvent the RoO altogether. Investors may simply choose to locate in the territory of the PTA partner where they can obtain the highest rents and service the market from within, rather than paying the high compliance costs of RoO that would be incurred when exporting to that market from the other PTA members under the PTA preferences. As such, stringent RoO can boost FDI inflows to the PTA area and the main PTA market, in particular. When compliance costs are high, the RoO-jumping investor would have a cost advantage vis-à-vis producers located in the other PTA partners, ceteris paribus.

Much as an upstream investor has an interest in the RoO governing downstream industries, a potential downstream investor may have incentives to consider RoO *upstream*. For one, restrictive RoO in the upstream industries that supply the downstream industry might signal to the downstream investor the presence of an uncompetitive upstream provider that itself is unable to access cheap inputs from ROW. Furthermore, downstream investors may see stringent RoO upstream as a proxy for high external tariffs in upstream industries—which is an additional signal of the existence of inefficient suppliers and which would further complicate the downstream investors' possibilities for tapping into cheap and

---

[8] See, for instance, Krueger (1993), Krishna and Krueger (1995), and Bond (2001). The specialization of inputs to the needs of the final goods producer creates a bilateral monopoly problem and the potential for opportunism when contracts between the parties are incomplete and when the parties are not tied by a vertically integrated firm. Even if intra- and extra-PTA supplies are compatible, switching suppliers involves a time lag in the presence of contractual obligations. De Silanes, Rutherford, and Markusen (1994) show that when foreign firms in a PTA area rely on imported inputs more than domestic industries do, RoO can reduce output and shift profits to domestic firms.

efficient supplies outside the PTA area. In short, downstream industries have incentives to invest in the PTA area when the RoO governing their industry and the upstream industries that supply them are flexible.

Third, flexible, nonbinding RoO are not necessarily conducive to FDI among all downstream investors. Consider downstream producers that have important existing intra-PTA links and are not globally the most competitive ones, yet are intent on exporting within the PTA area. Such producers might be attracted by RoO that are flexible enough to accommodate any of their existing extra-PTA supply links, yet restrictive enough to bar more competitive ROW downstream producers from immediately meeting the RoO and thus qualifying for the PTA-conferred preferences. In the presence of such RoO, ROW downstream producers would need to switch to intra-PTA input sources in order to obtain the PTA-provided preferential treatment: they would incur the costs beyond the increased cost of inputs, namely, the costs of locating suppliers with appropriate components and of altering production techniques to meet the RoO requirements, assuming that intra- and extra-PTA inputs are not perfect substitutes.[9]

Sufficiently stringent RoO can thus provide downstream producers that are not globally the most competitive ones with an edge over their more competitive ROW counterparts in exporting from one PTA partner to another. As such, RoO that are restrictive enough to bar the entry of globalized producers could boost investment by some downstream producers.

In sum, there are a number of ways in which product-specific RoO can arbitrate the incentives to invest in a particular PTA area. However, it is hardly clear whether restrictive RoO are more conducive to FDI than loose RoO are. There are five further considerations that obscure the effect of product-specific RoO on FDI.

First, most PTAs carry regime-wide RoO, such as cumulation and de minimis, that can ameliorate or accentuate the degree of restrictive-

---

[9] This assumes that intermediate and final goods producers are two separate, competitive firms engaged in arm's-length transactions with each other. The costs of inputs and the attendant bilateral monopoly problems will be reduced should the input and the final good be produced within a vertically integrated firm. In the presence of specialized production ties and/or vertical integration, RoO can raise the costs for the downstream producer's rivals.

ness of product-specific RoO (Suominen, 2004a). Capturing the effects of regime-wide RoO on FDI would inherently require a multi-PTA analysis.

Second, the incentives generated by RoO are filtered through firm-level factors, such as the downstream producer's geography of pre-existing sourcing and production linkages—which, after all, determine whether RoO are binding or not—and the completeness and duration of the existing contracts between the producer and its input suppliers.[10]

Third, the depth of tariff preferences can arbitrate RoO's investment effects.[11] If and when the benefits of the "carrot" of preferential market access exceed the costs of the "stick" of having to comply with the RoO—that is, incurring higher production and administrative costs—a firm with pre-PTA sourcing and/or production ties outside the PTA will post-PTA have incentives to shift its operations to the PTA area to source intermediate goods from and/or to perform RoO regime-mandated production processes there, and to subsequently serve the entire PTA market by exporting under the preferential regime. In other words, the higher the payoff of qualifying for preferential treatment, the greater the incentives for firms to adjust the geography of their production processes in order to meet the RoO requirements even if such an adjustment implies inefficiencies and raises their costs of production from the pre-PTA equilibrium.[12] By definition, this payoff has to be higher than that obtained by exporting to the PTA market under the partners' MFN regimes.[13]

Fourth, RoO are an endogenous instrument: in particular, firms operating in the slated PTA area can play an important role in designing the agreement's RoO regime. This implies that the restrictiveness of the

---

[10] See Thoening and Verdier (2006) for a nuanced pioneering treatment.

[11] See Krishna (2004) and Ju and Krishna (1998) for theoretical treatments of the long-term effects of RoO.

[12] This is a particularly feasible strategy for firms that are engaged in easily divisible multistage production and that are able to quickly terminate their contracts with the existing extra-FTA suppliers. RoO can induce a greater range of production processes for final goods to be diverted to the FTA than is the case in the pre-FTA equilibrium.

[13] Indeed, given that RoO hold the potential of increasing local sourcing, governments can use RoO to encourage investment in certain strategic or high-value sectors—for instance, in order to create lucrative jobs (Jensen-Moran, 1996; Hirsch, 2002).

resulting RoO for such firms may be immaterial. Endogeneity of RoO can also mean that RoO-jumping investment remains deterred: as hypothesized in the literature on endogenous tariffs, intra-PTA firms threatened by extra-PTA FDI flows may moderate their demands for restrictive RoO in order to keep RoO-jumping FDI at bay.

Fifth, in the longer term, the interplay of intermediate and final goods markets can alter the prices of intra-PTA inputs and/or production processes, changing the incentives for investment. For instance, any RoO-induced inflows of FDI in intermediates could eventually crowd out the market for inputs and, as such, reduce the possibilities for extracting surplus in intermediate production and reverse the prior incentives for both up- and downstream producers to invest in the PTA area. Or increases in production costs entailed by stringent RoO can reduce final goods producers' derived demand for intermediates, undermining the price of intermediates and again discouraging investment in the intermediate goods industries, while encouraging intra-PTA final goods production.

Effects of RoO on FDI: The Case of Mexico

That there are multiple equilibria in the presence of RoO renders the relationship between RoO and FDI an empirical matter. This section conducts an empirical investigation of the role of NAFTA RoO in the location of FDI in Mexican manufacturing industries. The first subsection discusses the cross-sectoral variation in FDI in Mexico. The second subsection specifies the construction of the independent variable, restrictiveness of RoO, and the third subsection puts forth the empirical specification and discusses the results. The fourth subsection raises some methodological issues and their implications for the results.

FDI Flows in Mexico in the NAFTA Era: Industry-Level Data

Mexico experienced impressive increases in inflows of FDI in the wake of the formation of NAFTA in 1994 (Figure 6.1). According to the Ministry of the Economy, aggregate flows shot up from an annual

Figure 6.1 | Total and Manufacturing FDI Flows to Mexico, 1994–2003

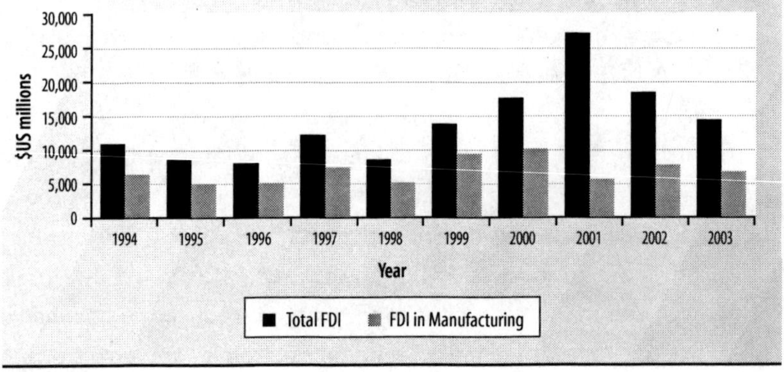

Source: Ministry of the Economy.

average of US$4.6 billion in 1989–93 to US$10.7 billion in 1994 and further to US$12.2 billion in 1997, reaching US$26.6 billion in 2001. The inflows leveled off in 2002 to US$13.3 billion; the estimated total in 2003 was US$9.4 billion. In 1994–2000, manufacturing inflows accounted for more than half of FDI in Mexico each year; however, the share of manufacturing in the total was less pronounced in the 2001–03 period. The main source of investment in the Mexican manufacturing sector was the United States, followed by, in order, the European Union, Canada, and Japan. The share of the United States and Canada, Mexico's NAFTA partners, in total FDI in Mexico rose from 54 percent in 1994 to 80 percent in 2001, leveling off somewhat to 63 percent in 2002 and 54 percent in 2003.

However, the distribution of FDI in the Mexican manufacturing sector has hardly been uniform. Table 6.1 presents the sectoral breakdown of investment flows in the Mexican manufacturing sector in the period examined in this chapter, 1994–2000, by division of the ISIC Revision 3 classification. We focus on this period because a change in 1994 in the Mexican classification system to exclude all intended investment from FDI data undercuts the compatibility between FDI data before and after that year. The highest average annual growth rates are in tobacco, wood, nonmetallic mineral products, publishing and printing, leather goods and

Table 6.1 FDI Flows to Mexican Manufacturing Industries, 1994–2000

ISIC division	Description	Total FDI 1994–2000 ($US thousands)	Share of total (%)	Annual average change (%)	Change 1994–2000 (%)
15.	Food and beverages	5,855,000	11.5	–8.6	–44.3
16.	Tobacco products	3,260,941	7.4	256,741.8	9,835.7
17.	Textiles	1,165,000	2.3	28.5	–12.0
18.	Wearing apparel	815,000	1.7	35.3	207.8
19.	Leather goods and footwear	86,461	0.2	149.4	–88.2
20.	Wood and wood products	56,199	0.1	366.2	–114.0
21.	Paper and paper products	700,600	1.4	73.2	54.5
22.	Publishing, printing, reproduction of recorded media	327,890	0.6	241.3	411.3
23.	Coke, refined petroleum products, nuclear fuel	247,742	0.6	42.3	–97.6
24.	Chemicals and chemical products	4,712,000	10.4	47.3	–56.9
25.	Rubber and plastics products	1,511,100	3.0	25.3	150.9
26.	Other nonmetallic mineral products	653,443	1.3	242.1	140.4
27.	Basic metals	2,454,900	5.1	49.0	–78.9
28.	Fabricated metal products	1,114,400	2.1	37.1	311.3
29.	Machinery and equipment	3,051,000	5.8	32.7	247.8
30.	Office and computing machinery	2,028,900	3.5	106.3	1,817.9
31.	Electrical machinery and apparatus	4,520,000	9.1	23.3	69.0
32.	Radio, TV, communication equipment	4,013,000	8.6	50.8	49.2
33.	Medical and optical instruments	300,900	0.6	19.9	15.8
34.	Motor vehicles, trailers, semi-trailers	8,829,000	17.3	53.1	65.0
35.	Other transport equipment	105,900	0.2	–10.0	–100.0
36.	Furniture; miscellaneous manufacturing	3,823,000	7.4	51.0	356.9

Source: Authors' calculations based on data from Mexico's Ministry of the Economy.

footwear, and office machinery. Tobacco, office machinery, publishing and printing, fabricated metal products, machinery and equipment, and apparel top the list for greatest increases in FDI inflows from the 1994 level to 2000.

NAFTA RoO

The NAFTA RoO regime is among the most complex RoO regimes in the world. Although the majority of the tariff lines in NAFTA are governed by change in chapter and change in heading rules, the agreement incorporates no fewer than 19 different RoO combinations in the 6-digit tariff universe of the Harmonized System (see Estevadeordal and Suominen, 2005). The greatest variation in RoO types is found in the manufacturing sector.

Have NAFTA RoO arbitrated the location of FDI flows in the Mexican manufacturing sector? This chapter strives to answer the question by operationalizing NAFTA's product-specific RoO. We employ Estevadeordal's categorical index for the restrictiveness of RoO (*RoO-RI*) presented in Chapter 3, which ranges from 1 (least restrictive) to 7 (most restrictive).[14] The index can be conceptualized as an indicator of how demanding a given rule of origin is for an exporter to comply with. The restrictiveness values are here coded at the HS 6-digit level of disaggregation and subsequently aggregated to the 4-digit level of the ISIC Revision 3 classification by taking simple averages. We employ the Mexican input-output table to calculate the restrictiveness of RoO also in up- and downstream industries. Table 6.2 summarizes the sectoral restrictiveness values of the three key independent variables by ISIC division.[15]

---

[14] See Estevadeordal and Suominen (2006a) for the observation rule and the behavior of restrictiveness values in the HS tariff universe governed by NAFTA.

[15] The average and standard deviation values at the bottom of the table are based on calculations at the 4-digit level.

Table 6.2 | Restrictiveness of RoO in NAFTA, by ISIC Division

Division	Description	*RoO-RI*	*RoO-RI-DOWN*	*RoO-RI-UP*
15.	Food and beverages	5.47	4.78	5.78
16.	Tobacco products	6.00	0.00	5.67
17.	Textiles	6.07	5.89	5.37
18.	Wearing apparel	5.44	5.83	5.38
19.	Leather goods and footwear	5.40	6.28	5.56
20.	Wood and wood products	4.13	4.99	4.89
21.	Paper and paper products	4.69	5.64	5.30
22.	Publishing, printing, reproduction of recorded media	5.00	4.89	5.05
23.	Coke, refined petroleum products, nuclear fuel	4.00	5.19	5.02
24.	Chemicals and chemical products	5.02	5.32	4.95
25.	Rubber and plastics products	4.46	5.10	5.46
26.	Other nonmetallic mineral products	5.61	5.14	5.59
27.	Basic metals	4.84	4.82	5.30
28.	Fabricated metal products	4.54	4.88	4.85
29.	Machinery and equipment	4.14	4.77	4.72
30.	Office and computing machinery	3.78	4.80	4.92
31.	Electrical machinery and apparatus	4.35	4.49	4.90
32.	Radio, TV, communication equipment	2.39	4.62	4.91
33.	Medical and optical instruments	4.32	5.14	5.00
34.	Motor vehicles, trailers, semi-trailers	4.51	4.99	4.78
35.	Other transport equipment	4.15	4.72	4.64
36.	Furniture; miscellaneous manufacturing	5.50	5.07	4.90
	Average	*4.81*	*5.00*	*5.13*
	Complexity (Standard Deviation)	*0.99*	*0.95*	*0.43*

Source: Authors' calculations.
Note: RoO-RI-DOWN and *RoO-RI-UP* refer to the restrictiveness of RoO in down- and upstream industries, respectively.

Empirical Specification

This section explores the relationship between NAFTA RoO and FDI in Mexico at the 4-digit level of disaggregation through estimation of the following equation in OLS:

$$\ln\left(FDI_{it}^{MX}\right) = \beta_0 + \beta_1 \ln\left(TARIFF_{it}^{MX}\right) + \beta_2\left(FDI\text{-}GLOBAL_i^{US}\right), \qquad (6.1)$$
$$+ \beta_3\left(SALARY\text{-}DUM2_i^{MX}\right) + \beta_4\left(SALARY\text{-}DUM3_i^{MX}\right)$$
$$+ \beta_5\left(PREFERENCE_{it}^{US}\right) + \beta_6\left(FDI\text{-}CAP_i^{MX}\right)$$
$$+ \beta_7 \ln\left(RoO\text{-}RI_i\right) + \varepsilon_{it},$$

where

$\ln\left(FDI_{it}^{MX}\right)$ is the log of FDI flows in Mexico in industry *i* in time *t*;

$\left(TARIFF_{it}^{MX}\right)$ is Mexico's weighted average of the tariff in Mexico's FTAs and Mexico's tariff applied on its FTA partners;

$\ln\left(FDI\text{-}GLOBAL_i^{US}\right)$ is the log of U.S. FDI flows to the world;

$\left(SALARY\text{-}DUM2_i^{MX}\right)$ is a dummy variable for the second tercile of salary levels in Mexico, measured as level of remunerations/number of workers;

$\left(SALARY\text{-}DUM3_i^{MX}\right)$ is a dummy variable for the highest tercile of salary levels in Mexico;

$\left(PREFERENCE_{it}^{US}\right)$ is the preferential margin offered by the United States to Mexico, expressed as the absolute difference between the U.S. tariff to the rest of the world and the U.S. preferential tariff to Mexico;

$\left(FDI\text{-}CAP_i^{MX}\right)$ is Mexico's imposed ceiling on sectoral FDI inflows under NAFTA, expressed as the percentage of ownership by foreign investors that is allowed in a sector;

$\ln\left(RoO\text{-}RI_i\right)$ is the log of RoO restrictiveness that takes values between 1 and 7; and

ε_{it} is a normally distributed error term.

All regressions include year dummies. The data on FDI flows into Mexico come from Mexico's Ministry of the Economy at the 6-digit level of the Clasificación Mexicana de Actividades y Productos (CMAP) classification and are deflated using the U.S. consumer price index.

Data on Mexico's external tariff are calculated on the basis of Ministry of the Economy data at the 6-digit-level CMAP. U.S. FDI flows to the world are at 3-digit-level U.S. Standard Industrial Classification (SIC) and come from the U.S. Bureau of Economic Analysis. Mexican salary levels are obtained from the 1994 census of Mexico's Instituto Nacional de Estadística Geografía e Informática. U.S. preferential margin is from U.S. International Trade Commission's 8-digit-level HS data. Mexico's cap on incoming FDI is obtained from the NAFTA text. All variables are converted into 4-digit-level ISIC Revision 3 classification using United Nations correspondence tables.

The main interest here is on the effect that RoO may have on FDI flows. We control for several other factors that can influence FDI. First, FDI may simply have been of the tariff-jumping kind, flowing into industries where Mexico's MFN tariff is high.[16] Second, the location of FDI in Mexico may simply have followed the global patterns in FDI flows, proxied here by the sectoral FDI outflows from the United States to the world. Third, FDI flows may have been of the efficiency-seeking kind, flowing to industries where Mexico has a comparative advantage—in labor-intensive, low-wage industries, such as apparel production.[17] Fourth,

---

[16] The most traditional explanation is that FDI is tariff-jumping: multinational corporations move to produce in the host in order to avoid the high tariff and to service the host market directly from within. FDI thus flows to industries most protected by tariffs, with trade and capital mobility becoming substitutes (Mundell, 1957; Corden, 1967; Johnson, 1967; Brecher and Diaz Alejandro, 1977; Bhagwati and Brecher, 1980; Bhagwati and Tironi, 1980). Trade liberalization in the host increases the incentives to export from home rather than servicing the host market through FDI: production consequently becomes centralized in the home market (Rugman and Gestrin, 1993).

[17] In the case of intraregional investment, this assumes that trade and investment are complementary, rather than substitutes—or that FDI is of the efficiency-seeking rather than the tariff-jumping type and thus geared to producing at lower costs in the host in order to export subsequently to third markets. Under this assumption, FDI flows to industries with low production costs and, should intermediate products need to be imported to the host from abroad, with low barriers to trade in intermediates. As such, trade and investment would be complementary—a view shared in a growing body of theoretical and empirical literature (Swedenborg, 1979; Lipsey and Weiss, 1981; Donnenfeld and Weber, 2000; Baldwin and Ottaviano, 2001). These findings have been found to hold even at the firm level (Blomström, 1988; Head and Ries, 1999) and product level (Blonigen, 2000).

a wide preferential margin from the United States to Mexico under NAFTA can be expected to have induced industries to locate in Mexico in order to use Mexico as an export platform to the U.S. market. Fifth, a low ceiling on the level of permitted FDI inflows into Mexico could be expected to dampen FDI.[18]

Table 6.3 shows the results. Columns I and II indicate that NAFTA has indeed played a central role in arbitrating the location of FDI in Mexico: investment has been drawn to sectors enjoying deep preferences from the United States and few Mexican restrictions on foreign investment under NAFTA. Meanwhile, the key independent variable, the restrictiveness of NAFTA RoO (*RoO-RI*), enters with a negative and significant sign. This is the first main result of this chapter: restrictive NAFTA RoO appear to have discouraged FDI in Mexico. This suggests that FDI in Mexico has flowed to sectors that allow flexibility in sourcing patterns, rather than tying the investors to purchasing intermediates and/or performing production processes in the NAFTA region. If flexible RoO are attractive to globally integrated industries in particular, the result could be interpreted to mean that it is globalized producers that have entered Mexico in NAFTA's early years. This interpretation is all the more compelling given that Mexico's tariff to the world ($TARIFF^{MX}$) has little effect on FDI flows: FDI in Mexico post-NAFTA does not appear to have been geared to jump either RoO or tariffs.[19]

Moreover, there is a correlation not only between FDI and exports of investor countries to host countries, but also between FDI and exports from host countries to investor ones (Gundlach and Nunnenkamp, 1996).

[18] Mexico's 1993 Foreign Investment Law (FIL) is inseparable from NAFTA: it was adopted on 27 December 1993, only five days before NAFTA's entry into force, as part of the legislation required to implement Mexico's NAFTA commitments. Conversely, Mexico incorporated in NAFTA Annexes I–III the provisions of FIL vis-à-vis foreign investment (and, in particular, investment provisions pertaining to national treatment, most-favored nation treatment, performance requirements, and senior management and board of directors). As such, NAFTA and FIL are highly compatible: the exceptions to national treatment under the two instruments are the same, as are the thresholds for the shares that foreigners can own of Mexican enterprises; investors responding to the FIL automatically responded to the incentives of NAFTA and vice versa.

[19] The result could well be different for FDI located in the United States, the largest NAFTA market.

Table 6.3 Restrictiveness of RoO and FDI in Mexican Manufacturing Sectors, 1994–2000

Independent variables	I 1994–2000	II 1994–2000	III IV, 1994–2000	IV 1994–2000	V 1994–2000
	Dependent variable: ln(*FDI*)				
TARIFF^{MX}	−0.015	−0.006	−0.003	−0.005	−0.003
	−1.69	−0.61	−0.25	−0.56	−0.27
FDI-GLOBAL^{US}	0.588	0.54	0.515	0.543	0.519
	(5.62)**	(5.21)**	(4.93)**	(5.24)**	(4.96)**
SALARY-DUM2^{MX}	0.313	0.496	0.406	0.506	0.417
	−1.01	−1.61	−1.31	−1.64	−1.34
SALARY-DUM3^{MX}	1.72	2.042	2.077	2.052	2.087
	(6.14)**	(7.08)**	(7.17)**	(7.11)**	(7.21)**
PREFERENCE^{US}	0.096	0.127	0.065	0.129	0.066
	−1.93	(2.55)*	−1.18	(2.58)*	−1.2
FDI-CAP^{MX}	0.048	0.032	0.032	0.032	0.031
	(2.36)*	−1.6	−1.55	−1.56	−1.51
ln(*RoO-RI*)		−2.11	−2.125	−0.838	−0.857
		(3.77)**	(3.70)**	−0.65	−0.66
ln(*RoO-RI*)*1995				−2.166	−0.66
				−1.2	−1.23
ln(*RoO-RI*)*1996				−1.005	−1.036
				−0.55	−0.57
ln(*RoO-RI*)*1997				−0.146	−0.189
				−0.08	−0.1
ln(*RoO-RI*)*1998				−3.751	−3.727
				(2.09)*	(2.07)*
ln(*RoO-RI*)*1999				−0.985	−0.886
				−0.54	−0.48
ln(*RoO-RI*)*2000				−0.827	−0.723
				−0.43	−0.38
Constant	2.104	7.138	7.638	5.196	5.7
	−0.84	(2.55)*	(2.71)**	−1.56	−1.7
Observations	439.00	439.00	439.00	439.00	439.00
Adjusted *R*-squared	0.25	0.27	0.27	0.27	0.27

Note: Absolute value of *t*-statistics in parentheses. All regressions include year dummies. IV (instrumental variables) regressions are instrumenting Mexican tariff and U.S. preferential margin.

* significant at 5 percent level; ** significant at 1 percent level.

The other control variables shed further light on the pattern of FDI in Mexico following NAFTA's enactment. The positive and significant sign on U.S. FDI to the world (*FDI-GLOBAL*^{US}) indicates that the trends in Mexico form part of a broader global pattern of sectoral distribution of FDI. Meanwhile, the positive and significant sign on the highest salary tercile (*SALARY-DUM3*^{MX}) indicates that foreign investment has sought out skilled labor—and, as such, potentially went to sectors where Mexico has not traditionally held a comparative advantage.[20] The result is driven in good part by the heavy FDI flows in the Mexican automotive sector, where the salaries also tend to be higher than in most of the country's other manufacturing sectors. To be sure, the results do not tell us anything about the number of employees affected by the growth of FDI: sectors with more-limited FDI inflows—particularly textiles and apparel—also employ important segments of the labor force.

Importantly from the methodological point of view, both the Mexican tariff and the U.S. preferential tariff can be viewed in part as endogenous to FDI flows to Mexico. For example, some investors driven to capture the Mexican market may have lobbied Mexico to increase its external tariff. Meanwhile, U.S. investors that located to Mexico may have called on the United States for deeper preferences for United States–bound exports from Mexico. We account for these possibilities by instrumenting Mexico's tariff and U.S. preferential tariffs with Mexican tariffs offered to all Mexico's FTA partners and the U.S. MFN tariff, respectively.

Column III shows the results. While instrumenting has very little effect on the behavior of the Mexican tariff variable, the U.S. preferential margin does lose its significance. Although the instrument is not necessarily optimal given its potential endogeneity to the FDI flows, the result

[20] We also explored the possibility that injury-prone and polluting industries in the United States may have moved to Mexico to take advantage of the laxer enforcement of labor and environmental regulations in that country; however, neither of the variables employed to test the effect of these two factors was significant or added to the explanatory power of the model. The data for the exercise were taken from the U.S. Environmental Protection Agency and U.S. Bureau of Labor Statistics.

is a disclaimer to the notion that the U.S. preferential margin alone has been a key factor propelling FDI inflows in Mexico.

Column IV extends the investigation to exploring the relationship between restrictiveness of RoO and FDI inflows over time vis-à-vis the base year of 1994. The results indicate that the effect of RoO on FDI has been relatively consistent over time: the effect is significantly different from that in 1994 only in 1998. The other variables behave as before. Column V displays the results of the regressions with the instrumented tariff variables. (Appendix 6.2 provides details concerning the separate annual regressions and instrumental variables regressions.)

However, there are grounds to believe that restrictiveness of NAFTA RoO is in part *a function of* the depth of preferences offered by the United States to Mexico: investors may be more willing to bear the potentially heightened production costs entailed by stringent RoO when the lure of preferences is strong. We explore this hypothesis by interacting RoO restrictiveness with the U.S. preferential margin as follows:

$$\begin{aligned}\ln\left(FDI_{it}^{MX}\right) = {} & \beta_0 + \beta_1 \ln\left(TARIFF_{it}^{MX}\right) + \beta_2\left(FDI\text{-}GLOBAL_i^{US}\right), \\ & + \beta_3 (SALARY\text{-}DUM2_i^{MX}) + \beta_4\left(SALARY\text{-}DUM3_i^{MX}\right) \\ & + \beta_5\left(PREFERENCE_{it}^{US}\right) + \beta_6\left(FDI\text{-}CAP_i^{MX}\right) \\ & + \beta_7 \ln\left(RoO\text{-}RI_i\right) + \beta_8 \ln\left(RoO\text{-}RI\right)*PREFERENCE_{it}^{US} + \varepsilon_{it},\end{aligned} \tag{6.2}$$

where $\ln\left(RoO\text{-}RI_i\right) + \beta_8 \ln\left(RoO\text{-}RI\right)$ is the interaction term of the log of RoO restrictiveness and the U.S. preferential margin. All other variables are as in (6.1).

Table 6.4 shows the results. They indicate that the interaction is indeed central to the pattern of FDI in Mexico.

Importantly, investors do not operate in a vacuum, but must also consider the trade policies, including RoO, in industries with which they interact. Most immediately, and as discussed above, upstream producers will be particularly interested in the restrictiveness of RoO in the downstream industries to which they sell, as stringent RoO downstream will compel downstream producers to limit their sourcing to the PTA area.

Table 6.4 Restrictiveness of RoO and FDI in Mexican Manufacturing Sectors, 1994–2000

Independent variables	Dependent variable: ln(*FDI*)
$TARIFF^{MX}$	–0.006
	–0.28
ln($FDI\text{-}GLOBAL^{US}$)	0.556
	(4.95)**
$SALARY\text{-}DUM2^{MX}$	0.417
	–1.13
$SALARY\text{-}DUM3^{MX}$	2.011
	(5.73)**
$PREFERENCE^{US}$	–0.504
	–1.68
$FDI\text{-}CAP^{MX}$	0.03
	–1.29
ln(*RoO-RI*)	–2.798
	(3.97)**
ln(*RoO-RI*)*$PREFERENCE^{US}$	0.366
	(2.23)*
Constant	8.344
	(2.50)*
Observations	439.00
Adjusted R-squared	0.30

Note: Robust *t*-statistics in parentheses. All regressions include year dummies.
* significant at 5 percent level; ** significant at 1 percent level.

Meanwhile, potential downstream investors may be concerned about restrictive RoO upstream, as such RoO might signal to the downstream investor the presence of an uncompetitive upstream provider with limited chances for accessing the least expensive inputs from ROW. Tariffs can be hypothesized to lead to similar considerations: a downstream investor that depends heavily on imported intermediate goods will likely be deterred from locating in a country that imposes high external tariffs on intermediates.

We investigate these possibilities through the following specification:

$$\begin{aligned}\ln\left(FDI_{it}^{MX}\right) = {} & \beta_0 + \beta_1 \ln\left(TARIFF_{it}^{MX}\right) + \beta_2\left(FDI\text{-}GLOBAL_i^{US}\right) \qquad (6.3)\\ & + \beta_3(SALARY\text{-}DUM2_i^{MX}) + \beta_4\left(SALARY\text{-}DUM3_i^{MX}\right)\\ & + \beta_5\left(PREFERENCE_{it}^{US}\right) + \beta_6\left(FDI\text{-}CAP_i^{MX}\right)\\ & + \beta_7\left(RoO\text{-}RI_i\right) + \beta_8 \ln\left(RoO\text{-}RI\text{-}DOWN_i\right)\\ & + \beta_9\left(SALES\text{-}TO\text{-}TRADABLES_i^{MX}\right)\\ & + \beta_{10}\ln\left(RoO\text{-}RI\text{-}DOWN_i\right)*\\ & (SALES\text{-}TO\text{-}TRADABLES_i^{MX})\\ & + \beta_{11}\ln\left(RoO\text{-}RI - UP_i\right) + \varepsilon_{it}\end{aligned}$$

where

$\ln\left(RoO\text{-}RI\text{-}DOWN_i\right)$ is the restrictiveness of RoO in downstream industries that industry *i* supplies;

$\left(SALES\text{-}TO\text{-}TRADABLES_i^{MX}\right)$ is the percentage share of the downstream industry's production that is traded rather than destined for domestic consumption;

$\ln\left(RoO\text{-}RI\text{-}DOWN_i\right) + \beta_9\left(SALES\text{-}TO\text{-}TRADABLES_i^{MX}\right)$ is an interaction term between the restrictiveness of RoO in industry *i*'s downstream industries and the percentage share of their production sold to the tradables sector; and

$\ln\left(RoO\text{-}RI - UP_i\right)$ is the restrictiveness of RoO in upstream industries from which industry *i* purchases supplies.

All the other variables are as in (6.1).[21]

The results in Table 6.5 indicate that restrictiveness of RoO in downstream industries is indeed significantly related to FDI flows. However, the negative sign on the variable *RoO-RI-DOWN* suggests that upstream inves-

[21] NAFTA's elimination of duty drawback mechanisms, under which Mexico's maquiladoras operated through 2000, can be seen as a further inducement for intermediate goods producers in particular to move operations to Mexico. Although signs of economic actors' anticipation of the end of the duty drawback program may be embedded in the data presented here, the analysis of the impact of the actual ending of the program at the beginning of 2001 remains beyond the scope of our data.

Table 6.5 RoO in Down- and Upstream Industries and FDI Flows in Mexico, 1994–2000

	Dependent variable: ln(*FDI*)			
Independent variables	**I**	**II**	**III**	**IV**
TARIFF[MX]	0.002	0	0.001	−0.002
	−0.17	−0.03	−0.07	−0.24
ln(*FDI-GLOBAL*[US])	0.542	0.559	0.542	0.561
	(5.30)**	(5.43)**	(5.29)**	(5.45)**
SALARY-DUM2[MX]	0.505	0.434	0.507	0.425
	−1.68	−1.42	−1.68	−1.39
SALARY-DUM3[MX]	2.108	2.165	2.121	2.197
	(7.41)**	(7.54)**	(7.44)**	(7.61)**
PREFERENCE[US]	0.138	0.125	0.14	0.126
	(2.78)**	(2.47)*	(2.82)**	(2.49)*
FDI-CAP[MX]	0.033	0.031	0.032	0.03
	−1.68	−1.58	−1.63	−1.49
ln(*RoO-RI*)	−1.889	−1.846	−2.031	−2.077
	(3.37)**	(3.25)**	(3.37)**	(3.41)**
ln(*RoO-RI-DOWN*)	−3.258	−3.384	−3.508	−3.76
	(3.04)**	(2.13)*	(3.08)**	(2.30)*
SALES-TO-TRADABLES		−0.05		−0.056
		−0.68		−0.75
ln(*RoO-RI-DOWN*)* *SALES-TO-TRADABLES*		0.027		0.03
		−0.6		−0.66
ln(*RoO-RI-UP*)			1.01	1.667
			−0.65	−1.04
Constant	11.892	12.205	10.954	10.624
	(3.76)**	(3.37)**	(3.15)**	(2.70)**
Observations	428.00	428.00	428.00	428.00
Adjusted *R*-squared	0.30	0.30	0.30	0.30

Note: Absolute value of *t*-statistics in parentheses. All regressions include year dummies.
* significant at 5 percent level; ** significant at 1 percent level.

tors that have located in Mexico have not done so in order to benefit from stringent RoO in downstream industries. Rather, upstream industries have entered sectors whose downstream purchasers have flexible RoO; this, in turn, suggests that it is upstream suppliers that are relatively efficient—able to competitively supply downstream customers that have the option of turning to suppliers outside the NAFTA region. Should that be the case, upstream producers would see few advantages in restrictive RoO downstream: efficient and competitive, they will be the most-preferred supplier for downstream industries regardless of whether RoO downstream are binding or not. Importantly, the results also indicate that the competitiveness of the upstream suppliers is likely in part due to the efficiency that RoO in the upstream sectors per se provides for them: the negative sign on the restrictiveness of RoO variable (*RoO-RI*) indicates that upstream investors are attracted to the Mexican market by loose RoO, which provide flexibility for them to procure *their own* supplies from outside the NAFTA theater. Although the result must be taken with a grain of salt because of the relatively high level of aggregation and the correlation between the two RoO variables, it allows for a preliminary conclusion that Mexico post-NAFTA has been marked by the entry of globalized, competitive, and efficiency-seeking FDI both up- and downstream.

There are also reasons to believe that flexible RoO downstream may have played a role in encouraging upstream producers to invest in Mexico. Flexible RoO downstream may signal to upstream producers the presence of a dynamic, globalized, and competitive—and hence high-demand—sector downstream, whereas restrictive RoO downstream may communicate the presence of a dying industry with low prospects for sustained demand.

Moreover, three unobserved firm-level factors may be at play. First, the negative sign on both the RoO restrictiveness and RoO restrictiveness downstream variables (*RoO-RI* and *RoO-RI-DOWN*, respectively) may simply indicate that the upstream supplier and downstream customer operate within the same firm. Competitive downstream investors may simply have brought with them their upstream operations when relocating into Mexico—and done so precisely because of the attraction of loose RoO both up- and downstream. Second, upstream industries providing to downstream industries with restrictive RoO were or have located in the United States rather than in Mexico and use NAFTA's preferential market access to export intermediates from the U.S. market to the downstream industries in Mexico rather than actually investing in plants in Mexico. Third, long and binding pre-existing contracts between up- and downstream firms may simply have opened fewer possibilities for new upstream providers to move to Mexico to supply downstream industries with restrictive RoO.

Column II of the table controls for the possibility that RoO are irrelevant to downstream producers, which could be the case if downstream producers are indifferent to exporting to the U.S. market and, rather, destine their produce for the domestic market only.[22] We do this by interacting the downstream RoO variable (*RoO-RI-DOWN*) with a variable that captures the share of downstream sectors' production that is traded rather than destined for domestic consumption (*SALES-TO-TRADABLES*). The result remains unchanged.

Columns III and IV investigate the possibility that restrictiveness of RoO in upstream industries has played a role in investor decisions to enter the Mexican market. However, the results indicate that downstream investors in the Mexican market have by and large been indifferent to the restrictiveness of RoO upstream.

Mexico's external tariffs in up- and downstream industries may also have figured in investors' considerations. For example, high tariffs in upstream industries could presage a high cost of imported intermediates for those industries and hence reduce incentives for investment. Meanwhile, high tariffs surrounding a potential investor's downstream customer might signal the presence of an import-competing downstream industry with a relatively limited future demand for intermediates.

We explore these hypotheses by running (6.3) with Mexican tariffs to the world in up- and downstream industries ($TARIFF\text{-}UP^{MX}$ and $TARIFF\text{-}DOWN^{MX}$, respectively). The results, presented in Table 6.6, are somewhat surprising in the case of the upstream tariff, which enters with a positive sign and is significant at the 5 percent level. However, the relationship is relatively unpronounced and dissipates altogether in column III. Moreover, even if the Mexican tariff on intermediates is high, downstream industries may be able to access duty-free inputs from U.S. upstream industries, so that the high Mexican tariff on upstream industries does not curb downstream producers' access to relatively cheap inputs upstream. In other words, the upstream tariff variable may only proxy

---

[22] Such producers could, to be sure, prefer stringent RoO in order to deter imports.

Table 6.6 Tariffs and RoO in Down- and Upstream Industries and FDI Flows in Mexico, 1994–2000

Independent variables	Dependent variable: ln(*FDI*) I	II	III
$TARIFF^{MX}$	–0.009	–0.005	–0.007
	–0.87	–0.51	–0.71
ln($FDI\text{-}GLOBAL^{US}$)	0.59	0.579	0.583
	(5.67)**	(5.61)**	(5.62)**
$SALARY\text{-}DUM2^{MX}$	0.435	0.521	0.522
	–1.4	–1.7	–1.64
$SALARY\text{-}DUM3^{MX}$	2.2	2.162	2.228
	(7.47)**	(7.41)**	(7.47)**
$PREFERENCE^{US}$	0.124	0.148	0.141
	(2.46)*	(2.93)**	(2.74)**
$FDI\text{-}CAP^{MX}$	0.027	0.03	0.03
	–1.36	–1.52	–1.49
ln(*RoO-RI*)	–2.41	–2.071	–2.098
	(4.00)**	(3.35)**	(3.37)**
$TARIFF\text{-}DOWN^{MX}$	–0.014	0.015	0.01
	–0.54	–0.53	–0.35
$TARIFF\text{-}UP^{MX}$	0.028	0.028	0.023
	(2.16)*	(2.06)*	–1.6
ln(*RoO-RI-DOWN*)		–3.624	–3.066
		(3.08)**	–1.79
ln(*RoO-RI-UP*)		–1.267	–0.57
		–0.7	–0.29
SALES-TO-TRADABLES			0.011
			–0.13
ln(*RoO-RI-DOWN*)* *SALES-TO-TRADABLES*			–0.01
			–0.19
Constant	7.256	14.062	12.351
	(2.62)**	(3.78)**	(2.91)**
Observations	422.00	422.00	422.00
Adjusted R-squared	0.29	0.31	0.31

Note: Absolute value of t-statistics in parentheses. All regressions include year dummies.
* significant at 5 percent level; ** significant at 1 percent level.

for a deep preferential margin in Mexico. Overall, the results indicate that the single most relevant trade policy variable affecting investors' considerations in regard to locating to Mexico has been NAFTA RoO in their *own* sector.

Methodological Issues

Five methodological issues should be considered when interpreting the results of this chapter. First, the relatively high level of aggregation may obscure some nuances in the RoO-investment nexus. NAFTA RoO were negotiated at up to 8- and 10-digit levels of disaggregation. Moreover, as discussed previously, FDI flows are also driven in part by firm-level considerations. A further complication stems from changing all our variables into the ISIC classification from other schemes.

Second, the relationship between RoO and FDI is not necessarily linear but possibly quadratic, so that FDI may flow only to sectors with very stringent and very loose RoO—which would indicate heterogeneous trade policy preferences among the set of companies that have invested in the Mexican market. Indeed, some regressions with a quadratic RoO restrictiveness variable suggest that both relatively loose and stringent RoO may have attracted FDI.

Third, the empirical exercises here do not account for transportation costs, another variable that arbitrates the effect of RoO on FDI. Transportation costs prohibitive of exporting to a PTA region from ROW can encourage extra-PTA producers to invest in the PTA market. And high transport costs within a PTA market can, much like stringent RoO, encourage investors to jump the transport cost via locating in the largest market among the signatories to the PTA to serve the PTA market from within.

Fourth, the patterns of FDI in Mexico may be affected by domestic policies pursued by that country, many of which precede NAFTA. For example, NAFTA merely extended Mexico's unilateral reforms of the 1980s in FDI regulations in automotives, textiles, and apparel. Furthermore, FDI in textiles and apparel may also be affected by the 1989 U.S. elimination of some quotas and expansion of others on

Mexican textiles and apparel, and on U.S. expansion of Mexican steel quotas.[23] Moreover, Mexico's 1989 sweeping domestic reforms of investment regulations may have affected the glass, iron, steel, cellulose, automotives, auto parts, electronic components, furniture, and textiles and apparel industries in particular.[24] However, the unavailability of FDI data for the pre-NAFTA era that are compatible with the data in the

---

[23] The United States and Mexico concluded bilateral agreements on trade and investment between 1985 and 1989. These general agreements were accompanied by sectoral accords on steel and textiles (Hufbauer and Schott, 1993). In October 1989, the United States doubled Mexico's annual steel import quota from 400,000 to 800,000 tons. In February 1990, the United States agreed to eliminate quotas on 52 textile and apparel products from Mexico and to expand quotas by an average of 25 percent for products that remained under quota restrictions. The improvement in Mexico's market access was accentuated by the fact that the United States had concurrently been tightening or creating quotas on the imports of the main textiles and apparel exporters to the U.S. market.

[24] The 1989 reforms, carried out under Regulation of the Law for the Promotion of Mexican Investment and the Regulation of Foreign Investment, to the regulations designed to implement the 1973 Law to Promote Mexican Investment and Regulate Foreign Investment extended to a number of activities previously sheltered by restrictions (so-called classified activities) and activities marked by less restrictive rules (unclassified activities) (Hufbauer and Schott, 1993: 76–77). They provided for an automatic approval of FDI of up to US$100 million and also permitted 100 percent foreign control in companies in the unclassified economic activities as long as a number of conditions were met, such as that the project at hand guaranteed an equilibrium in its balance of foreign exchange over the first three years, generated employment for Mexicans, and was not located in Mexico City, Guadalajara, or Monterrey. The unclassified activities were subsequently expanded to previously restricted areas of the glass, iron, steel, and cellulose industries.

The regulations also abolished the requirement for foreigners to obtain the National Foreign Investment Commission's approval prior to participating in or acquiring Mexican maquiladoras—in-bond production facilities involved in the processing or secondary assembly of imported components for re-export. The in-bond arrangement entails that imported inputs can enter Mexico duty free as long as the finished products are re-exported afterwards; in practice, the importer posts a bond to ensure that the finished products will be exported rather than sold on the domestic market. U.S. imports of Mexico's maquiladora products particularly in the automotive, auto parts, electronic components, furniture, and textiles and apparel sectors had boomed in the 1980s under the U.S. Generalized System of Preferences and the U.S. Harmonized Tariff Schedule items 9802.00.60 (metals of U.S. origin) and 9802.00.80 (goods containing U.S.-made components) (Hufbauer and Schott, 1993: 96). The HST provisions allowed any maquiladoras, including third-country ones, as well as other Mexican industries to receive duty-free treatment for the value of the U.S. content of their exports to the U.S. market; moreover, Mexico's duty drawback allowed third-country maquiladoras to avoid paying duties on imported components when the final product was being exported.

NAFTA years and the high correlation between Mexican policies and NAFTA's provisions complicates efforts to disentangle the respective contributions of these two sets of variables.

Fifth, the empirical exercises do not consider the (several) other PTAs into which Mexico has entered during the NAFTA era. RoO, preferential tariffs, and investment provisions in these agreements can plausibly have had an effect on FDI inflows into Mexico. To be sure, these agreements were signed with other Latin American countries, and thus their effects likely pale in comparison with those of NAFTA. The EU-Mexico FTA, a major PTA with plausibly important effects on FDI in Mexico, entered into force only in July 2000 and thus remains outside the temporal scope of this chapter, except for the case of potential investments made in anticipation of the agreement.

Conclusion

The proliferation of PTAs has been accompanied by a surge in FDI flows around the world. However, both theoretical and empirical studies have yet to establish a clear causal relationship between the two phenomena. This chapter has sought to connect PTAs and FDI by focusing on a central market access provision embedded in virtually all PTAs, rules of origin. We have explored the various theoretical ways in which RoO can regulate FDI flows. Our empirical exercises suggest that foreign investment in Mexico during the NAFTA era has been attracted to sectors with flexible RoO—RoO that allow industries to establish production and supply networks of global reach. Should flexible RoO attract globalized and competitive industries, the news would be good for Mexico: NAFTA has paved the way for the entry of globalized and efficiency-seeking investors into the Mexican market. There are, however, various methodological limitations to the conclusiveness of the evidence; the results are also not immediately generalizable beyond the case of Mexico. This study has nonetheless illustrated ways to apply RoO in empirical work, and it is hoped that it will inspire further work on the effects of RoO on FDI.

PTA provisions other than RoO can also arbitrate investment flows in a PTA partner. We have found that Mexican manufacturing sectors that enjoy deep NAFTA preferences in the U.S. market and are governed by liberal investment rules under NAFTA in Mexico have seen an increase in FDI. These findings are instructive and generalizable beyond NAFTA to other North-South PTAs, many of which, like NAFTA, are marked by a high degree of sectoral selectivity. Moreover, much like Mexico, many developing-country PTA members have experienced impressive surges in FDI inflows in selected industries. By operationalizing PTAs, this study has provided a fresh interpretation for cross-sectoral variation in FDI flows.

The need for further work on the effects of PTA provisions on FDI is compelling given the rapid proliferation of PTAs—and of PTAs with distinct and detailed market access and investment regimes. Three avenues of investigation would be particularly fruitful: consideration of FDI inflows in *entire* PTA areas rather than single PTA members; exploration of the determinants of FDI in the pre- and post-PTA eras; and an analysis of the ultimate welfare effects of FDI spurred by PTAs.

Appendix 6.1 Descriptive Statistics

Table 6A.1 ▌Descriptive Statistics

Variable	Observations	Mean	Standard Deviation	Minimum	Maximum
ln(*FDI*)	689	15.984	2.602	–0.055	21.414
$TARIFF^{MX}$	777	10.512	13.951	0.000	136.317
ln($FDI\text{-}GLOBAL^{US}$)	510	14.474	1.199	10.389	17.746
$SALARY\text{-}DUM1^{MX}$	784	0.339	0.474	0.000	1.000
$SALARY\text{-}DUM2^{MX}$	784	0.339	0.474	0.000	1.000
$SALARY\text{-}DUM3^{MX}$	784	0.321	0.467	0.000	1.000
$PREFERENCE^{US}$	758	2.243	2.649	–5.856	17.933
$FDI\text{-}CAP^{MX}$	739	97.321	13.009	0.000	100.000
ln(*RoO-RI*)	725	1.549	0.218	0.780	1.931
ln(*RoO-RI-DOWN*)	833	1.629	0.099	1.230	1.885
ln(*RoO-RI-UP*)	854	1.633	0.082	1.489	1.787
TARIFF-DOWN	826	10.742	4.971	3.040	47.037
TARIFF-UP	854	10.237	9.791	2.477	75.080
SALES-TO-TRADABLES	854	25.980	23.005	2.186	93.512

Appendix 6.2 Annual Regressions

Table 6A.2 Restrictiveness of RoO and FDI in Mexican Manufacturing Sectors, 1994–2000

	Dependent variable: ln(*FDI*)						
	I	II	III	IV	V	VI	VII
Ind. var.	1994	1995	1996	1997	1998	1999	2000
$TARIFF^{MX}$	0.032	−0.077	−0.063	0.050	0.039	0.035	0.022
	(1.27)	(4.09)**	(3.53)**	(2.35)*	(1.20)	(1.46)	(0.54)
ln($FDI\text{-}GLOBAL^{US}$)	0.831	−0.124	0.430	0.957	0.371	0.889	0.742
	(2.75)**	(0.53)	(2.13)*	(4.17)**	(1.04)	(3.92)**	(2.91)**
$SALARYDUM2^{MX}$	−0.228	1.167	−0.252	0.023	1.825	0.473	0.632
	(0.26)	(1.50)	(0.39)	(0.03)	(1.78)	(0.72)	(0.82)
$SALARYDUM3^{MX}$	1.552	2.758	1.643	1.001	3.061	1.630	1.901
	(1.91)	(3.88)**	(2.73)**	(1.52)	(3.24)**	(2.70)**	(2.69)**
$PREFERENCE^{US}$	−0.173	0.320	0.175	0.074	0.307	0.163	0.150
	(0.77)	(1.82)	(1.74)	(0.71)	(1.80)	(1.68)	(1.36)
$FDI\text{-}CAP^{MX}$	0.010	−0.007	−0.112	0.019	0.101	−0.059	0.027
	(0.20)	(0.15)	(0.45)	(0.49)	(1.74)	(0.25)	(0.66)
ln(*RoO-RI*)	−1.101	−1.507	−0.618	−1.104	−5.969	−2.196	−2.089
	(0.73)	(1.05)	(0.55)	(0.88)	(3.27)**	(1.91)	(1.39)
Constant	4.310	19.567	22.010	1.124	6.566	11.889	5.304
	(0.59)	(3.03)**	(0.86)	(0.19)	(0.76)	(0.48)	(0.82)
Observations	63.00	62.00	63.00	64.00	66.00	60.00	61.00
Adjusted *R*-squared	0.20	0.36	0.40	0.33	0.29	0.39	0.28

Note: Absolute value of *t*-statistics in parentheses.

* significant at 5 percent level; ** significant at 1 percent level.

Table 6A.3 Restrictiveness of RoO and FDI in Mexican Manufacturing Sectors with Instrumented Mexican Tariff and U.S. Preferential Margin, 1994–2000

	Dependent variable: ln(*FDI*)						
	I	II	III	IV	V	VI	VII
Ind. var.	1994	1995	1996	1997	1998	1999	2000
TARIFF[MX]	0.020	−0.060	−0.040	0.054	0.046	0.040	0.003
	(0.62)	(2.60)*	(1.97)	(2.27)*	(1.16)	(1.36)	(0.06)
ln(*FDI-GLOBAL*[US])	0.759	−0.182	0.456	0.984	0.424	0.939	0.684
	(2.41)*	(0.76)	(2.14)*	(4.20)**	(1.12)	(3.91)**	(2.60)*
SALARY-DUM2[MX]	−0.175	0.778	−0.594	0.028	1.632	0.416	0.524
	(0.20)	(0.97)	(0.91)	(0.04)	(1.58)	(0.63)	(0.67)
SALARY-DUM3[MX]	1.662	2.797	1.662	0.945	3.082	1.659	1.973
	(1.98)	(3.80)**	(2.67)*	(1.42)	(3.22)**	(2.73)**	(2.75)**
PREFERENCE[US]	−0.324	−0.001	0.036	0.101	0.182	0.150	0.081
	(1.54)	(0.00)	(0.31)	(0.82)	(1.04)	(1.40)	(0.66)
FDI-CAP[MX]	0.025	−0.006	−0.092	0.018	0.105	−0.046	0.034
	(0.47)	(0.13)	(0.36)	(0.46)	(1.80)	(0.19)	(0.81)
ln(*RoO-RI*)	−0.090	−2.425	−0.970	−1.210	−5.870	−2.138	−1.464
	(0.05)	(1.60)	(0.81)	(0.95)	(3.14)**	(1.82)	(0.94)
Constant	2.739	22.404	20.406	0.960	5.590	9.823	4.816
	(0.36)	(3.36)**	(0.78)	(0.16)	(0.63)	(0.39)	(0.73)
Observations	63.00	62.00	63.00	64.00	66.00	60.00	61.00
Adjusted *R*-squared	0.13	0.32	0.38	0.33	0.29	0.38	0.25

Note: Absolute value of *t*-statistics in parentheses.

* significant at 5 percent level; ** significant at 1 percent level.

References

Balasubramanyam, V. N., and D. Greenway. 1992. "Economic Integration and Foreign Direct Investment: Japanese Investment in the EC." *Journal of Common Market Studies* 30:175–93.

Baldwin, R. E. 1989. "The Growth Effects of 1992." *Economic Policy* 9:247–81.

Baldwin, R. E., and G. I. P. Ottaviano. 2001. "Multiproduct Multinationals and Reciprocal FDI Dumping." *Journal of International Economics* 54:429–48.

Behrman, J. R. 1972. "Sectoral Elasticities of Substitution Between Capital and Labor in a Developing Economy: Time Series Analysis in the Case of Postwar Chile." *Econometrics* 40:311–26.

Bhagwati, J., and R. A. Brecher. 1980. "National Welfare in an Open Economy in the Presence of Foreign-Owned Factors of Production." *Journal of International Economics* 10:103–15.

Bhagwati, J., and E. Tironi. 1980. "Tariff Change, Foreign Capital, and Immiserization: A Theoretical Analysis." *Journal of Development Economics* 7:71–84.

Blomström, M. 1988. "Labour Productivity Differences Between Foreign and Domestic Firms in Mexico." *World Development* 16(11):1295–98.

Blomström, M., and A. Kokko. 1997. "Regional Integration and Foreign Direct Investment: A Conceptual Framework and Three Cases." Policy Research Working Paper No. 1750. Washington, DC: International Trade Division, International Economics Department, World Bank.

Blomström, M., A. Kokko, and S. Globermann. 1998. "Regional Economic Integration and Foreign Direct Investment: The North American Experience." Working Paper Series in Economics and Finance No. 269. Stockholm: Stockholm School of Economics.

Blonigen, B. A. 2000. "Tariff-Jumping Antidumping Duties." NBER Working Paper No. 7776. Cambridge, MA: National Bureau of Economic Research.

Bond, E. W. 2001. "Commercial Policy in a 'Fragmented' World." *American Economic Review* 91(2):358–62.

Brecher, R. A., and C. F. Diaz Alejandro. 1977. "Tariffs, Foreign Capital and Immiserizing Growth." *Journal of International Economics* 7:317–22.

Bulmer-Thomas, V. 1982. "The Central American Common Market." In A. El-Agraa (ed.), *International Economic Integration*. London: Macmillan.

Chudnovsky, D. (ed.). 2001. *El boom de inversión extranjera directa en el Mercosur*. Buenos Aires: Siglo Veintiuno.

Corden, W. M. 1967. "Protection and Foreign Investment." *Economic Record* 43:209–32.

De Silanes, F., T. F. Rutherford, and J. R. Markusen. 1994. "Complementarity and Increasing Returns in Intermediate Inputs." *Journal of Development Economics* 45(1):101–19.

Donnenfeld, S., and S. Weber. 2000. "Do Rising Tariffs Trigger Foreign Direct Investment? A New Look at the Tariff Jumping Argument." *Journal of Economic Integration* 15(1):100–126.

Dunning, J. H. 1992. *Multinational Enterprises and the Global Economy*. Wokingham, U.K.: Addison-Wesley.

Eden, L. 2001. "Regional Integration and Foreign Direct Investment: Theory and Lessons from NAFTA." Unpublished.

Estevadeordal, A. 2000. "Negotiating Preferential Market Access: The Case of the North American Free Trade Agreement." *Journal of World Trade* 34(1):141–66.

Estevadeordal, A., J. E. López-Córdova, and K. Suominen. 2006. "How Do Rules of Origin Affect Investment Flows? Some Hypotheses and the Case of Mexico." IDB-INTAL Working Paper No. 22. Buenos Aires: IDB-INTAL.

Estevadeordal, A., and K. Suominen. 2005. "Rules of Origin in Preferential Trading Agreements: Is All Well with the Spaghetti Bowl in the Americas?" *Economia* 5(2):63–103.

Franko, L. G. 1976. *The European Multinationals: A Renewed Challenge to American and British Big Business*. Stamford, CT: Greylock.

Gundlach, E., and P. Nunnenkamp. 1996. "Falling Behind or Catching Up? Developing Countries in the Era of Globalization." Kieler Diskussionsbeiträge 263. Kiel: Institut für Weltwirtschaft.

Hanson, G. H. 1996. "Economic Integration, Intra-industry Trade, and Frontier Regions." *European Economic Review* 40:941–49.

———. 1998. "North American Economic Integration and Industrial Location." *Oxford Review of Economic Policy* 14:30–44.

Head, K., and J. Ries. 1999. "Rationalization Effects of Tariff Reductions." *Journal of International Economics* 47(2):295–320.

Hirsch, M. 2002. "International Trade Law, Political Economy and Rules of Origin: A Plea for a Reform of the WTO Regime on Rules of Origin." *Journal of World Trade* 36(2):171–81.

Hufbauer, G., and J. Schott. 1993. *NAFTA: An Assessment*. Washington, DC: Institute for International Economics.

ITC (U.S. International Trade Commission. 1997. *The Impact of the North American Free Trade Agreement on the US Economies and Industries: A Three-Year Review.* Washington, DC: ITC.

Jensen-Moran, J. 1996. "Trade Battles as Investment Wars: The Coming Rules of Origin Debate." *Washington Quarterly* 19(1):239–53.

Johnson, H. G. 1967. "The Possibility of Income Losses from Increased Efficiency or Factor Accumulation in the Presence of Tariffs." *Economic Journal* 77:151–54.

Ju, J., and K. Krishna. 1998. "Firm Behavior and Market Access in a Free Trade Area with Rules of Origin." NBER Working Paper No. 6857. Cambridge, MA: National Bureau of Economic Research.

Krishna, K. 2004. "Understanding Rules of Origin." Unpublished.

Krishna, K., and A. O. Krueger. 1995. "Implementing Free Trade Areas: Rules of Origin and Hidden Protection." In A. Deardorff, J. Levinsohn and R. Stern (eds.), *New Directions in Trade Theory.* Ann Arbor: University of Michigan Press.

Krueger, A. O. 1993. "Free Trade Agreements as Protectionist Devices: Rules of Origin." NBER Working Paper No. 4352. Cambridge, MA: National Bureau of Economic Research.

Lipsey, R. E. 1990. "American Firms Facing Europe: 1992." In M. Feldstein and Y. Kosai (eds.), *U.S.-Japan Economic Forum*. Cambridge, MA: National Bureau of Economic Research.

Lipsey, R., and M. Y. Weiss. 1981. "Foreign Production and Exports in Manufacturing Industries." *Review of Economics and Statistics* 63(4): 488–94.

Little, J. S. 1996. "U.S. Regional Trade with Canada during the Transition to Free Trade." *New England Economic Review* (January–February):3–21.

Markusen, J. 1983. "Factor Movements and Commodity Trade as Complements." *Journal of International Economics* 13:341–56.

Mayes, D. G. 1983. "EC Trade Effects and Factor Mobility." In A. M. El-Agraa (ed.), *Britain within the European Community: The Way Forward*. London: Macmillan.

Molle, W., and R. Morsnik. 1991. "Intra-European Direct Investment." In B. Burgenmeier and J. L. Muccielli (eds.), *Multinationals and Europe 1992: Strategies for the Future*. London and New York: Routledge.

Mundell, R. A. 1957. "International Trade and Factor Mobility." *American Economic Review* 47:321–35.

Mytelka, L. K. 1979. *Regional Development in a Global Economy: The Multinational Corporation, Technology, and Andean Integration*. New Haven, CT: Yale University Press.

O'Farrell, P. N. 1983. "Ireland." In L. H. Klaassen and W. T. M. Molle (eds.), *Industrial Mobility and Migration in the European Community*. Aldershot, U.K.: Gower.

Pelkmans, J. 1984. *Market Integration in the European Community*. The Hague: Martinus Nijhoff.

Rodriguez, P. 2001. "Rules of Origin with Multistage Production." *World Economy* 24(1):201–20.

Rugman, A. M., and M. Gestrin. 1993. "The Strategic Response of Multinational Enterprises to NAFTA." *Columbia Journal of World Business* 28(4):18–29.

Suominen, K. 2004a. "Rules of Origin in Global Commerce." Ph.D. diss., University of California, San Diego.

———. 2004b. "Selective Liberalization in Response to Globalization: Rules of Origin as Determinants of Market Access Provisions in PTAs." *Integration and Trade Journal* 19:153–85.

Swedenborg, B.1979. *The Multinational Operations of Swedish Firms: An Analysis of Determinants and Effects.* Stockholm: Industriens Utredningsinstitut.

Thoening, M., and T. Verdier. 2006. "Rules of Origin: IO Perspectives." In O. Cadot, A. Estevadeordal, A. Suwa-Eisenmann, and T. Verdier (eds.), *The Origin of Goods: A Conceptual and Empirical Assessment of Rules of Origin in PTAs.* Washington, DC: Inter-American Development Bank and London: Centre for Economic Policy Research.

Waldkirch, A. 2001. "The 'New Regionalism' and Foreign Direct Investment: The Case of Mexico." Working Paper. Corvallis: Department of Economics, Oregon State University.

Winters, L. A. 1996. "Lebanon's Euro-Mediterranean Agreement: Possible Dynamic Benefits". Paper presented at Lebanese Center for Policy Studies' "Conference on Lebanese-EU Relations," July 1–2, Beirut.

———. 2000. "Regionalism and Multilateralism in the Twenty-First Century." Paper presented at the "High-Level Regional Policy Dialogue," Inter-American Development Bank, November 20–21, Washington, DC.

World Bank. 2000. *Trade Blocks*. Oxford: Oxford University Press.

PART IV
WHERE TO GO FROM HERE?

CHAPTER 7

Multilateralizing Preferential Rules of Origin?*

Antoni Estevadeordal, Jeremy Harris, and Kati Suominen

Chapter 5 showed that restrictive rules of origin can be consequential to, and even prohibitive of, trade in any one regime. However, in light of the proliferation of PTAs, RoO regimes today also feature a *systemic* problem of divergence across the various different regimes. There are two potential RoO divergence problems.

First, RoO divergence can balkanize the global trading system. If the various PTAs carry widely distinct RoO, they can impose undue transaction costs on traders, investors, and governments dealing in several PTA markets simultaneously. Firms dealing on different PTA fronts may need to alter their production patterns to comply with the idiosyncratic rules of origin and meet other requirements of each of the different PTAs; customs administering imports from numerous PTA partners may have to refer to multiple divergent sets of rules instead of a single document applicable to all PTAs.

What is more, problems at customs can boomerang to hurt traders. For example, complications in customs can result in delays in shipments' clearing customs, which increases time to market for finished goods and can increase inventory costs when the delayed shipments are intermediates. Administrative complexities also increase the chance for error in the application of rules and thus potential denial of preference

---

*This chapter draws on the final part of Estevadeordal, Harris, and Suominen (2007).

for originating products, which can disincentivize efforts to meet RoO requirements.

In general, these problems can increase uncertainty for traders, depressing trade. And they will likely affect traders in developing countries disproportionately, as developing-country customs are more likely to be unprepared to handle the complicated administrative tasks associated with divergent rules of origin.

The second problem with divergence is that it risks the rise of de facto hub-and-spoke systems built around a few hub countries, where the potential cost savings from cumulation of production among the spokes remains untapped. Although this arrangement may hold some benefits for the hub country, the spokes will be at an increasing disadvantage, as they will be unable to use inputs from other spokes when producing for the hub market. Even in cases where the hub-and-spoke pattern is less clear (i.e., where all bilateral pairs have PTAs, and there are multiple "hubs"), the barriers to cumulation can generate significant inefficiencies and reduced trade.

In short, then, whereas restrictive RoO can introduce undue barriers to trade between PTA members and nonmembers, thus dampening PTAs' trade-creating potential, divergences across RoO regimes can increase the transaction costs for countries and companies dealing on two or more PTA fronts simultaneously, especially as they may not cumulate inputs across agreements. An important insight is that these two issues are intricately linked: divergence matters more when RoO are binding—that is, when restrictiveness is consequential for economic decisions and shapes firms' production functions. Nonbinding RoO around the world would eliminate the importance of divergence. Thus, both balkanization and hub-and-spoke become increasingly relevant when RoO are binding *and* when the various RoO regimes differ from one another.

Figures 7.1a and 7.1b illustrate this. Restrictive RoO effectively set up walls around PTA members that prevent the use of some inputs in each product produced in the member countries. Multiple overlapping PTAs with divergent origin regimes thus entail many such walls to free and efficient sourcing of inputs. The more restrictive the rules are, the

Figure 7.1a | Divergence with High Restrictiveness

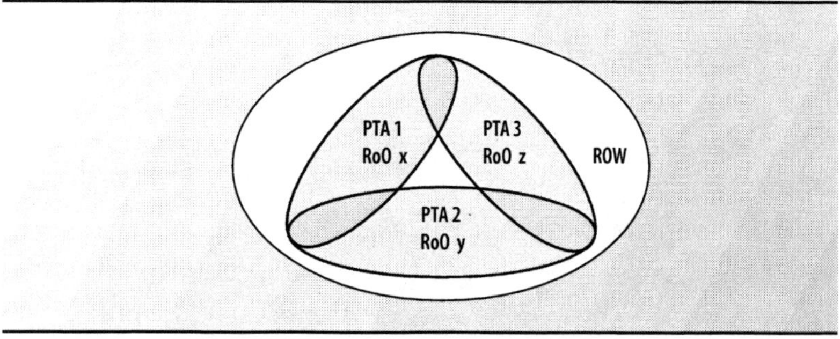

Figure 7.1b | Divergence with Low Restrictiveness

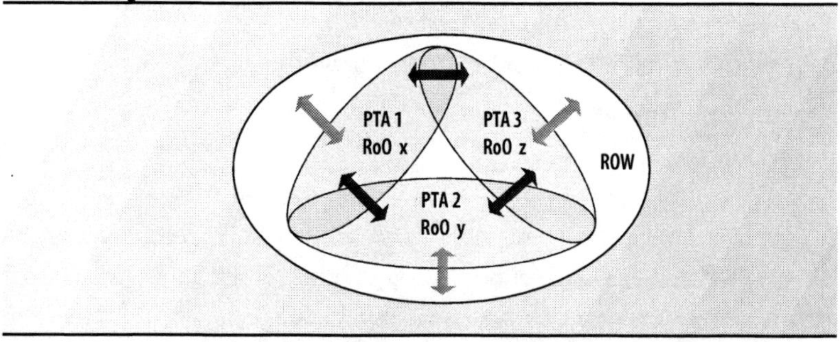

higher the walls are (as depicted by the heavier lines around each PTA in Figure 7.1a), and the more difficult is efficient allocation of resources. In this sense, then, more restrictive rules of origin will accentuate the divergence problem for countries that have entered into multiple PTAs, as both the number and height of the walls will be higher.

Figure 7.1b depicts the same set of PTAs, but with lower restrictiveness. In this case the RoO barriers to trade are lower, both across PTAs and between members and ROW. Inputs can be sourced efficiently, raising the global gains from trade.

The purpose of this chapter is to measure RoO divergence around the world and to propose concrete ways for reducing it. In particular, we (1) quantify the extent of restrictiveness in and divergence among some 58 RoO regimes around the world (which contain 74 sets of product-specific rules; Appendix 7.1) and (2) put forth a number of policy options—including multilateralizing RoO at the global level, inducing convergence across RoO regimes in the main world regions, and some combination of the two—for facilitating trade and efficient production around the world.

We define "multilateralizing" RoO as the establishment of multilateral disciplines on preferential rules within the WTO framework that set guidelines to minimize the systemic harm that can be caused by the current uncoordinated approach. "Convergence" here is a process of establishing a common RoO regime that covers a set of PTAs and subsequently permits cumulation among their members. Conversely, "divergence" here refers not only to the existence of different rules across agreements, but in cases of overlapping agreements, also to the absence of cumulation of production across the agreements. We reach two main conclusions:

- The prospects for bridging the differences in RoO regimes vary from region to region. There are marked divergences across RoO regimes around the world: on average about one-third of all agreements' rules coincide on any given product. Nonetheless, there are clear RoO families centered on the United States, the European Union, and Mexico, in particular, which suggests potential for some form of regional RoO convergence. Moreover, there are some signs of a de facto cross-regional harmonization of RoO, as U.S.-style agreements are spreading toward Asia via the recent transpacific agreements.
- The most ideal solution to the RoO tangle is a multilateral-cum-regional harmonization strategy: putting in place some global guidelines for preferential RoO that would serve to counteract the tendency of larger cumulation zones to erect higher barriers to extrazone inputs, while also striving to harmonize RoO at megaregional levels in order to promote cumulation of production across the subject PTAs. In simple terms, global "capping" of RoO is crucial so as not to "converge" into trade-diverting megablocs.

This chapter has applications beyond RoO. It is hoped that it will inspire further thinking about the key problem of the spaghetti bowl of PTAs—that of multiple overlapping regimes, which would be nonexistent in the presence of a single global set of trade rules. To our knowledge, although there are some studies analyzing the use of various trade disciplines in PTAs,[1] there are no empirical attempts to actually *measure* differences across PTAs. The only effort to our knowledge to measure costs of divergence across PTAs is a firm-level study by the IDB (forthcoming) in eight countries in the Americas and Asia. This chapter paves the way for rigorous efforts to understand the overlap problems and find ways to attenuate their putative economic costs.

The following section sets out various analytical measures of the degree of divergence across RoO regimes. The chapter's third section makes policy recommendations for reducing or eliminating the divergence. The fourth section concludes.

Measuring Divergence

Divergence is due to the different needs of different producers in different cumulation zones, not carelessness in negotiation. However, it can also be expected to generate costs and uncertainty in practice. But how divergent are the various agreements among countries of the world? We strive to answer this question by comparing RoO regimes to one another, product by product, using Harris's (2007) restrictiveness index, which is detailed in Chapter 2.

Figure 7.2 reports the frequency with which the most common rule of origin, that is, the "mode rule," for each product within a "family" of agreements is applied across those agreements. For example, if four out of five agreements within a family specify the same rule for product *x*, then that implies an 80 percent similarity across those agreements for that product. The average of this measure across all products for each family of agreements is reported in the figure.

---

[1] For the most comprehensive compilation, see Estevadeordal, Suominen, and Teh (forthcoming).

Figure 7.2 | Similarity within Families: Average Percentage of Agreements in Each Family Sharing the Mode Rule

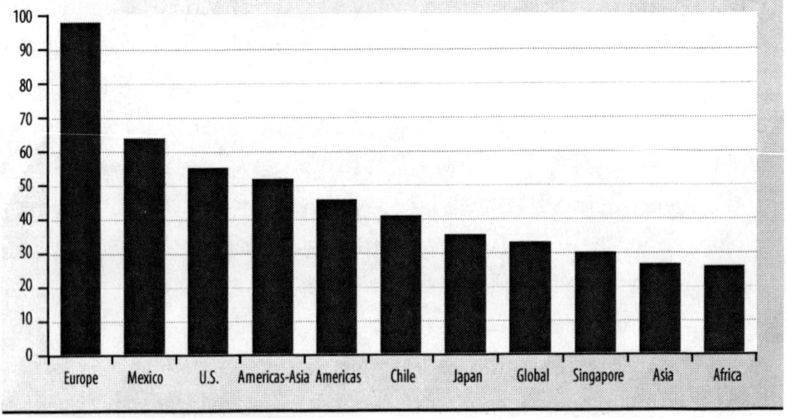

Source: Authors' calculations on the basis of PTA texts.

In the Pan-Euro family of agreements on average nearly all of the agreements apply the same rule[2] for a given product. In the U.S. family, on the other hand, just over half of the agreements apply the same rule for any given product. In the African agreements, the 25 percent similarity actually implies complete divergence, as there are only four agreements included in the analysis, and their rules never coincide. The Americas-Asia family of transcontinental agreements and the Mexico family as well show significant similarities, with over half and nearly two-thirds of agreements coinciding on average, respectively. For the full global set of agreements, on average about one-third of agreements' rules coincide on any given product.

How relevant are these families in economic terms? Figure 7.3 shows the share of world trade covered by the agreements included in

[2] By "the same rule" we thus mean "rules with the same level of restrictiveness," which is not necessarily the same thing. Containing 28 different measures for RoO restrictiveness, and thus abstracting from the RoO typology (with 211 RoO), the index provides a solid and in our view sufficiently nuanced basis for capturing cross-regime divergences. See Appendix I for a list of agreements included in each group.

Figure 7.3 | Percentage of World Trade Covered by Agreements, by Family, 2004

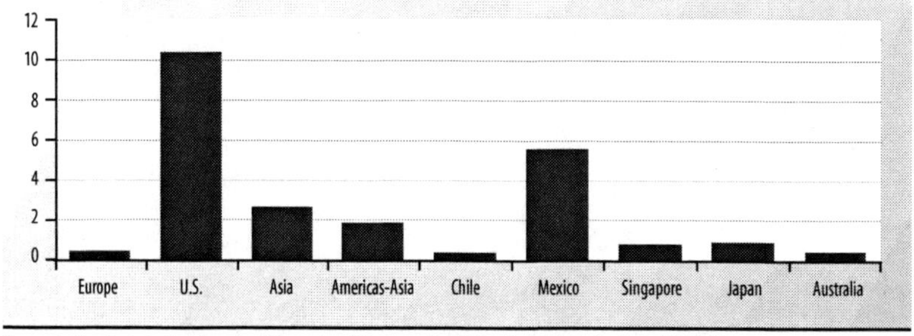

Source: Authors' calculations based on International Monetary Fund Direction of Trade Statistics (IMFDOT).

each family. Intra-European trade is not counted as part of the Europe family, as this trade is not subject to rules of origin in the customs union. The U.S. and Mexico families both include intra-NAFTA trade.

To be sure, in the countries around which these families of PTAs are defined, some PTAs are more important than others. Mexico is a prime example. Approximately two-thirds of Mexican imports are from the United States, and nearly 85 percent of Mexican exports are destined for the U.S. market.[3] Thus, the bulk of Mexico's trade is conducted under a single origin regime. Nonetheless, a third of Mexico's imports and a sixth of its exports must still be administered under MFN and a significant variety of differing origin regimes. Even among agreements with regimes modeled on NAFTA, there is meaningful variation in rules. On average three of Mexico's nine agreements have rules that deviate from the "mode" rule. Among the United States's 12 agreements, this fraction is closer to one-half. Even though some PTAs will be more important than others for a given country, except in the case of agreements with EU-imposed uniformity, firms wishing to take advantage of multiple PTAs will most likely have to confront different rules.

Table 7.1 extends the analysis of rule of origin divergence by showing the number of agreements and the average frequency of the mode rule

[3] Based on 2004 International Monetary Fund Direction of Trade Statistics (IMFDOT) figures.

Table 7.1 | Similarity of RoO within Families

	Number of agreements	Average frequency of mode	Average restrictiveness of mode	Average deviation from mode
Africa	4	1.0	3.80	−0.02
Americas-Asia	7	3.6	7.48	−0.15
Americas	39	17.6	5.43	0.37
Asia	11	2.9	6.47	0.84
Chile	8	3.3	7.29	−0.72
Europe	4	3.9	6.92	0.00
Japan	4	1.4	7.10	0.58
Mexico	9	5.7	8.52	−0.48
Singapore	4	1.2	8.71	0.30
United States	12	6.5	7.63	−0.39
Global	69	22.4	6.27	−0.14

Source: Authors' calculations on the basis of PTA texts.

within agreement families. It also displays a measure of the restrictiveness of the mode rules (a restrictiveness of 6 is equivalent to a change in heading rule or a VC requirement of 50 percent), as well as the average deviations from the mode.

This average deviation from the mode gives an indication as to how these rules are negotiated. In the analysis of the complexity of RoO in Chapter 2, we showed that countries tend to have more selective rules of origin when they trade more products and hence have more product-specific interests to satisfy internally. Here, we can see whether satisfying these interests tends to lead to more or less restrictive rules on average.

Divergence from the mode rule within a family in the Chilean, Mexican, and U.S. cases is on average toward less restrictive rules. This is also true for transpacific agreements and in the overall global case, though to a lesser degree. The opposite is the case in the Singapore, Japan, Asia, and Americas families. In the case of the Asian, Japanese, and Singaporean families, the relatively low frequency of the mode rules makes generalizations even more difficult. The tendency to deviate upward in restrictiveness here may arise from the fact that these countries often have origin regimes that consist of a fixed rule that applies to all products that is generally fairly lax[4] and apply exceptions to this rule only in cases where additional protection is desired.

Although speculation on explanations for these results oversimplifies reality, some informed hypotheses can be advanced. The U.S., Mexican, and Chilean agreements generally follow a NAFTA-like model. Since negotiation of product-level rules in this model can be quite tedious, rules for products of no special interest to either party are likely simply to be copied from one or the other party's previous agreements. Deviations from the rules of previous agreements are likely to occur mainly in the cases of products that are of particular interest to one or the other party. What is interesting here is that these deviations are generally toward less restrictive rather than more restrictive rules. This could be because the "default" rules tend to be sufficiently restrictive to begin with, so that no upward deviations in restrictiveness are usually necessary. However, this probably also indicates that in these cases, the task of negotiators is geared more toward ensuring that their exporters will be able to meet the requirements than to seeking extra protection for domestic producers. In short, political economy may provide less of an explanation than do inertia and transaction costs of negotiating new rules.

Divergence at the Sectoral Level

What sectors drive the average observed divergences and similarities in RoO *within* families? This is a policy-relevant question: the sectors where divergence within the families is least should be the low-hanging fruit for negotiators of any attempts to bridge differences in RoO across regimes.

Figure 7.4 shows the degree of similarity in RoO within PTA families of the Americas, Asia, Europe, and United States. The only divergences in the homogeneous European family arise from RoO in plastics (Section 7), textiles and footwear (Sections 11 and 12) and machinery and electrical equipment, transport equipment, and precision instruments (Sections 16–18). The

---

[4] Except in the case of Japan-Singapore, where the default rule is effectively a wholly obtained requirement except where otherwise stipulated.

Figure 7.4 Similarity by HS Section within PTA Families of the Americas, Asia, Europe, and United States (percentage of agreements by family with the same RoO)

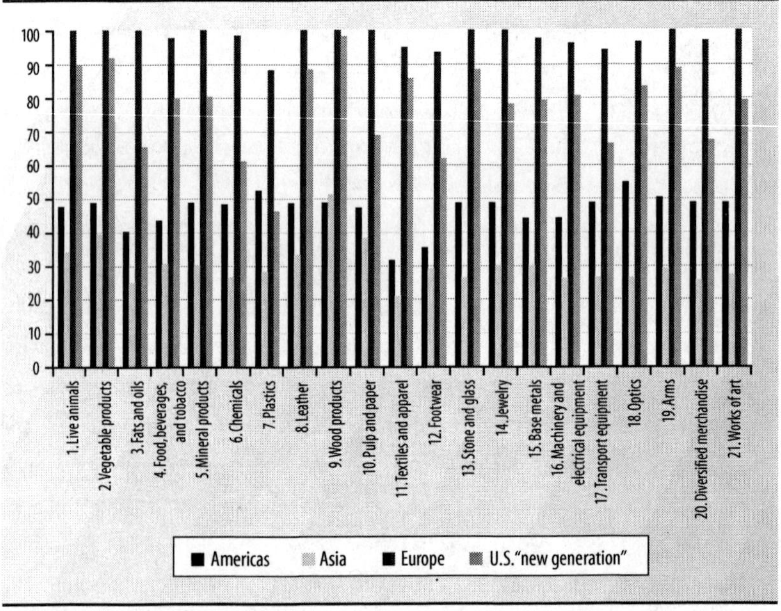

Source: Authors' calculations on the basis of PTA texts.

"new-generation" U.S. agreements (i.e., U.S. agreements excluding those with Middle Eastern countries with across-the-board VC rules) are still rather diverse, with 80 percent or more of the U.S. agreements featuring the same RoO in only 8 of the 21 sectors. The Americas and Asia are even less homogeneous, with the average share of regional agreements that coincide rarely exceeding 50 percent.

Comparing U.S., EU, and Nonpreferential RoO

Given that the United States and the European Union are the two global poles in setting RoO in preferential agreements, they would also hold the keys to any effective multilateral process to tackle RoO. In principle, the more similar their RoO regimes are, the more likely they would be to find common ground in any RoO negotiation.

How divergent are U.S. and EU RoO? Figure 7.5 compares the most common rule for each product within the set of U.S. agreements with the rule for that product in the Pan-Euro RoO.

The overall average levels of restrictiveness of these two sets of rules are quite similar (a difference of less than 0.15 using the Harris [2007] scale). This overall average, however, masks some significant differences in certain sectors (indeed the standard deviation of the difference across all products is 5.5).

At the HS section level, the differences that stand out are in basic animal and vegetable products (Sections 1 and 2), animal and vegetable oils (3), chemical products (6), furs and hides (8), wood and paper (10), textile products (11), stone and its manufactures (13), common metals (15), and precision instruments (18).

The most dramatic of these differences—in live animals (Section 1), vegetable products (2), and textiles and apparel (11)—are perhaps overstated by the comparison methodology, as the EU relies heavily in Sections 1 and 2 on a "wholly obtained" criterion, whereas the United States applies rules

Figure 7.5 Comparing Average Restrictiveness of U.S. and EU RoO by Section, US - EU (Harris 2007)

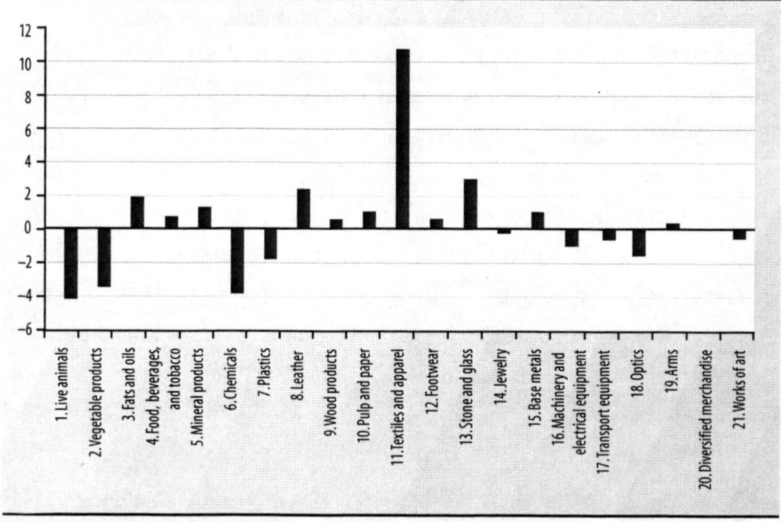

Source: Authors' calculations on the basis of PTA texts.

based on the change in classification component of the substantial transformation criterion, which for these products in fact give a similar effect. In textile products, the differences are somewhat overstated, again because of differences in approach to defining the rules, with the United States again relying on CTC and the EU relying on specifying production processes. In this case the differences boil down to the United States requiring that material inputs be originating starting with yarn, whereas the EU generally requires that material inputs be originating starting with fabric.

Of the other HS sections, 10 out of the 21 show a difference of less than one point (equivalent to the difference between an exception to a CTC in a heading and an exception to a CTC in a subheading).

Despite recognizing that the differences in some sectors are somewhat overstated because of "stylistic" differences in the definition of the rules, we must also emphasize the importance of stylistic differences. Agreement on the substance of a matter does not always lead easily to agreement on the particulars of implementation. The fact that the average difference in 10 of the 21 HS sections is less than one point on the Harris scale, though encouraging in that differences may not be as large as one might think, does not imply that reaching an agreement on how to eliminate those differences would necessarily be simple. Recall that CAFTA relies on criteria other than CTC as the first rule for less than 3 percent of products, whereas the Pan-Euro rules eschew CTC as the first rule for nearly 15 percent of products. Even if the observed restrictiveness is quite similar in many cases, these stylistic differences, which derive from fundamentally different understandings of the best way to approach market access issues, are significant.

Another potentially useful analysis involves comparing the U.S. and EU preferential RoO families, respectively, to the nonpreferential RoO as they stand to date. Although the nonpreferential rules generally seem to be a compromise position between the U.S. and EU standard preferential positions, there are a number of sections where this is not the case. In seven sections (most notably, food and beverages, mineral products, transportation equipment, and arms), the nonpreferential rules are more demanding than either the standard U.S. or EU preferential rules. In another four sections (plastics, jewelry, base metals, and machinery and equipment), the nonpreferential rules are less demanding than either of these.

Note that the ostensible purpose of nonpreferential rules is different from that of preferential rules. Whereas preferential rules must simply allow a determination of whether a good originates in a particular PTA member or not, the nonpreferential rules must allow a determination of the good's "official" originating country when this is not the country of export. These differing purposes may be the cause of the deviations just noted.

Beyond Geographic Families?

The foregoing exercises studied RoO hubs and families ex ante defined. One could certainly ask whether there are sets of PTAs that frequently coincide in their origin requirements despite not falling in the same families—that is, whether there are families across the geographical families examined above. Such an exercise could help identify "global RoO coalitions," or clusters of PTAs sporting common product-specific RoO. In essence, it would help illustrate the divergence within the global bar in Figure 7.2. Figure 7.6 strives to get at such global families by looking at the frequency with which origin requirements coincide in different numbers of agreements across products.

Unsurprisingly, we find that there are no large unexpected coalitions. The peak at 21 coinciding agreements is due to the large group of agreements in South America that follow the LAIA model, with a general rule that gives the alternative of a change in heading or a 50 percent VC. There are virtually no large global coalitions of PTAs outside the expected families. Nonetheless, in the presence of global "RoO caps" that would limit the number of types of RoO, the number of PTAs with common RoO should expand.

In sum, the foregoing exercises have revealed marked divergences across RoO regimes around the world: on average about one-third of all agreements' rules will coincide on any given product. Nonetheless, there are clear RoO families centered on the United States, the European Union, and Mexico, in particular, which suggests potential for bridging RoO regimes in some fashion at the regional levels.

Figure 7.6 | Frequencies of Agreements with Coinciding Origin Requirements

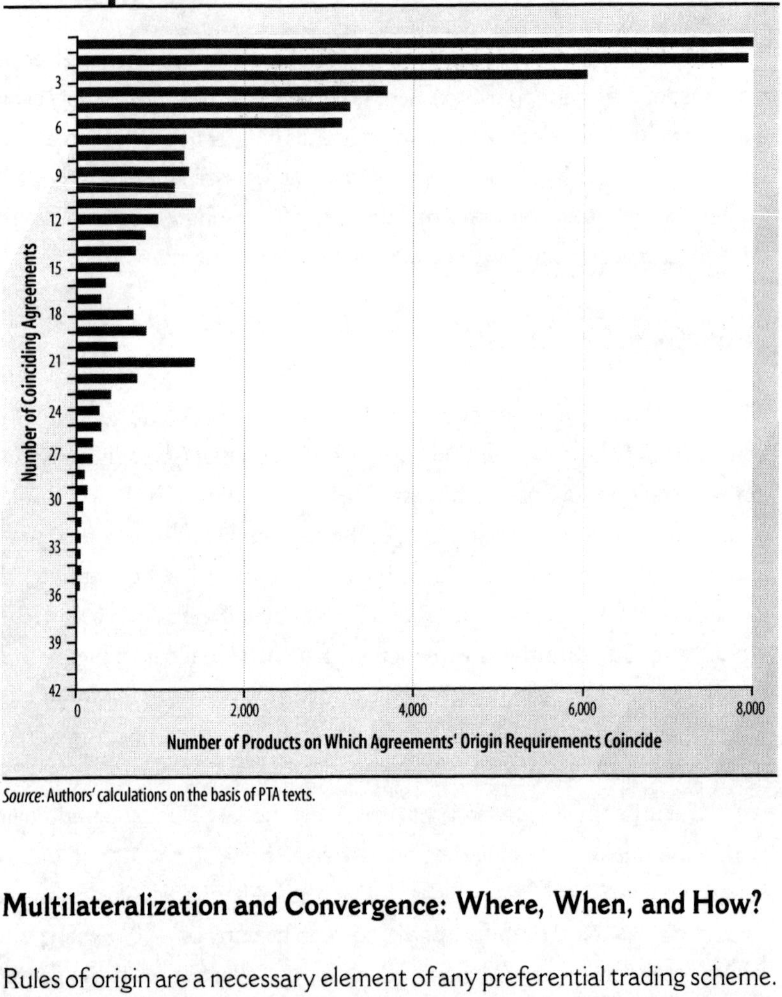

Source: Authors' calculations on the basis of PTA texts.

Multilateralization and Convergence: Where, When, and How?

Rules of origin are a necessary element of any preferential trading scheme. Indeed, "preferences" and "RoO" go hand in hand: by precluding free-riding, the latter enables the former. Taking as given that PTAs, either individually or collectively, can fuel and further the multilateral trading system, it must be recognized that they could not have been agreed to without origin regimes that to a sufficient degree limited the benefits of each agreement to its constituent members. As such, discussion of "eliminating" rules of origin from preferential trading arrangements is nonsense.

Furthermore, if we accept the "building-block" hypothesis that successive and overlapping PTAs are the most viable path to global free trade, then the elimination of preferential origin regimes will itself be a stumbling block. After all, under the building-block hypothesis, preferential origin regimes are the mechanisms that make PTAs viable by allowing the participating countries to focus on eliminating intraregional trade barriers without concerns about inadvertently undertaking a broad unilateral liberalization.

We have shown that restrictive and divergent RoO are facts in the PTA universe. We have also discussed the reasons why restrictiveness accentuates the importance of divergence and described the potential transaction costs ensuing from the restrictiveness-divergence combination. Although RoO per se in any given agreement are not necessarily "bad" for sound economic decisions, restrictive RoO can be, as shown in Chapters 5 and 6. Furthermore, at least in theory, differences *between* RoO regimes can make a difference in the decisions of economic actors in favor of less efficient outsourcing and investment strategies even in a simplified bi- or tripolar RoO world. How, then, can the RoO tangle be tamed?

One way to relegate RoO to irrelevance—and, indeed, to produce the same effects as by multilateralizing regionalism—is by bringing MFN tariffs to zero globally. However, since this is something that is unlikely to be accomplished in the near future, there are four options as to where to go from here in regard to curbing the divergence in RoO worldwide.

The first is doing nothing: status quo PTA proliferation and a likely de facto bipolarization of the global RoO world map into regimes following the U.S. and EU RoO models, respectively—and with many countries sporting both, à la Chile and Mexico. This option, however, does nothing to alleviate the problems with the RoO discussed thus far. The remaining three options have the potential to solve, or at least ameliorate, the problem. The second and third are multilateralization and convergence. A fourth option is a combination of these two. We discuss these three potentially effective options in turn.

Multilateralizing Preferential Rules of Origin

Full harmonization of preferential RoO would be as politically unfeasible as it would be technically unpalatable to producers around the world. Not only could the technical process of harmonization be hampered by the often marked differences in RoO across regimes, but even the more subtle differences could be difficult to overcome as a result of political resistance by sectors benefiting from the status quo. Meanwhile, it is unlikely that an industry lobby would materialize to voice demands for harmonization. Perhaps most importantly, neither the European Union nor the United States would likely be willing to adopt the other's RoO. Both would likely also be concerned about the other's striving for RoO that would allow it to transship via the parties' common PTA partners, such as Mexico.

Moreover, harmonization could be harmful in that it could accentuate restrictiveness. If harmonization implied "upward" adjustment—increased restrictiveness—in some PTAs, it could prohibit the use of nonoriginating materials by the PTA members even when those materials did not exist within the PTAs' respective cumulation zones. This would effectively cancel liberalization of the affected products in that PTA. In short, harmonization can be straitjacketing.

A better option than harmonizing is, then, multilateralizing preferential RoO. Multilateralizing is different from harmonizing and here refers to the establishment of multilateral disciplines on preferential rules within the WTO framework that will set some limits on the restrictiveness and complexity of rules of origin in preferential agreements. Such a RoO cap, perhaps best conceived of as a limited range of potential RoO options (which would truncate the existing vast repertoire of RoO combinations implied in Figure 7.2), would ensure that at least the qualifying production methods in a given sector remained relatively similar across export markets. Although such a cap would likely have to be set relatively high in order to accommodate the various preset RoO in existing PTAs, it could serve as a useful reference point in the same way as the benchmark rules discussed later in the chapter.

A complementary approach could be for PTAs to agree to "bind" their rules of origin at existing levels of restrictiveness and then consider reductions of these bindings in future negotiations. Importantly, this kind of a capping process ought to be couched in a principle of "common flexibilization": multilateralization of RoO, like that of other disciplines, should not result in increased restrictiveness of RoO—and thus potentially harming trade as well as violating GATT Article XXIV—but preferably should work toward loosening both observable and, by extension, effective restrictiveness of RoO.

There are various ways to conceive of the technical process of multilateralizing RoO. For example, once agreement is reached on harmonization of the nonpreferential rules of origin, these could be taken as a benchmark. Then some mechanism could be employed for quantifying the net deviation of each agreement's preferential rules of origin from this benchmark, perhaps using some variant of the indices employed in this book.

PTA member countries would then be assigned the task of ensuring that their rules of origin produce a net deviation from the nonpreferential benchmark or cap that did not exceed an agreed-upon amount. Having established this target reduction in net deviation, the member countries of each agreement would be free to negotiate modifications to their rules of origin to meet the target in a way that is mutually acceptable and that respects the availability of inputs within their respective cumulation zones. Note again that such a mechanism does not aim at harmonizing rules per se, but rather, at reducing the restrictiveness of the rules of origin relative to a fixed benchmark and thus achieving a greater openness of each bloc to the rest of the world. As blocs become more open to inputs from ROW, the distortionary effects of RoO would be reduced.

In this the net deviation method of multilateralization, agreements could compensate for rules that are more restrictive than the benchmark on some products with rules that are less restrictive than the benchmark on other products (note that the concept here is the observed restrictiveness, not effective restrictiveness). It would also make sense, perhaps, for deviations from the benchmark in an agreement to be weighted by the average external tariff of the countries party to the agreement, as more restrictive rules distort more in more-protected sectors.

A further technical fix might be to attack the general RoO instead of the product-specific RoO: for instance, increasing de minimis and/or creating innovative cumulation-like methods in PTAs around the world as is done in Singapore's FTAs. These methods could make RoO nonbinding (nonrestrictive), thus eliminating the relevance of divergence, as well.

Besides the technical "what," there are the political "hows" and "whos" of the process toward multilateralization. The first step might be the launching of a global mechanism—perhaps a technical group of RoO experts—that monitors and catalogues preferential RoO and reports to WTO members on the existing rules. Alternatively, the task could be accomplished by an existing WTO venue, such as under the auspices of the Committee on Regional Trade Agreements, although this might be more time-consuming. The technical group could also serve as a forum for consultations wherein countries and/or companies could communicate their concerns about being excessively restricted and/or excluded from markets by RoO. As a starting point, this could bring increased transparency to RoO by giving countries excluded from PTAs a (nonbinding) voice on the issue, while also helping to gauge the relevance of multilateralizing RoO to companies and the potential designs of such multilateralized RoO.

Another potential institutional mechanism for addressing RoO multilateralization would be Transparency Mechanism on PTAs approved by the WTO General Council in December 2006, which mandates that the "WTO Secretariat, on its own responsibility and in full consultation with the parties, shall prepare a factual presentation of the [notified] PTA."[5] The mechanism entails that PTAs be subject to similar, albeit much lighter, examination by the WTO as national trade policies are in the context of the Trade Policy Review Mechanism. Although this function of the WTO has no enforcement capacity, a rigorous and objective review of preferential RoO in the factual presentation of the PTA would bring added transparency to preferential RoO.

Who should join the multilateralization process? PTAs have evolved from intraregionalism to transcontinentalism, engaging some rather unlikely partners such as Chile and Korea, or Mexico and Israel. This trend is far from abating; given that PTAs are increasingly transcontinental in nature and that all countries but one, Mongolia, are members of at least one PTA, effective multilateralization would seem to require all WTO members to step up to the plate, and on equal terms: everyone

[5] See http://docsonline.wto.org/DDFDocuments/t/WT/L/671.doc.

should play, and with a level playing field. Indeed, the drive toward less restrictive RoO inherent in multilateralization should be acceptable to developing countries: among RoO regimes currently in force, there are certain ones that provide developing countries with more flexibility to fulfill their RoO requirements than is afforded to the more-developed country members (see Suominen, 2004). Developing countries are thus likely to gain from these regulations, as any of the mechanisms previously described would likely have relatively little effect on their RoO, whereas reductions in the restrictiveness of developed-country PTA rules would provide openings to developing-country products. Moreover, it would also be immensely useful to include RoO end-users, that is, private sector actors, from the beginning in the process, perhaps as a consultative committee. Indeed, if globalized industries bought into the idea, they would help build political support for the negotiation and implementation of any outcome.

Getting the process moving toward actual multilateralization as understood here is a broader challenge. One major stumbling block is that the train has left the station. Revising the manifold existing RoO regimes would generally require resubmitting existing PTAs for legislative approval and thus be politically unpalatable in many capitals. One way to overcome the need to reopen negotiations regarding product-specific RoO could thus be a variable geometry approach—a simple capping process, such as a commitment to increase de minimis, in existing regimes, accompanied by a cap for product-specific RoO in forthcoming PTAs. An alternative (or complementary) mechanism might be to adopt two optional (capped) multilateralized RoO for any given product, much as is done in the European Union, United States, and several other countries' RoO regimes. This would help accommodate the entrenched RoO regimes and help push the process forward.

To be sure, one facilitator of multilateralization could be an external shock, such as a push toward RoO convergence in a major world region, such as Asia or the Americas, as this might hasten nonregional parties to the multilateralization table. Overall, the process should be much more streamlined than that of harmonizing nonpreferential RoO, which has dragged on for more than a dozen years.

What would multilateralizing mean to GATT Article XXIV? As formulated here, multilateralization does not appear to necessitate a revision of the article, but rather, some independent agreement among the WTO members. Regardless of the method for doing so, the process of multilateralizing RoO could have positive externalities at the bilateral and national levels. Rules of origin are not regularly renegotiated for a variety of good reasons (predictability and stability of the trading rules) and bad reasons (inertia, negotiation costs, externalities, and information gaps and asymmetries). One benefit of establishing negotiations to govern preferential rules is that it would generate an opportunity to open such negotiations, thus overcoming the negotiation inertia and creating technical awareness of the negative aspects of restrictive RoO. This objective could be made explicit by establishing mandatory review mechanisms whereby PTAs would have to revisit their RoO every 5 to 10 years. In the context of Baldwin's (2006) "juggernaut effect," such an iterative renegotiation would be likely to result in falling levels of protection: in this case, less restrictive rules of origin in regional trade agreements.

Convergence

The second potential path to taming the RoO tangle is convergence. Before entering into what is implied by convergence, it is helpful first to define what it is not. Simply harmonizing rules of origin across PTAs is not "convergence" and in fact would not even necessarily be particularly helpful. Recalling that RoO are in part determined by the availability of inputs within the relevant cumulation zone, the imposition of a standardized set of rules would likely result in *increasing* the restrictiveness, both observed and effective, of some rules in some PTAs—which would be counterproductive.

Furthermore, having similar rules across PTAs would not, in itself, actually result in more openness, except where the harmonization process resulted in rules' moving to lower observed restrictiveness. This is because without changing the borders of PTAs' cumulation zone(s), there would be little gain in market access.

Figure 7.7 | Three-PTA Cumulation Zone

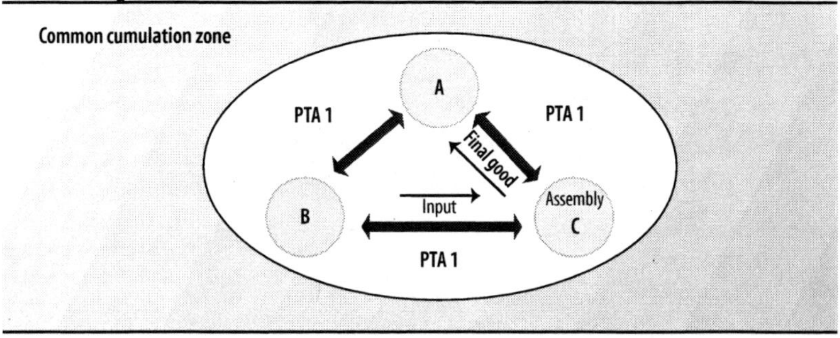

What convergence would have to mean, then, is the unification of multiple overlapping existing PTAs into a single cumulation zone with a new, single list of rules of origin.[6]

One instance of convergence so defined was the creation of the Pan-Euro system in Europe; the process involved harmonizing and connecting RoO regimes that were already very similar, if not fully alike, in many instances. In a more diverse context, convergence would require multiparty negotiation of a new list, as well as negotiation of tariff elimination for any bilateral relationship where it has not been established by an existing PTA. The latter requirement is important, as cumulation would not be viable if there are residual tariffs on either the final good or the inputs to be cumulated in any of the countries in which these originate: such differences could lead to distortions of trade and production patterns, with trade likely flowing through the lowest-tariff channels and production agglomerating in the hub country that faces lowest tariffs in the other participating countries. In the simple example depicted in Figure 7.7, then, convergence would enable C to import inputs free of duty from B under the B-C PTA and use the inputs for final goods destined for A's market under the A-C PTA all governed by the new, mutually agreed-upon, single list of RoO.

When seeking to encourage harmonization (or, for that matter, multilateralization) of RoO, it is important to be aware that a rule that

[6] See Cornejo and Harris (2007) and IDB (forthcoming) for a detailed treatment.

establishes the exact same requirement in two different PTAs can have dramatically different effects on firms' cost structures in the different contexts given the differences in scale and efficiency of production of inputs within the geographic and input pools of the two agreements. As such, while the analysis of RoO divergence is important in that it highlights the degree to which any kind of coordination is absent from the development of this discipline, the fact that rules differ across PTAs does not mean that they are necessarily suboptimal in any particular case.

In practice, initial interest in expanded cumulation is implicit in recent U.S. agreements (apparel provisions in CAFTA, for example). Though their agenda is still vague, the Pacific Basin Forum of 11 countries in Latin America has formed a work agenda to study, among other things, trade convergence and integration.[7] The EU's new PTAs will likely carry the Pan-Euro rules, expanding the uniformity conducive to expanded cumulation. Finally, the growing discussion on a Free Trade Area of the Asia-Pacific might entail some form of convergence rather than a full-blown megaregional negotiation.

However, bridging RoO regimes is bound to be complex and would involve at least six significant considerations. First, what should be the country and sectoral coverage of a negotiation aimed at a common regime? Obviously, for any one country, the decision to join such a negotiation is ultimately a political one, but a number of factors can make such a negotiation more useful. These include an existing set of PTAs that cover the majority of the bilateral relationships within a given group of countries and a similar trade policy strategy among these countries. To be sure, there can be a tipping point effect, produced either by a major economy joining or launching such a process or by a sheer cascading in numbers of participants, such that the payoffs of remaining outside at that point could turn very negative.[8]

[7] See http://www.rree.gob.pe/portal/enlaces.nsf/3f08cf720c1dbf4805256de20052913d/e0380a5ecc82f6800525733f0077e87e/$FILE/Declaracion_de_Lima.pdf and http://www.rree.gob.pe/portal/enlaces.nsf/3f08cf720c1dbf4805256de20052913d/608d2fa8bc449f260525733f007806df/$FILE/Programa_Trabajo.pdf.

[8] That is, the "Domino Effect" of Baldwin (2006).

Second, and of fundamental importance, what exact format should the common RoO regime take so as to be agreeable to all countries and so as not to jeopardize the existing degree of liberalization in a region?[9] Although in this chapter we do not address questions of whether CTC rules are preferable to VC rules, or whether self-certification is preferable to public certification, these questions remain important and worthy of further study, especially at the empirical level, before any new regional (or global) standard is set.[10]

Third, how would a new common origin regime relate to the existing bi- and plurilateral regimes? Would it replace the existing regimes altogether, or would it coexist with them? Under the former model, traders would be able to use the common regime only; under the latter, they could choose between the common regime (and reap the benefits of cumulation) or the existing bi- or plurilateral RoO (and forego cumulation). In the pasta metaphor, the individual spaghetti strands of the PTAs would continue to exist but would be covered also by a large flat piece of lasagna in the form of the convergent origin regime.

Fourth, and critically, how would a common regime interface with extraregional PTAs? A rapidly growing share of the PTAs countries are forming is with extraregional partners. Most countries should thus have an interest in a common regime that is both compatible with the extraregional PTAs and amenable to trading with extraregional partners, rather

---

[9] Restrictive and complex RoO regimes have been shown to undercut PTAs' liberalizing potential. See Suominen (2004), Estevadeordal and Suominen (2006), and Cadot and de Melo (2007).

[10] Gasiorek, Augier, and Lai-Tong (2007) propose a reform mechanism composed of value-added tariffs, VC RoO, and full cumulation that would provide better access for developing-country exports to developed countries. The value-added tariff here is the key, as it levies the tariff only on the nonoriginating components of the final good. These ideas are very useful, especially for GSP-type preferences, where the primary objective is to foment development of export industries in the developing country. The mechanism proposed by Gasiorek et al. could also serve as an add-on to the more standard determination of origin, which is very binary. Generally, when a good is found to be nonoriginating, there is no preference granted at all, regardless of the fact that there may be significant originating content, though insufficient to meet the requirements of the rule of origin. The proposed mechanism would allow something of a sliding scale of preference that would allow some but not full tariff elimination for such goods, thus promoting the development of production capacity in the partner countries.

than sealing them off from a given region.[11] And surely all extraregional players have an interest in continuing to see their market access expand rather than be cut off in these new overarching agreements.

Fifth, who would do the talking? Although governments are necessary for forming and redefining international agreements, considerations of cumulation, like those of multilateralizing, call for private sector participation, not least given that private sector actors are the end users of PTAs and thus hold the best information about the operation of PTAs and the relevance of the hypothetical problems posed by the PTA spaghetti bowl. Indeed, these are the actors responsible for the unbundling of production that leads to the political feasibility of such endeavors as PTAs in the first place. As such, any process aimed at bridging PTAs should inherently involve public sector–private sector partnerships.

Sixth, and finally, what is the role of the multilateral trading system (and the WTO) in such a process? One of a dispassionate (or impotent) observer, or one of a player in the process? This is a question we turn to next.

Multilateralism-cum-Convergence: A "Cap-Con" Strategy

The issue of sequencing of multilateralization and convergence is crucial, should the two concepts mean what they refer to in this chapter—"capping" RoO at the multilateral level while establishing single origin regimes at the regional (or some other group/family) levels to permit the formation of larger cumulation zones. Recall from Chapter 2 that there is a natural theoretical tendency for larger cumulation zones to negotiate rules of origin with higher observed restrictiveness. Granted, any expansion of the U.S. or EU cumulation zones would imply only marginal proportional increases in their size, and thus in the degree to which the rules would be likely to become more restrictive. However, other regions, such as groupings within Latin America (Pacific Basin Forum), Asia (ASEAN+6), or Africa, should they follow convergence paths, would be well advised

[11] For a mapping of RoO in PTAs around the world, see Suominen (2004) and Estevadeordal and Suominen (2006).

to take care to resist pressures to establish more restrictive rules than those prevailing in their existing regimes. Although any multilateral cap on RoO restrictiveness is unlikely to bind on such arrangements, as it would have to be agreed to by the larger players as well, the existence of such a reference point could help restrain protectionism in the negotiation of new origin regimes.

Moreover, the argument that larger cumulation zones could mean greater restrictiveness in RoO assumes away (1) ongoing MFN tariff liberalization among the members; (2) potential RoO loosening by some members or a major member (as per the NAFTA relaxation of RoO); and (3) the rise of an export lobby in the midst of a convergence process to push for decreasingly restrictive RoO. Indeed, that such a process could be launched at all would likely suggest the consolidation of the globalized industry lobbies (and weakening of the import-protecting industries)—while of course not precluding stepped-up efforts of protectionist lobbies aiming at expanding rent-seeking opportunities in the convergence talks.

In any case, expansion of the zone governed by a RoO regime could lead to greater RoO complexity. Moreover, to the extent that countries wish to pursue convergence on the hope that it also leads to more liberal global trade, it could be important to basically all countries to first have in place, at a minimum as an insurance policy against the theoretical rise in restrictiveness, some global guidelines for (the convergent) preferential RoO. Such guidelines would simply serve to counteract the theoretical tendency of larger cumulation zones to create complex RoO and to erect higher barriers to extrazone inputs, and thus would entail simultaneous global capping and regional convergence processes.[12] This could be termed a "cap-and-con strategy," and it is based on a notion that global "capping" of RoO is useful so as to prevent "convergence" into trade-diverting megablocs.

---

[12] Note that the argument presented earlier that the effective restrictiveness of such rules is lower in larger blocs applies to the effects that rules have on the production costs of members, as the globally low-cost producer is more likely to be included within the cumulation zone as that zone becomes larger. This attenuating effect is of no help to suppliers left outside the expanded cumulation zone, and it is this distortion that we seek to minimize through multilateral rules governing preferential origin regimes.

The proposed optimal outcome is shown in Figure 7.8. Countries that are party to a group of overlapping PTAs decide to establish a convergent origin regime that will allow cumulation among all of them under a newly negotiated set of rules of origin. This new origin regime risks moving them up line A following the natural tendency for larger groupings to move toward more complex and more restrictive regimes. In the presence of multilaterally agreed-upon guidelines (a cap), this movement would be counteracted with a move down line B.

Whether the guidelines would serve to promote one type of criteria over another (CTC over VC or vice versa, for example) is a distinct question from whether such guidelines function to limit the erection of new barriers to global trade. As discussed previously, it is preferable that limitations on additional trade barriers be imposed on some aggregate calculus and not product by product, as flexibility at the product level would be indispensable for political economy reasons within each convergent group.

The important danger to keep in mind when establishing global caps, however, is that they must be set in such a way as to avoid reducing the incentive for convergence. Bringing groups of countries with multiple, overlapping PTAs into a single cumulation zone has the potential to greatly increase trade, especially among those that might be considered spokes, as well as to create trade, as long as the zone in question is grounded on open regionalism. As such, convergence of the right, nonrestrictive kind should be encouraged, not stifled. The wrong type of convergence—that

Figure 7.8 | Effects of "Cap-and-Con"

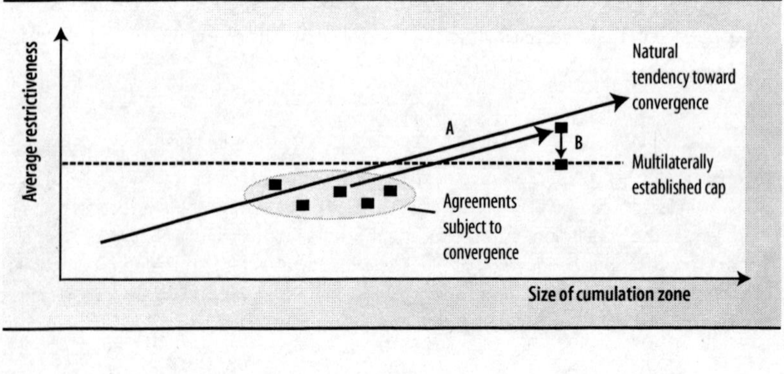

which produces trade-diverting megablocs that silo global commerce, something that cap-and-con is intended to pre-empt—should be opposed with the most stringent of measures.[13]

Although optimally some global capping would take place before the convergence processes begin, it already seems too late for that, as evinced by the current policy debates on some regional bridging of PTAs in the Americas and Asia and the EU's entrenched Pan-Euro regime. The Pan-Euro architecture implies that all of the EU's new PTAs will have the potential to continue the expansion of the Pan-Euro cumulation zone, though at least in that case the prospect for increasing restrictiveness of the rules is reduced, as new EU agreements tend to carry identical rules to the previous agreements.

Where Are We Headed?

Having described what we consider to be the optimal path for both regional and multilateral treatment of rules of origin, let us step back and re-engage with reality. What is optimal is one thing, but what is likely? We see four potential scenarios.

In the first potential scenario, one where nothing changes, countries continue to negotiate PTAs bilaterally or in small groups, with no convergence of origin regimes and no rules established at a global level to regulate the origin regimes of current or future PTAs. This is a "worst-case scenario" in which many small, overlapping PTAs channel preferential trade in narrow paths that prevent many producers from sourcing inputs efficiently and others from producing at all, as no cumulable inputs are available.

In the second possible scenario, convergence, groups of countries with overlapping PTAs begin to negotiate convergent origin regimes, but in the absence of any multilateral guidelines that would limit the theoretical natural tendency of larger cumulation zones to apply more restrictive rules. The gains to be had from allowing expanded cumulation within these

[13] Krugman (1991) finds that the globally most suboptimal trade bloc formation would be the rise of three megablocs. That extreme scenario is not likely in its theoretical form, as there are already many transbloc PTAs that would make Krugman's megablocs quite "leaky."

groups of countries are likely to be quite significant.[14] However, these groupings could, at least in theory, accentuate observed restrictiveness, hurting suppliers in excluded countries.

The third possible scenario, one where multilateralization of preferential rules occurs, but there is little convergence of existing regimes, is somewhat better than the worst-case scenario just discussed. It would still, however, exclude any gains to be had from expanding cumulation.

In the fourth potential scenario, the "cap-and-con" outcome we described in the previous section, regional convergence is accompanied by multilateral limitations on rules of origin. This would capture the benefits of both expanded cumulation and relatively less restrictive RoO.

The final relevant scenario is one in which there is successful multilateral tariff liberalization. The conclusion of a round of tariff reductions that results in the binding of MFN tariffs at zero or very low levels for nearly all products would make all preferential origin regimes irrelevant, as there would be no meaningful tariff preferences to qualify for. However, there seems to be little likelihood of such significant tariff reductions in the current global trade round.

Of these five scenarios, the second is probably the most likely. Initial movements toward convergence are already in evidence in such regions as the group of 11 Pacific countries of Latin America, as described previously. Most of the significant bilateral relationships in world trade are already subject to PTAs (certainly among countries prone to liberalization), and the unbundling of production within these PTAs is leading the "juggernaut" forces for liberalization, currently frustrated at the multilateral level, to push on regional levers.

This is not the worst-case scenario, but it is not optimal either. The outcome is likely to involve multiple overlapping "lasagna plates," the largest of which would be centered on the United States and Europe, with additional Latin American and Asian bits. A bipolar RoO world is likely welfare superior to a fully balkanized RoO world, as larger cumulation zones increase trade, especially among the current spoke countries. But it is not too difficult to

[14] Gasiorek, Augier, and Lai-Tong (2007) estimate that the implementation of the Pan-Euro system increased spoke-spoke trade by between 14 and 72 percent.

imagine that such zones could end up with highly restrictive rules of origin that would serve to isolate production within each zone, with attendant losses for global efficiency. Some mechanism is needed to limit the degree to which such production blocs are closed to outside trade.

Conclusion

The path to global free trade could proceed on several fronts. First, there is the standard front of multilateral tariff reductions. Second, there could be a gradual opening of preferential blocs via reduction of the restrictiveness of preferential rules of origin. This could occur either via regulation at the global level or via autonomous reform. Third, a path might be found through expansion of the cumulation zones of the preferential blocs in ways that at the same time promote further bloc-to-bloc liberalization. Finally, we might see some combination of these three mechanisms.

This chapter has analyzed the feasibility, utility, and mechanics of global trade liberalization via these fronts, focusing in particular on PTA rules of origin. We have described RoO regimes around the world, detailed the degree of restrictiveness within regimes and divergence across regimes, and elaborated why these two dimensions matter for economic outcomes. We have subsequently discussed policy options for reducing restrictiveness and divergence around the world and shown that such a reduction might be most likely at the regional level. Nonetheless, in our view, such processes should be complemented by a multilateral process of RoO capping, though it is important that such caps do not discourage regional convergence.

More specifically, this chapter has made three recommendations:

- At the multilateral level, there should be a process toward capping RoO—an effort to establish a common and limited set of RoO that can be employed in forthcoming, and perhaps also in currently existing, PTAs.
- At the regional level, groups of countries with multiple, overlapping PTAs should pursue avenues to establish inclusive origin regimes that permit cumulation in larger zones to promote trade

among spokes—yet do so in order to further open regionalism.

- At the level of individual PTAs, the appropriateness of the RoO should be re-evaluated on a regular basis, with an eye to reducing barriers to the use of third-country inputs in the production of originating goods.

To be sure, opening a full renegotiation of an origin regime, or worse, regimes for several PTAs at once and reconciling differences across regimes either at the regional or global levels certainly feels like lifting the lid on a Pandora's box of endless troubles. Nonetheless, the prospect of incorporating lessons learned over the past decade or more of operation of so many PTAs, bringing the regimes up to date with the commercial and technological realities of the 21st century, certainly makes such an effort seem worthwhile. The way these issues are addressed, both regionally and globally, will determine how, when, and if we arrive at global free trade.

Appendix 7.1 PTAs Considered in the Study

Table 7A.1 PTAs Considered in the Study

	Family assignment											
Agreement	Europe	Americas	U.S.	U.S. "new generation"	Asia	Africa	Americas-Asia	Chile	Mexico	Singapore	Japan	Australia
Pan-Euro	x											
EU-Chile (EUCHL)	x							x				
EU-Mexico (EUMEX)	x								x			
EU-South Africa (EUZAF)	x											
U.S.-Chile (CHLUSA)		x	x	x				x				
NAFTA		x	x	x					x			
U.S.-Colombia (USACOL)		x	x	x								
U.S-Panama (USAPAN)		x	x	x								
U.S.-Peru (USAPER)		x	x	x								
Argentina-Brazil-Peru (ARGBRAPER)		x										
Paraguay-Peru (PRYPER)		x										
Uruguay-Peru (URYPER)		x										
Argentina-Colombia (ARGCOL)		x										
Argentina-Ecuador (ARGECU)		x										
Argentina-Venezuela (ARGVEN)		x										
Brazil-Colombia (BRACOL)		x										
Brazil-Ecuador (BRAECU)		x										
Brazil-Venezuela (BRAVEN)		x										
Paraguay-Colombia (PRYCOL)		x										
Paraguay-Ecuador (PRYECU)		x										
Paraguay-Venezuela (PRYVEN)		x										
Uruguay-Colombia (URYCOL)		x										
Uruguay-Ecuador (URYECU)		x										
Uruguay-Venezuela (URYVEN)		x										
CACM		x										

(continued on next page)

Table 7A.1 ▌PTAs Considered in the Study *(continued)*

Agreement	Family assignment											
	Europe	Americas	U.S.	U.S. "new generation"	Asia	Africa	Americas-Asia	Chile	Mexico	Singapore	Japan	Australia
CACM-Dominican Republic (CACM-DR)		x										
CAFTA-Dominican Republic (CAFTA-DR)		x										
Canada-Costa Rica (CANCRI)		x										
Andean Community (ANDEAN C)		x										
CARICOM		x										
Chile-Canada (CHLCAN)		x						x				
Chile-CACM (CHLCACM)		x						x				
Chile-Mexico (CHLMEX)		x						x	x			
Chile-Peru (CHLPER)		x						x				
G3		x										
MERCOSUR		x										
MERCOSUR-Bolivia (MERCOSURBO)		x										
MERCOSUR-Chile (MERCOSURCH)		x										
Mexico-Bolivia (MEXBOL)		x							x			
Mexico-Costa Rica (MEXCRI)		x							x			
Mexico-Nicaragua (MEXNIC)		x							x			
Mexico-Northern Triangle (MEXNT)		x							x			
Mexico-Uruguay (MEXURY)		x							x			
Chile-Colombia (CHLCOL)		x										
Chile-Ecuador (CHLECU)		x										
U.S.-Australia (USAAUS)			x	x			x					x
U.S.-Bahrain (USABAH)			x									
U.S.-Israel (USAISR)			x									
U.S.-Jordan (USAJOR)			x									
U.S.-Korea (USAKOR)			x	x			x					

(continued on next page)

Table 7A.1 ▌PTAs Considered in the Study *(continued)*

Agreement	Family assignment											
	Europe	Americas	U.S.	U.S. "new generation"	Asia	Africa	Americas-Asia	Chile	Mexico	Singapore	Japan	Australia
U.S.-Morocco (USAMOR)			x									
U.S.-Singapore (USASING)			x	x			x			x		
U.S.-Oman (USAOMN)			x									
ASEAN					x							
ASEAN-China (ASEANCHN)					x							
ASEAN-Korea (ASEANKOR)					x							
Australia-New Zealand (ANZCERTA)					x							x
Australia-Singapore (AUSSING)					x					x		x
Australia-Thailand (AUSTHA)					x							x
Bangkok					x							
Chile-China (CHLCHN)							x	x				
Chile-Korea (CHLKOR)							x	x				
COMESA						x						
ECOWAS						x						
Japan-Malaysia (JPNMYS)					x						x	
Japan-Singapore (JPNSING)					x					x	x	
Japan-Thailand (JPNTHA)					x						x	
Mexico-Japan (MEXJAP)							x		x		x	
P4							x			x		
SADC						x						
SAFTA						x						
Thailand-New Zealand (THANZ)					x							
Peru-Thailand (PERTHA)							x					
GCC												

Table 7A.2 Percentage Similarity of Rules in Selected Families (percentage of agreements coinciding at the product level)

Section	Africa	Americas-Asia	Americas	Asia	Chile	Europe	Japan	Mexico	Singapore	U.S.	U.S. "new generation"	Global
1. Live animals	25	67	47	34	56	100	74	69	39	55	90	31
2. Vegetable products	27	77	48	39	61	100	61	81	40	58	92	34
3. Fats and oils	27	61	40	25	26	100	66	45	26	39	65	26
4. Food, beverages, and tobacco	31	36	43	30	43	98	55	56	29	51	79	28
5. Mineral products	25	55	49	29	43	100	35	88	40	49	80	29
6. Chemicals	25	29	48	26	29	99	47	49	27	41	61	32
7. Plastics	25	30	52	27	29	88	45	46	30	32	46	35
8. Leather goods	25	54	49	32	37	100	54	46	32	56	88	30
9. Wood products	25	84	49	51	59	100	67	75	48	60	98	37
10. Pulp and paper	25	59	47	38	48	100	29	68	42	43	68	30
11. Textiles and apparel	29	57	31	20	43	95	36	60	25	67	86	27
12. Footwear	25	45	35	28	42	94	39	71	33	42	61	25
13. Stone and glass	25	57	49	25	48	100	27	88	35	53	88	31
14. Jewelry	25	60	49	29	47	100	42	74	31	45	78	30
15. Base metals	26	46	44	30	45	98	27	69	35	49	79	29
16. Machinery and electrical equipment	25	42	44	26	43	96	30	74	31	49	81	31
17. Transportation equipment	25	41	48	26	40	94	28	64	27	52	66	34
18. Optics	25	50	54	26	53	96	31	69	30	56	83	37
19. Arms and ammunition	25	47	50	28	58	100	26	76	50	67	88	34
20. Diversified merchandise	26	42	48	25	42	97	29	81	29	55	67	32
21. Works of art, miscellaneous	25	46	49	26	25	100	25	89	25	48	79	30

References

Baldwin, R. 2006. "Multilateralizing Regionalism: Spaghetti Bowls as Building Blocs on the Path to Global Free Trade." NBER Working Paper No. 12545. Cambridge, MA: National Bureau of Economic Research.

Cadot, Olivier, and Jaime De Melo. 2007. *Why OECD Countries Should Reform Rules of Origin*. London: Centre for Economic Policy Research.

Cornejo, Rafael, and Jeremy Harris. 2007. "Convergence in the Rules of Origin Spaghetti Bowl: A Methodological Proposal." IDB/INTAL Working Paper No. 34. Washington, DC: Inter-American Development Bank.

Estevadeordal, Antoni, Jeremy Harris, and Kati Suominen. 2007. "Multilateralizing Rules of Origin around the World." Paper presented at WTO/HEI/NCCR Trade/CEPR Conference "Multilateralizing Regionalism," September 10–12, Geneva.

Estevadeordal, Antoni, and Kati Suominen. 2006. "Trade Effects of Rules of Origin." Unpublished.

Estevadeordal, Antoni, Kati Suominen, and Robert Teh. Forthcoming. *Regional Rules and the Global Trading System*.

Gasiorek, Michael, Patricia Augier, and Charles Lai-Tong. 2007. "Multilateralising Regionalism: Relaxing Rules of Origin, or Can Those PECS Be Flexed?" Paper presented at WTO/HEI/NCCR Trade/CEPR Conference "Multilateralizing Regionalism," September 10–12, Geneva.

Harris, Jeremy. 2007. "Measurement and Determinants of Rules of Origin in Preferential Trade Agreements." Ph.D. diss., University of Maryland, College Park.

IDB (Inter-American Development Bank). Forthcoming. *Coping with the Spaghetti Bowl of FTAs in LAC and Asia: Effects of FTAs on Company Strategies.*

Krugman, Paul. 1991. "The Move toward Free Trade Zones." *In Policy Implications of Trade and Currency Zones: A Symposium Sponsored by the Federal Reserve Bank of Kansas City, Jackson Hole, Wyoming, August 22–24*, 7–42. Kansas City: Federal Reserve Bank of Kansas City.

Suominen, Kati. 2004. "Rules of Origin in Global Commerce." Ph.D. diss., University of California, San Diego.